Building a Salesforce-Powered Front Office

A Quick-Start Guide

Rashed A. Chowdhury

Apress®

Building a Salesforce-Powered Front Office: A Quick-Start Guide

Rashed A. Chowdhury
Marietta, GA, USA

ISBN-13 (pbk): 978-1-4842-6675-5   ISBN-13 (electronic): 978-1-4842-6676-2
https://doi.org/10.1007/978-1-4842-6676-2

Managing Director, Apress Media LLC: Welmoed Spahr
Acquisitions Editor: Susan McDermott
Development Editor: Laura Berendson
Coordinating Editor: Rita Fernando

Cover designed by eStudioCalamar

Cover image designed by Pixabay

Distributed to the book trade worldwide by Springer Science+Business Media New York, 1 New York Plaza, New York, NY 10004. Phone 1-800-SPRINGER, fax (201) 348-4505, e-mail orders-ny@springer-sbm.com, or visit www.springeronline.com. Apress Media, LLC is a California LLC and the sole member (owner) is Springer Science + Business Media Finance Inc (SSBM Finance Inc). SSBM Finance Inc is a **Delaware** corporation.

For information on translations, please e-mail booktranslations@springernature.com; for reprint, paperback, or audio rights, please e-mail bookpermissions@springernature.com.

Apress titles may be purchased in bulk for academic, corporate, or promotional use. eBook versions and licenses are also available for most titles. For more information, reference our Print and eBook Bulk Sales web page at http://www.apress.com/bulk-sales.

Any source code or other supplementary material referenced by the author in this book is available to readers on GitHub via the book's product page, located at www.apress.com/9781484266755. For more detailed information, please visit http://www.apress.com/source-code.

Printed on acid-free paper

Table of Contents

About the Author

Rashed A. Chowdhury is currently a Sr. Principal at Infosys, where he consults to many Fortune 500 companies on Salesforce strategy and Front Office development. Rashed is a part-time Adjunct Faculty in the Robinson College of Business, Georgia State University, where he teaches master's level students Customer Relationship Management (CRM) and digital platform courses.

Rashed Chowdhury was the Global VP of Salesforce Development at Crawford & Company, the largest insurance claim management company based out of Atlanta, responsible for high-level design, strategy to implement cloud technology, marketing automation, and Front Office platform.

He sits on the Executive Leadership Board and leads the Marketing committee for Cheatham Hill Educational Foundation, a nonprofit organization that aims to engage interested stakeholders, gain volunteer support, secure financial aid, and interact within the West Cobb Marietta.

Rashed is also a Miller Heiman certified Sales and Business Development professional. He holds an MBA from Newman University and a bachelor's degree in Computer Information System from St. Cloud State University.

About the Technical Reviewer

Jarrod Kingston is a Salesforce MVP and Director of Solution Engineering with 7Summits. He has 12 Salesforce certifications and 10+ years of experience in the support, training, and advancement of Salesforce. He has extensive experience in providing presentations, solution demonstrations, and training. Jarrod has a dynamic ability to provide valuable content in an engaging way. Outside of work, Jarrod enjoys woodworking, house remodeling, and spending time with his family. He lives in Kansas City and is an avid Jayhawks (#RCJH), Chiefs (#ChiefsKingdom), and Royals (#RaisedRoyal) fan. You can follow him on Twitter at @jarrodmichael.

Introduction

The Front Office is the face of your business, where your company directly interacts with customers and where your revenue is instantly generated. In a hotel, the Front Office is the lobby – where guests are greeted, their problems are handled, and room payments are made. At a coffee shop, the Front Office is the employee taking your order or serving your drink. It doesn't matter what your business is; the Front Office is essential. The Front Office is the customer's first impression of your business. You want to make sure that your Front Office is sending a positive message to the public.

As we all know, it's difficult to overcome a wrong first impression. Preparing your Front Office correctly to make an excellent first impression is essential in the business world. After all, the Front Office is where the customers directly connect with your company. Your whole company should be ready to make a good impression on the customer. All parts of your company, including the sales and marketing departments and service and support personnel, should be focused on making a good impression on every customer (see Figure 1). Salespeople connect to customers by selling your company's goods or services, while marketing connects with them through advertising and promotional activities. Your service and support staff assists customers with problems and provides help with products. If customers have a good experience with your company, you can bet that they will be back again and again.

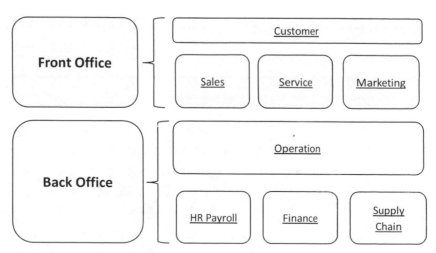

Figure 1. *Front Office diagram*

Repeat customers are likely to refer their friends to your company. Repeat customers will help you build your client contact list, also known as consumer data. Consumer data is generated as a company does business and may be in emails, spreadsheets, databases, or other data spread across different systems. Salesforce is one tool that can be used to consolidate that data into a single place to gain better insight into your business and more efficiently manage data. The tools available on Salesforce will make it easier for you to keep in contact with your customers. Throughout this book, we will be discussing the different ways Salesforce can help you manage your consumer data and grow your business.

What Is Salesforce?

Salesforce, a Customer Relationship Management (CRM) software service, was established in 1999. Today, it is the most popular CRM tool on the market. Salesforce exists as a Software as a Service (SaaS) model, meaning users pay a subscription fee to use the software each month. The software itself is hosted and maintained remotely and user-accessed through a website.

CRM software is a tool to manage relationships and interactions not only with current customers but with potential customers as well. It includes tools to reach out to potential customers. Contacting these potential customers gets your company name and product or service in front of more people. Over time, this process has been proven to very effectively grow businesses.

It includes tools to stay connected with customers and increase profits. CRM systems store customer data, such as contact information, opportunities, marketing campaigns, sales data, and more.

CRM software also makes it easy to stay connected with customers. Send out newsletters, coupons, sales info, and other specials to your current customers, and it helps keep your company in your customer's minds. Staying connected with customers like this has been proven to increase profits. One way this happens is when customers come back when you run sales or specials. The other profits can grow when customers refer friends to your company because your name is in the front of their minds. Either way, the result is an increased profit for you. CRM systems make it easy for you to store customer data. It allows you to break this data into categories such as contact information, opportunities, marketing campaigns, sales data, and more.

Salesforce is a large platform with various features suitable for businesses ranging from small- to medium-sized (SMBs) to international enterprises. SMBs may benefit from other tools in the Salesforce ecosystem outside of CRM, such as ecommerce. At the same time, big enterprises can enjoy various third-party plugins found in the Salesforce AppExchange and developer support and online training.

Salesforce creates a 360-degree view of your customers, allowing you to view customer data in one place and gain valuable business insights. This single point of engagement renders analytics more effective and easier to use and will enable users to manage customer relationships more efficiently.

For employees using the CRM platform, like Salesforce, it's hard to imagine a world without it. The structure and organization that the CRM software offers help keep everything related to your business organized and in one place. This makes managing your customer relationships easier because all the data, notes, metrics, and more are in one place.

To access Salesforce, open up a browser (I prefer Google Chrome or the latest Internet Explorer) window of your choice with Internet on and type `https://login.salesforce.com`. You will be presented with the login screen, as shown in Figure 2.

Figure 2. *Salesforce login screen (https://login.salesforce.com)*

INTRODUCTION

Once you are presented with the login window, go ahead and enter your login credentials (typically your email address and password when you set up the system). The home screen (Figure 3) will appear after entering the login credentials, which is your organization's instance of Salesforce.

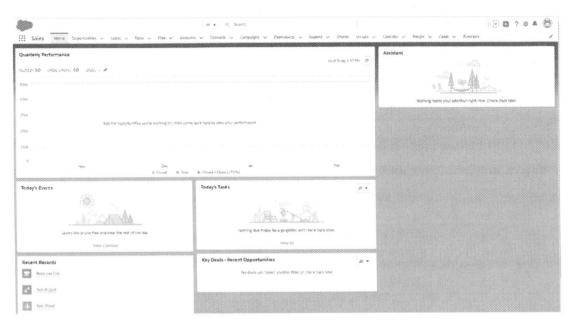

Figure 3. *The Salesforce home screen*

This is Salesforce's new and improved user interface called the Lightning Experience. The previous version of the system is often referred to as the Salesforce Classic. It is a good idea to reset your password during the initial login and make sure to complete the security questions that can verify your identity if you forget your password.

Salesforce keeps track of whether you are trying to log in to the system from each device and browser so that in the event any security concerns arise, the system emails or text-messages a confirmation code to validate that you are who you say you are.

The homepage is the main area when you access Salesforce and has standard components like events, tasks, recent records, and Salesforce performance metrics that specifically apply to the authenticated user. From the homepage, the user can navigate throughout the application using the navigation menu bar (Figure 4) that has standard tabs like Home, Account, Leads, Contacts, Opportunities report, and dashboard. If you don't see an item, check the more drop-down menu.

Figure 4. *The navigation*

Your admin has chosen which items should appear and the order in which they should appear. If something you need is missing or prefer a different arrangement, personalize the navigation that works for you by simply dragging the items around.

Favorites are a shortcut for top Salesforce pages. If you have favorite pages and want them to be in front and center, add them to the navigation bar.

Salesforce apps are a set of items that are bundled together to meet a specific business need. The navigation bar shows the name of the app you are using and the items that are assigned to the app. If you open a different app, the navigation bar changes to show that app's assigned tab items.

Key Salesforce Terminology

Salesforce is a valuable CRM tool, with many features and options for a variety of businesses. Because of this variety within Salesforce, users must learn new terminology and vocabulary. Here are a few of the important ones:

- Account: A company, person, prospect, partner, and so on with whom your company does business or plans to do business.

- Lead: A Lead is a potential sales opportunity. Prospective buyers, email communications, and website visitors are all considered Leads. They have not yet made purchases but have expressed an interest in your business.

- Opportunities: Qualified Leads that are working as a potential sale. These are linked to Contacts and can be generated whenever a deal is closed.

- Contacts: A person with whom your company does business. Contacts are linked to an Account in Salesforce.

- Activities: Activities may be events or tasks and are tied to records in Salesforce, such as Contacts or Accounts. Events are marked on the calendar and may include meetings, appointments, or presentations. Tasks may include follow-up calls with prospects or finishing a request for proposal (RFP).

- Record: A record consists of several fields that make up a Salesforce object. For example, a Contact record would include the contact's name, phone number, email address, and so on.

- Reports: Reports are real-time data analysis of accounts, contacts, opportunities, activities, and so on. It is used to compare sales goals to actual figures and measure company performance.

- Dashboard: Dashboard is a visual representation of data within Salesforce, which shows report data.

- Object: An object is how information is stored within Salesforce. An object is similar to a worksheet within Excel. Objects contain Records.

- App: A collection of objects and components within Salesforce, such as tabs, reports, or dashboards.

- AppExchange: An interface provided by Salesforce wherein users can access Apps created by other users. Apps integrate with Salesforce.

Salesforce Data Organization

Within Salesforce, data is split into objects and records. An object can be likened to a spreadsheet tab, with accounts, Leads, or contacts (Figure 5). A row of data in a spreadsheet is a record. Salesforce comes standard with several different objects available for use, including Accounts, Contacts, Leads, and Opportunities. Figure 6 shows the core data elements of the Salesforce Sales Cloud and lists corresponding attributes of standard objects.

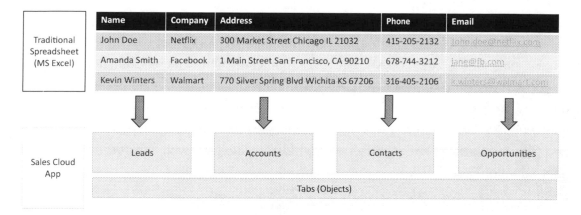

Name	Company	Address	Phone	Email
John Doe	Netflix	300 Market Street Chicago IL 21032	415-205-2132	john.doe@netflix.com
Amanda Smith	Facebook	1 Main Street San Francisco, CA 90210	678-744-3212	jane@fb.com
Kevin Winters	Walmart	770 Silver Spring Blvd Wichita KS 67206	316-405-2106	k.winters@walmart.com

Traditional Spreadsheet (MS Excel)

Sales Cloud App — Leads | Accounts | Contacts | Opportunities — Tabs (Objects)

Figure 5. *How data table overlays from traditional spreadsheet to Salesforce Cloud app*

Figure 6. *Core objects of Salesforce Sales Cloud (CRM ORG)*

An Account is a company or person (such as a contractor) with whom you currently do business. This account object contains a variety of fields, including the ID and the owner of the account, billing information, contact information, revenue, industry, and more.

Contacts are the people who work for companies with whom you are currently doing business (your Accounts). Examples of fields in this object include phone numbers and other contact information, Do Not Call status, names, titles, and department information.

Leads are business prospects. They are potential buyers who have not yet made a purchase or decided on a product. Leads contain some similar fields as Contacts, such as contact information and names, but Leads also include data fields such as a Lead rating and whether they have been converted. Salesforce will permit you to sort the Leads dependent on measures with the goal that you can make sense of how to best market to them. As we know, companies can't change Lead regularly over to clients in the short term. It takes reliable contact over some undefined timeframe, generally three to five connections, before the Lead is changed over.

Finally, Opportunities are proposals created when a Lead is converted into an account or person. It includes fields indicating sales amounts, dates the sale has been or will be made, and type of opportunity (e.g., new business or existing business).

These are just a few of the most used standard objects that come with Salesforce, but there are several hundred more available. Also, users may create custom objects to represent data as they need it if a standard object is not available, which fits their needs.

Salesforce makes managing this data simple, linking together objects and records to allow for more effortless information flow. For example, when qualified, a Lead can be converted to an Account object, with Contact and Opportunity objects linked with the Account, so all the data related to the sale is available in one place and is easy to find (see Figure 7).

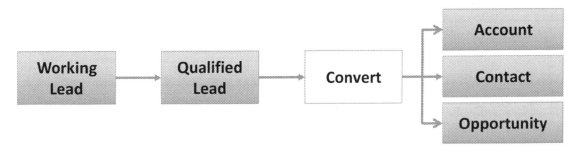

Figure 7. *The standard Lead conversion process*

We've covered a lot of material and technical terms already, and we're just getting started! Each chapter that follows will break down the tools Salesforce offers so you can build your business and create a robust Front Office.

Global Search Bar – Finding Records

The global search bar is located at the top of the page, and for the most part, you will be able to find most of the information using this search capability.

When you search for information in the search fields, a search result appears, as shown in Figure 8. The search results are organized following major types of records that include contacts, accounts, Leads, opportunities, people, and files.

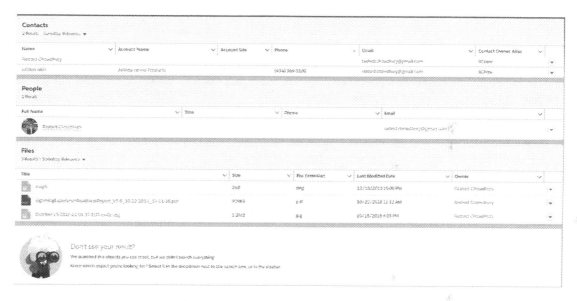

Figure 8. *Search result page*

If you are satisfied with the result sets, the linked record will lead you to the record details page, which would allow you to view the record details.

If you are unable to find what you are looking for, you need to add the * wildcard before and after to expand the search.

If you don't see your result, that's because Salesforce searched the objects you use most but didn't search for everything. If you know which object you're looking for, you can select it in the drop-down next to the global search box or in the sidebar.

CHAPTER 1

Lead to Cash: Front Office Process Tower

This chapter starts with an overview of the Front Office process tower and typical activities for each of those towers. We will discuss various concepts related to Front Office processes and tools consideration to support those processes. By the end of this chapter, you will have learned the fundamentals of an integrated Front Office powered by various solutions and modules from the Salesforce ecosystem. The following topics will be covered in this chapter:

- Front Office process tower
- Lead generation
- Tools for Lead generation
- Marketing automation
- Tools for marketing automation
- Sales management
- Tools for sales management
- Configure Price Quote (CPQ)
- Tools for CPQ
- Contract Lifecycle Management (CLM)
- Tools for CLM
- Order fulfillment
- Customer service
- Revenue management

© Rashed A. Chowdhury 2021
R. A. Chowdhury, *Building a Salesforce-Powered Front Office*, https://doi.org/10.1007/978-1-4842-6676-2_1

External-Facing Customer and Lead Interaction

The Front Office is where revenue is directly generated for your company, so ensuring you have a fair process for it is essential. As with anything, developing a strategy is key to success, as shown in Figure 1-1. Whether you are a new business or an existing one, get to know your market and develop a business strategy around it. Analyze the current market, gather business intelligence, and investigate marketing programs such as Partnership Growth Program or SPIFF, where salespeople are immediately rewarded through bonuses for sales.

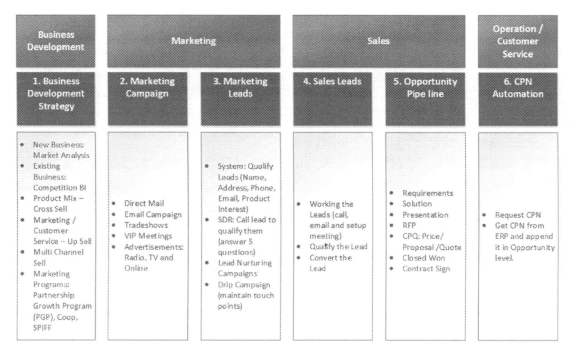

Figure 1-1. *Front Office process tower*

With your business strategy developed, it is time to delve into marketing. To make sales in the first place, customers need to know you are an option. Get the word out there through a marketing campaign. Advertise your business through the Web, TV, or radio, attend trade shows, launch email campaigns, and send direct mail to potential consumers. Once the word is out, Sales Development Representatives (SDRs) should work to organize potential Leads for the sales team.

Sales are next in the Front Office Process. Use the Leads which marketing has created and convert them into sales. Configure Price Quote software, or CPQ, may be used to generate accurate quotes for potential customers in real time for a salesperson to have a quote readily available to convert a Lead.

When a sale has been made, track that order using your Enterprise Resource Planning (ERP) software. This will help the Front Office Process by allowing salespeople to look at existing orders when maintaining clients or converting new Leads.

Now that you have had an overview of the Front Office Process Tower, you will find more details on each area within the tower in the following chapters.

Lead Generation

Lead generation is the process of converting someone from being a stranger to being someone interested in your company and the products and services you provide. There are many ways you can generate Leads across different platforms (see Figure 1-2). Good web content and marketing campaigns are two such ways. Keep your website up to date with quality content to attract new Leads. Marketing campaigns should direct people to your website or sales representatives, so having engaging content when they make it that far is essential. The landing page of your website is the page to which prospects are first brought when they visit your site for a specific product or service, so make sure that page is well done.

Emails are also an essential tool in Lead generation. You can use email templates to save time writing a lot of emails by hand, but be sure those templates may be personalized for each client. Drip and nurture campaigns can each be used to help generate Leads. Drip campaigns are emails sent out at set intervals. They are useful for keeping your company fresh in the minds of prospects or Leads. Nurture campaigns involve emails sent based on Lead behavior. They are typically used with people who have already become Leads to help send them further along the sales path.

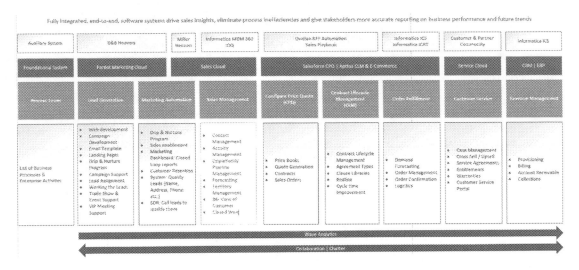

Figure 1-2. *Lead to cash – digital transformation blueprint*

Physical events may also be used to gather Leads. Trade shows are a great way to make new connections. Have a tablet or laptop at your booth where visitors can sign up with their email after viewing whatever it is you have to offer. Offering a drawing for a free product or service can entice people to sign up for your email list. Or perhaps you might host face-to-face VIP meetings with influential people who may be interested in your products. Such discussions are another critical place to have a tablet or laptop available so that you can get people's contact information.

Tools for Lead Generation

There are quite a few useful Lead generation tools you can use that are a part of Salesforce. One such tool is *Pardot Marketing Automation*, which can be used to build landing pages and create forms. It can also manage social media postings and provide insights to see how your marketing efforts are going. Pardot can track visitors to your website with cookies. Information such as what parts of the site they visit or what content they interact with can be saved, and when they become reasonable prospects, that information is automatically appended to their record. This information can also help you decide how to market to each customer. Typical key performance indicators (KPIs) to consider in the Lead stage are as follows:

- Lead by status (Open, Contacted, Qualified, Converted)

- Lead conversion rate

- Converted Lead by week, month, and quarter

- The top sales rep (Sales Development Representative, SDR)

It is necessary to calculate the return on investment (ROI) on a marketing campaign and quantify opportunity influence from campaign activities to understand marketing effectiveness. It is also essential to track the conversion rate of the Marketing Qualified Lead (MQL) to Sales Qualified Lead (SQL) and then benchmark them against an industry vertical to outline improvement opportunities (see Figure 1-3).

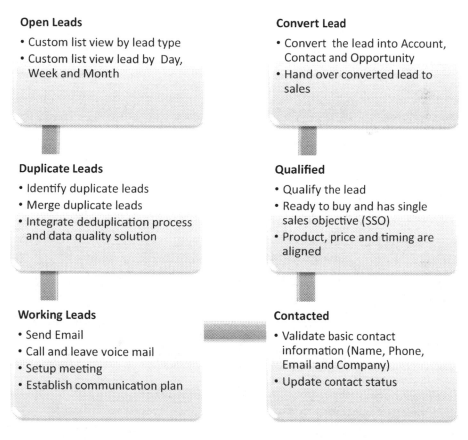

Open Leads
- Custom list view by lead type
- Custom list view lead by Day, Week and Month

Convert Lead
- Convert the lead into Account, Contact and Opportunity
- Hand over converted lead to sales

Duplicate Leads
- Identify duplicate leads
- Merge duplicate leads
- Integrate deduplication process and data quality solution

Qualified
- Qualify the lead
- Ready to buy and has single sales objective (SSO)
- Product, price and timing are aligned

Working Leads
- Send Email
- Call and leave voice mail
- Setup meeting
- Establish communication plan

Contacted
- Validate basic contact information (Name, Phone, Email and Company)
- Update contact status

Figure 1-3. *Lead lifecycle and stages*

It is recommended to create a vital closed-loop follow-up process so that Leads don't disappear or be displaced. Also, it is a common practice to establish a Lead qualification process for the entire organization, especially for the sales team, to make sure all sales reps use the same consistent methodology as Miller Heiman, MEDDIC, and so on.

Salesforce Pardot can also be used to create campaigns. One thing to keep in mind is that a Pardot Campaign is different than a traditional marketing campaign. A Pardot Campaign is a grouping of prospects. Grouped prospects may then be tracked together, and you can report on them as well. For example, all prospects who complete a form may be grouped into a Pardot Campaign (see Figure 1-4).

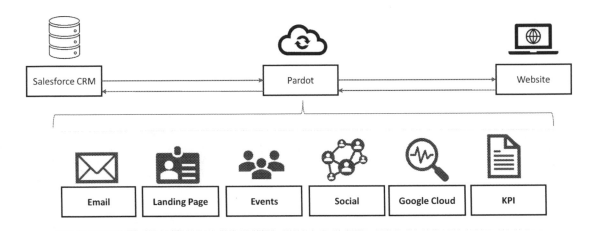

Figure 1-4. *Pardot integrates email, landing page, marketing events, social channel, and Google Cloud with Salesforce CRM and company website*

Another commonly used tool/provider is the Salesforce *Marketing Cloud*. Although Pardot is more typically used for B2B marketing, Salesforce Marketing is usually used for B2C marketing. Salesforce Cloud is all about supporting the customer journey through email, social media, content, and advertising. It helps to guide a customer through their interactions with your company and keep them engaged.

Salesforce Marketing Cloud allows you to have a one-on-one relationship with your customers to personalize their experience. It gives you a 360-degree view of your customers, pulling in data from multiple sources to one place. All interactions with your customers are easy to see and are grouped for visibility.

Another valuable feature of Salesforce Marketing Cloud is called triggered events. The triggered events section of the Salesforce Cloud allows you to set up actions that take place based on the action a customer takes. For example, a confirmation email can be sent to a customer after they make a purchase. Another example is "we miss you" emails. These can be set up by the triggered event spurred by time passing since the customer's last visit. Or you can send a "we miss you" email with a coupon or special offer. This type of email will keep your company in front of the customer. Most likely, when the customer sees this email, it will result in a sale from that customer. These events can also be set up to update one set of data when a different set of data changes.

Marketing Automation

Generating Leads is just one part of marketing automation. The business processes that go into marketing automation do have some overlap with Lead generation, but there are several unique processes. For instance, drip and nurture programs may be used to generate a Lead, but they are usually focused on someone who is already a leader.

Sales enablement is the process of helping your sales and marketing teams work together to maximize sales. It means getting marketing material and tools in the hands of your sales team to engage buyers better. Automating this process as best you can saves you time and improves sales. For example, interactions with customers may be input into Salesforce CRM and then automatically viewed throughout the sales pipeline. Information related to a deal can be pulled automatically through a Salesforce CRM app, saving the rep a lot of time. It can make sure that representatives are also following up with the customer in the stated or set timeline, so the customer doesn't lose interest.

Closed-loop marketing is also made possible through technology. Closed-loop marketing is marketing that uses data from sales team reports, in which the sales team tells marketing what happened with the Leads they were given. That way, marketing can see which sources are the best or the worst. Using Salesforce to track a prospect through the sales process may help with closed-loop marketing. For instance, you place a cookie on a visitor to your website and see what actions they take. After they fill out a form, you add them as a Lead in Salesforce and carry that data over. Later on, if they are converted by your sales team, you can look back and see where they came from initially. The records of Lead conversion will take the guesswork away from wondering how you got new customers or how to increase new customers. You will have a history of what does and doesn't work for your company.

Marketing automation is also used to improve customer retention. Using triggered events, you can automatically welcome new customers or subscribers with an email to give an excellent first impression. Use these emails to thank them when they sign up for different services. You can also automatically send out emails when events or promotions are coming up to offer discounts or other incentives to encourage early buyers. In general, you can keep in contact with a customer more easily through automated emails while at the same time increasing their loyalty.

Determining whether a Lead is qualified can also be done for you through marketing automation. As your visitor engages with your website and its content, their Lead score will change. If they fill out a form and you now have their contact information and name, their Lead score automatically increases. This allows you to easily filter out who needs to be nurtured and who is ready to send to the sales team.

Marketing automation ensures Leads get passed along to your Sales Development Representatives. They, in turn, do more work to qualify the Lead before passing it on to your sales team. Passing only truly ready Leads to your sales team allows your sales team to work more efficiently. Your marketing automation tool, SDRs, and sales team working together will improve your sales and conversion rates.

Salesforce Sales Cloud, Salesforce's CRM platform, is integral to marketing automation. If you can't find a specific process you need in the base application, it is easy to go to the AppExchange and to explore. The AppExchange is a marketplace for Salesforce apps, components, and consulting services. It is the gateway that connects your business to customers.

Tools for Marketing Automation

Like Lead generation, both Pardot and Salesforce Marketing Cloud may be used for marketing automation. They include many tools for qualifying and tracking Leads, such as automated emailing and automatic Lead qualification based on a set criterion.

Pardot scores and grades your Leads to make sure you are reaching out at the right time. It also supports closed-loop reporting, making it easy to track where your Leads are coming from and your target market.

Salesforce Engage is a Pardot Salesforce solution for marketing automation. Use it to create an Engage campaign to drive sales. Before kicking off your campaign with Engage, do some planning and research. Gather the requirements for your campaign. What milestones or criteria must be met to have the campaign be considered successful? Work with your team to figure that out in advance and begin the creation of your marketing material before starting your campaign.

Before you use Engage to roll out to a broad audience, try it out with a small control group. Ensure all marketers are kept on the same page by creating and distributing training guides and support resources. Launch your Engage campaign with that small group of early adopters and observe them closely to see how the campaign plays out.

Use the knowledge you gained from your test group to iterate on your Engage campaign. Take their feedback and update your training guides, material, and resources. Then you can alter the campaign as necessary before you run it on the larger group. Once the campaign is redesigned, you can gain the support of your sales leadership. Create communication plans and promotions for your launch.

With all your iterations finished and your launch materials ready, it's time to kick off your Engage campaign fully. Leverage your pioneer group and have them be the "hype men" or supporters of your campaign. They've already been introduced to your campaign and can tell others about it. Offer these supporters special offers or discounts for every new customer that they refer to you. Set up a way that you can track where these new customers originate.

Also, encourage adoption through leaderboards. Have office hours dedicated to product support so users feel as if they can always get the help they need with their new purchase. Use Chatter, another Salesforce feature, to keep your reps communicating with each other and to assist with onboarding and training. The more consistent your team is in marketing and talking with the customers, the stronger your company image will appear.

Salesforce Lightning Dialer allows you to gain back hours of productivity by communicating more efficiently with Leads, prospects, and customers. It all begins by logging details right from within Salesforce. The Lightning Dialer allows you to call prospects with one click on their phone number within Salesforce.

It also reduces data entry and increases productivity because the phone number is in one place, not on sticky notes or scrap pieces of paper. You can also streamline the sales process with automatic call logging, voicemail drop, and call lists. This allows you to power through calls and connect with Leads and contacts faster.

Lightning Dialer's ability to multitask allows deals to move faster. All the answers you need are in front of you. You can find call history, take notes, and finalize details while talking to the prospect. All this can be done without switching apps or devices. Lightning Dialer allows your business to turn inbound calls into personalized sales calls. It helps you to build more trust with your customers with incoming calls because it will enable customers to reach a personal dedicated number and voicemail.

Salesforce Sales Cloud, Salesforce's CRM platform, is integral to marketing automation. If you cannot find a specific process you need in the base application, it is easy to go to the AppExchange and research.

Sales Management

There are several different areas you need to keep in mind when managing your sales. These are your contacts, activities, opportunity pipeline, and territories.

Contact management is vital for keeping your contacts organized and ensuring you can easily make deals using accessible data. It's essential to keep all of the data you can about your contacts, including communication history, contact information (of course), and their relationships with members of your company. Keep this data in your CRM system, so it is easily accessible, and ensure the data is kept up to date. This allows multiple members of the sales team to work together on more complex deals, and everyone works with the same information.

Managing your activities (events and tasks) is easier than ever with tools like Salesforce. Activities include tasks such as weekly meetings, phone calls, and practically anything which needs to be done with a date. By ensuring your tasks are tracked, you'll have an easy view in Salesforce of what needs to be done and at what time.

Activities are often tied to opportunities, and managing those is essential as well. Opportunity pipeline management is all about tracking, organizing, and managing all your business opportunities. With software like Salesforce, this is very easy to do. Your opportunities should have any data related to them tracked. For example, an opportunity might have a specific contact or task associated with it. Make sure that the relationship is represented within Salesforce.

A sales territory is a grouping of accounts that belongs to a specific sales representative to whom they support and sell. These accounts are separated based on offset characteristics. For example, a salesperson may get a territory based on the postal codes of accounts or their revenue. Set up different rules to fit your organization and the needs of your sales team. Territories may also be broken up into hierarchies. For example, the top level of a geographical territory could be the world, which then gets broken down into regions, countries, and states/provinces.

Salesforce Sales Cloud CRM ORG provides a single place for updating all the deal-related information and enabling rep to close deals faster. Also, tracking opportunity milestones and recording customer interactions, meetings, tasks, and all notes in the opportunity level make an agent more efficient and make the organization more collaborative. Sales leaders can easily analyze the sales pipeline to quickly identify the highest value opportunity and remove any impediments within the sales cycle (See Figure 1-5).

Typical key performance indicators (KPIs) to consider an opportunity stage are as follows:

- Top 10 deals

- Closed won by month, quarter, and year

- The top sales rep and leader board

- Month to date trending

Figure 1-5. *Opportunity lifecycle and stages*

Lost opportunity goes back into the remarketing funnel to further engage the prospects by reevaluating customer needs and timing to position the right product at the right price when onboard a new customer. Salesforce provides your entire company a 360-degree view of your customers and facilitates collaboration across the organization as a whole, thus transforming into a customer-centric organization.

Tracking accounts, activities, opportunities, and territories are all current records. But managing the future is also essential. That's where forecast and forecast management come in. A sales forecast is simply an estimate of an expected future revenue, and, yes, Salesforce can help you there too. Use these forecasts to plan your sales cycle and to set goals. You can adjust your sales forecast goals by months. Many businesses have meager sales in January, as compared to later months. Also, some corporations make most of their sales during a particular season; it could be summer or in the fall before the holidays. This forecast model lets you compare your actual revenue at different points to the forecast, so you can see how well you're doing.

With all this data, you will have a 360-degree view of your customers in Salesforce. This means all your information is consolidated, and you will have a unified view of your customer. With this, you can tailor your customer's experience on a case-by-case basis and better personalize your sale. This information can then be used to predict your customer's behavior and improve their satisfaction.

Tools for Sales Management

Salesforce should be your primary tool for managing sales and customers that can handle accounts, activities, opportunities, territories, forecasting, and more. It provides you with a 360-degree customer view.

Another useful tool you may wish to consider is Informatica Cloud Customer 360. This ties into Salesforce and is a Master Data Management (MDM) tool that keeps your data regulated, deduplicated, and up to date to ensure the 360-degree customer view is maintained. Customer 360 for Salesforce has several features, including eradicating duplicate, inaccurate, and incomplete account, person, and contact records. It provides clean, trusted data and a real-time view into the quality and completeness of your Salesforce data through a user-friendly interface. This tool will verify the client's email, phone, and address information and track it in real time. It will eliminate duplicate clients based on matching information, so your sales team is not annoying the client with multiple emails or phone calls.

Customer 360 also automatically detects and corrects erroneous data found in your Salesforce organization. The Customer 360 tool ties everything up for your team into an excellent Salesforce-wrapped package. It is a Master Data Management tool that keeps your data regulated, eliminates duplicate copies of repeat data (often time refers as deduplicated), and up to date to ensure the 360-degree customer view is maintained. This tool will help you manage your customer's information efficiently so you and your team can spend more time selling.

Configure Price Quote

Configure Price Quote (CPQ) is a sales tool used to generate a quote for an order automatically (Figure 1-6). You set rules within your CPQ software, considering several pieces of data such as quantities or discounts. This is very useful to your sales team as it allows them to generate a quote quickly when they need it, so they will not keep the Lead waiting. Salesforce itself can perform CPQ.

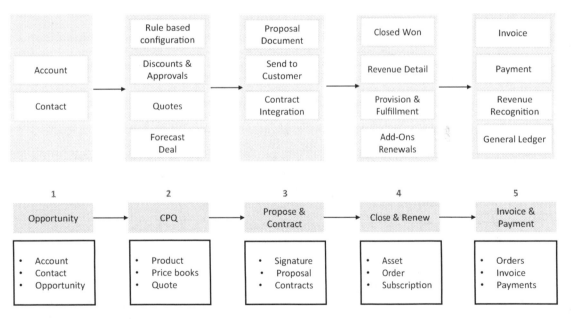

Figure 1-6. *Quote to Cash – key process flow and Salesforce objects*

Price books are one of the enterprise activities which go into CPQ. Simply put, a price book is a list of all your products and their prices. To start with, you should have a price book that contains default prices for all your products. From there, if necessary, you may create custom price books for your different market segments to tailor your costs.

Quotes are generated to give your potential buyers information about their purchase, its price, what they will be receiving, any discounts they will receive, and any other terms or agreements. Create a template for your quotes to help maintain a stable, consistent company brand image. If your CPQ tool uses this template when generating your quotes, it will save your sales team time; they can then use it to sell more.

Contracts are another object in Salesforce, which can generate quotes for new contracts and renewals as with other opportunities. When it's time for a customer's contract to be renewed, your CPQ will automatically make a unique quote for you. It will consider any products being added to the contract, as well as price changes, simplifying the renewal process (See Figure 1-7).

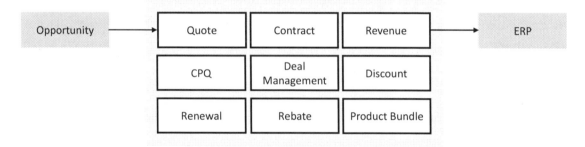

Figure 1-7. *Salesforce streamline Quote to Cash (QTC) process*

Orders are created after your quote. They are used to track the products a customer has purchased. Quote data will automatically be placed into the Order object within Salesforce. Multiple orders may also be created from a single quote if necessary. By letting Salesforce automate this data entry, you ensure your orders are more accurate.

Tools for CPQ

Salesforce itself will be your bread and butter when dealing with CPQ. It contains Contract, Quote, and Order objects ready for you to use. Managing your Quotes and Orders in Salesforce is easy, and it automates much of the process for you. Apttus is another tool useful in this area available to be integrated within the Salesforce platform natively and streamline the Quote to Cash process (See Figure 1-8). From Opportunity to ERP, Apttus modules can further automate the Front Office processing including the quote, contract, and revenue. From rebate management to e-commerce solutions, Apttus platforms can bring additional values to contract lifecycle management (CLM).

DocuSign is typically used to collect customer signatures and automatically add them to contract documents. You can get the DocuSign for Salesforce app from the Salesforce app exchange and integrate it into your Salesforce environment with ease. Informatica Cloud provides integration services and ETL (extract, transform and load) capabilities to Salesforce users. Informatica Cloud could be used to synchronize order details between Salesforce and your ERP (Enterprise Resource Planning) solutions such as SAP.

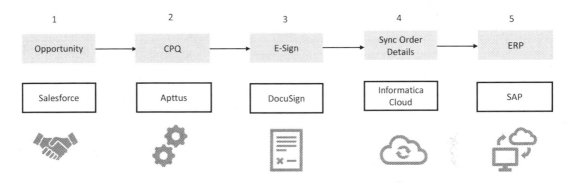

Figure 1-8. *Salesforce streamline Quote to Cash process using Salesforce and apps from ecosystem*

Qvidian RFP platform automates creating proposals and request for proposal (RFP) responses. Qvidian fills in responses to RFPs for you or will give you suggestions to choose from, speeding up the process. It analyzes your projects and content to maximize productivity. It integrates with Salesforce as well, ensuring your data stays centralized. Qvidian also automates proposals for you using a centralized content repository. It supports proposal templates and can measure the performance of your content or team members.

Conga is another CPQ tool that works with Salesforce. It provides guided selling in the CPQ process. It utilizes drop-down menus where the user can select discovery questions and receive best-case product selections using its rule-based configuration engine. Finally, it streamlines and standardizes your pricing using tied pricing, automated approvals, and discount criteria.

Contract Lifecycle Management

Contract Lifecycle Management (CLM) is aptly named. It is the process of managing your contract across all the points of its lifecycle, from when you are first planning it out to when the contract expires. Using some sort of CLM system is essential, especially when you manage many contacts at once.

Step 1 of CLM (See Figure 1-9) is ensuring all your contract data is in one place. You cannot manage a contract you do not know exists, so make sure wherever you keep your contracts is visible. Figure out your most essential data and track it. Track this data for all contracts – past, present, and future.

Next, streamline your contract creation process. Utilize templates to make sure you can create contracts quickly and accurately and following company guidelines. Tie in your organization's different libraries, so contracts pull in data automatically when filling in your templates. Make the process of creating a contract easy for your user. Templates help with this and ensure to complete contracts in a few clicks.

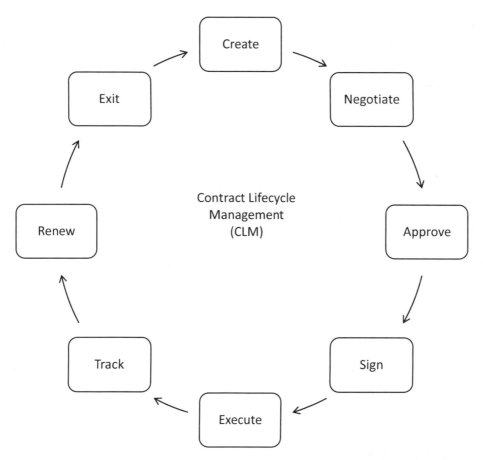

Figure 1-9. *Contract Lifecycle Management (CLM)*

The next stage of a contract is getting approval. Some less risky contracts may be preapproved automatically, but other contracts are going to need to go through an approval process. Send the contract to the appropriate department, whether that be

Legal, Management, or some specialized team. Track these approvals, as well, in case of future audits and for compliance purposes.

Some parts of the contract can pull in clauses from a clause library. A clause library contains preapproved sections of text to be placed into future contracts. Using a clause library saves time by contributing prewritten frequently used clauses. Your legal team does not have to spend time approving these clauses after the first time.

The contract will then be negotiated. The chances are that the first revision is not going to be the accepted one. Ensure all differences between revisions are highlighted and flagged. Redlining is an integral part of the negotiation process. Both parties involved with the contract mark the contract with their additions, deletions, or changes. When redlining, do your research beforehand and communicate with the other party. Make sure your changes are well reasoned out and are well communicated.

Ensure your sales playbooks assist with contract negotiations by including strategies. After your negotiations have been finalized, it is time to sign off. Everyone relevant must sign the contract before it is safely stored. Also, make sure it is not edited before copies get sent out. Check all changes with your legal team to make sure the contract is still approved.

Finally, all your existing contracts need to be easy to access and analyze. Automation is useful. You do not want your company to forget about a contractual obligation because the contract is in a filing cabinet and has been forgotten, which could lead to financial and legal issues that could have been avoided.

Tools for CLM

Intelligent CLM is a contract management software created by Apttus. It is powered by artificial intelligence to improve your contract management processes. It is easy for the user as they can talk to the AI through text or speech interactions. It integrates with Salesforce, Skype, Slack, and SMS.

Conga Contracts is another CLM tool that integrates with Salesforce. It speeds up the creation, negotiation, and signing processes to create contracts faster. Conga uses data analytics to show you how to improve your arrangements and find problem areas. It supports creating clause libraries to save time on the approval process as well. It also uses automated version control to make sure your data stays consistent and clear.

A third CLM tool is SpringCM. It automates several contract management processes and integrates with Salesforce as well. SpringCM creates a central repository for your contracts, as well as having the ability to generate contracts. This repository is intuitive to navigate and accessible from a variety of devices on demand.

Order Fulfillment

After a customer has placed an order with you, the next process is getting the purchased items into their hands. This is the order fulfillment process. As an example, an order is created. Information from the order is entered into different systems throughout your organization – such as accounting – as well as outside your organization, such as notifying the customer the order has been placed. The warehouse receives this information as well, and the items are gathered and shipped to the customer with an order notification. Managing this process, the logistics that are involved, and the planning for future demand are the key.

Salesforce supports order management right out of the box. Quote information is automatically placed into orders for ease of management. Whenever you use any order fulfillment tool, try to ensure it integrates with Salesforce (or whatever order management software you choose) to confirm your entire order lifecycle (See Figure 1-10) is visible and easier to manage.

Part of managing order fulfillment well means planning for future demand. This process is called demand forecasting. Using historical customer data, you make estimations about future direction. Use modern technology to automate this process as much as you can to optimize your inventory, budget better, and respond to an ever-changing market.

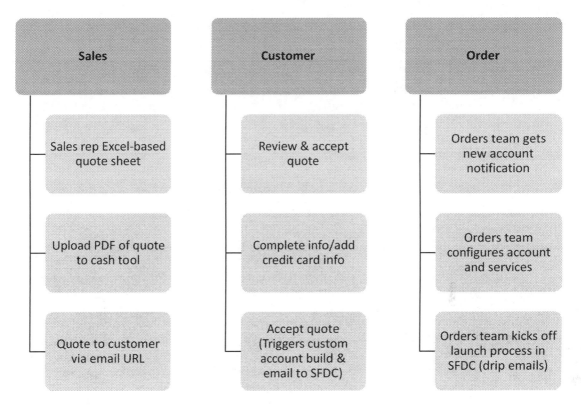

Figure 1-10. *Example of real-world sales order process flow*

The process of getting your items to your customer safely and efficiently, called logistics, is another concern. Intelligently group your products in your warehouse to speed up the time it takes to move them. If an item is frequently ordered, it should be easily accessible. Automate the process wherever you can, such as scanning inbound and outbound goods as they enter or exit your warehouse to keep your information up to date.

Tools for Order Fulfillment

Salesforce Commerce Cloud Order Management is an excellent place to start. It comes packed with a lot of features to assist with order management. It can help you allocate inventory, manage order lifecycles, and make sure all order is consistent and unified. It is customizable and has an API you can use to integrate with other commerce platforms.

Apttus B2B E-Commerce is an ecommerce buying experience tool that integrates with Salesforce. It can ensure that users are shown products they are most likely to buy through robust analytics driven by real-time activities. It makes it easy for buyers to make their purchases anywhere at any time whenever they are ready.

Customer Service

So, you have gotten the Leads, converted them into sales, and completed your orders. But the sales cycle does not end there. Customers may have issues or needs which need to be addressed after the sale has been made. This is where good customer service comes in. And the first step to achieving that is to have good case management.

Case management is the process of managing your communications and issues customers have across all your channels (See Figure 1-11). Use case management software to make this process as pain-free as possible. In today's world, customers will reach out to you in a few different ways, including multiple social media platforms, email, contact forms, phone calls, and in person. All these cases should be viewable from one location, typically a cloud-based platform.

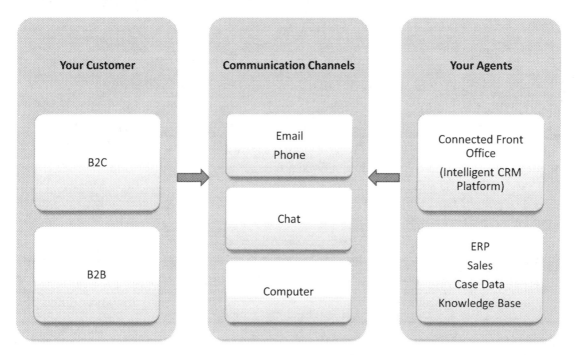

Figure 1-11. *Customer, communication channels, and customer service agent data flow*

Grouping your cases is not the end, however. Have a knowledge base with Frequently Asked Questions and solutions to problems that crop up a lot. Let your customers solve their problems before they ever need to create a case with you. If cases do occur, ensure your management software can keep them organized and filterable. For example, support representatives may need to organize cases by high priority or subject.

Consider cross-selling and upselling as well. Selling to a customer who has already purchased from you (or will be purchasing from you) is a great way to improve their loyalty and gain more revenue. Cross-selling involves selling additional items that are related to a customer's purchase. Make sure the extra things go well together and that they provide good value to the customer.

Upselling is like cross-selling in that it seeks to increase sales revenue from a specific customer. However, instead of offering similar products, the strategy is to provide an upgraded or improved version of the original product. Again, you should ensure the actual value is being provided to the customer. No one wants to feel like a sleazy car salesman who is trying to sell them a luxury car they do not need. Research your customer's needs and recommend additional products or services which match them. Not only does this increase revenue, but if the customer feels like they genuinely received better value than they initially expected out of the purchase, it improves customer loyalty as well.

The customer service provided to a customer can be limited based on entitlements. The service-level agreements they may sign will tell them what service they should expect from you. For example, they may receive an entitlement (creatable in Salesforce), which gives them access to phone or web support. Keeping track of your entitlements through Salesforce ensures your customer gets the support to which they agreed, and you do not spend time and money on unnecessary support. To simplify, link your entitlements to something else in Salesforce, such as an account.

Through Salesforce, you can even include support steps for your agents to follow and apply to entitlements. This is known as an entitlement process. Through this, you can make a timeline with steps the support team needs to complete to resolve a support request.

Entitlement management also allows you to set up warranties for your customer's products. A warranty is just another type of customer support agreement. Consequently, warranties fall under the entitlement management umbrella. Simple warranty entitlements may be created, but so can more complex ones involve real contracts.

Keep in mind that the modern customer wants to be able to research problems on their own before turning to contact support, so enable customers to have the ability to help themselves within your ecosystem. This can be done through a customer portal or a self-service portal. A self-service portal allows customers to view information such as their past orders or current order status and view support documentation. If they have a ticket open, they can view it here and check the status. Before even going through the process of opening a sales ticket, consumers can search for other cases that may be like their own. This saves your company time and money by enabling the customer to solve problems on their own.

Customer service portals can use the power of communities even further to empower self-service. Organizations are a place where users can ask questions and get answers from other users. Company agents may step in where necessary to answer questions, clear things up, or moderate.

Adding self-service to your customer support processes saves time and money and adds customer loyalty as they can solve their problems much faster than waiting for email or phone responses from the company during business hours.

Tools for Customer Service

Salesforce Service Cloud is going to be your one-stop shop to fulfill all your customer service requirements. It allows you to create self-service portals with communities, create and manage cases, and offer support across different digital channels.

Your Salesforce organization can use the community's user licenses to allow external users to access only the data you wish them to have available to them. For example, the Customer Community license may be used to give consumers access to a knowledge base or their cases, while a Partner Community license may be used to provide other businesses access to sales data.

Revenue Management

Revenue management (See Figure 1-12) is using analytics to help predict customer behavior and better price your products, as well as handle future demand. It is selling the right product to the right customer at the right time for the right price through the right channel. This is an often-used practice in hotels and airlines but can be equally applied to other businesses.

Using a hotel as an example, if they are selling a room for one night and it does not sell, they cannot ever sell the space for that night again. Therefore, they must use revenue management to ensure their pricing best matches the supply and demand of the market.

Revenue management also includes all the tasks which must be taken after a quote is made, a contract is signed, or an order is placed. Whenever any of these things happen, data is sent to different departments, such as Operations or Accounting. Operations need to know what items are being packed and where they are being shipped. Accounting needs to know about price details for invoicing. While both departments are doing their work, Finance is figuring out what revenue is currently available and when revenue is going to be received in the future.

Provisioning is a crucial accounting process that gives a more accurate balance for the year. A provision is a money set aside in the balance sheet for future uncertain but probable liabilities. As an example, a bad debt may be provisioned. The chance that a debt is not going to be paid may be estimated by using historical data from both your company and the industry. If it is high, a provision can be made to account for it using the expected expense.

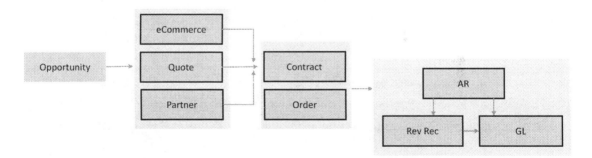

Figure 1-12. *High-level Quote to Cash workflow from opportunity through the contract and to revenue recognition (Rev Rec)*

Managing your billing is also a part of good revenue management. Billing management software makes it easy to integrate billing with the rest of your systems, such as generating invoices automatically from contract or quote data. Since all this data can be stored in the same place and read from different places, you will ensure other areas of your business are using accurate, up-to-date data.

Accounts receivable, the money owed to your organization for any goods or services you have supplied to customers, is also part of revenue management. It is vital to keeping track of specific data, such as how long it takes to receive money from accounts receivable or if any turn into bad debts. The more you know about accounts receivable, the better predictions you can make about cash flow and your budget.

Collections are the processes involved with getting money from a customer who is currently overdue on payments. Some examples include sending reminders of the outstanding balance through the mail, phone calls, or email or imposing late fees in addition to the reminder. Additional steps may be taken if the account remains overdue, such as stopping service or sending the account to a collection agency. Note that if the amount is small enough, your organization may find it costs more to collect it than to ignore it.

Tools for Revenue Management

If you need to decide between two types of customers to whom to sell something, CRM tools such as Salesforce can help with that. Salesforce helps track customers who are the most loyal and most likely to continue to bring in revenue in the long term. When forecasting demand, it may be necessary to factor in the more loyal customers differently.

Salesforce CPQ and CLM are also useful tools for revenue management. Creating quotes and contracts through centralized data means they are more accurately made. They can be made faster, as well, saving time in a variety of different departments. When you need to create an invoice for your customer, it is much easier if your contract or quote data is all in one place.

Apttus Revenue Management is a revenue and billing management tool which puts information from the back office into the Front Office for more accurate invoices. It, too, will use quote and contract data to create orders or billing schedules to ensure consistency. Apttus Revenue Management integrates with Salesforce and ERP software to work well with your enterprise's needs.

Summary

In this chapter, we have gone through various concepts related to Front Office processes and discussed tools consideration to support those processes. We started with the activities of a typical Front Office process tower that includes business development strategy, marketing campaign, and Marketing Qualified Leads, sales Leads, opportunity pipeline, and customer service automation. We also covered tools and concepts for Lead generation, marketing automation, sales management, Configure Price Quote (CPQ), Contract Lifecycle Management (CLM), order fulfillment, customer service functions, and revenue management. In the next chapter, we will go through the concept of Lead, Lead qualification process, Lead stage, what action to take in each stage of the Lead process, and detailing the Lead conversion process.

CHAPTER 2

Leads

In the previous chapter, we had an overview of various Front Office related concepts and Salesforce tools to support them. We discussed the core concepts of sales, marketing, services, and operational concepts. We discussed tools and critical Front Office concepts for Lead generation, marketing campaign, marketing automation, sales management, Configure Price Quote (CPQ), Contract Lifecycle Management (CLM), order fulfillment, customer service functions, and revenue management. In this chapter, we will be focusing on Lead and its processes, how to qualify the Lead and convert them to create an account, contact, and opportunity from Salesforce's point of view. We will review what action to take during each stage of the prospect journey in the Lead object.

The following topics will be covered in this chapter:

- Prospecting Leads

- Lead process

- Qualify the Lead – programmatically

- Lead qualification process

- Timeline for Lead qualification

- Lead management

- Lead assignment rules

- Lead settings

- Web to Lead

- Social account

- Contact overview

© Rashed A. Chowdhury 2021
R. A. Chowdhury, *Building a Salesforce-Powered Front Office*, https://doi.org/10.1007/978-1-4842-6676-2_2

Prospecting Leads and Potential Customer Journey

Leads are typically the building blocks of driving company growth and sales. In Salesforce terms, a Lead is a person in a company that might be interested in your products and services. A Lead can be in one of four stages, ideally progressing through each stage until they become an opportunity.

At the *open stage*, the Lead has shown some sort of interest in the product. No personal involvement has occurred at this point, but the Lead may have gone to your website or viewed an ad for your product aimed at them.

The next stage of a Lead involves the customer having made personal contact with the company. This can be through an email, a phone call, a meeting, and so on. Using data collected about open Leads will help determine which Leads to connect with first.

Throughout contact with a Lead, the end ideal stage is a sales-ready opportunity. This is the stage at which the Lead is ready to be passed to the sales. A qualified Lead should have a budget and the decision-making power to purchase from your company.

Track prospects apart from your contacts and opportunities with Salesforce Lead records. After you have qualified your Lead records, convert them to contacts and create accounts for them (if you don't already have the accounts in Salesforce). And create opportunities to bolster your pipeline. Figure 2-1 exhibits the different stages of a Lead and lists typical activities during each stage.

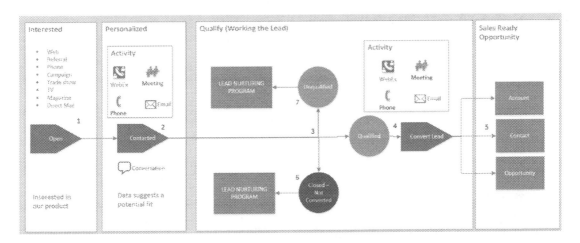

Figure 2-1. *Lead stages and activities*

Lead stages are customizable to suit an organization's unique business needs and can be customized using the Lead process definition from the Lead setup. In this exhibit, we divided them into four categories:

- Interested: During this stage, a prospect could be interested in your products or services. Anyone interested in your company can submit their information through the following marketing campaigns:

  - Web

  - Referral

  - Phone

  - Campaign

  - Trade show

  - TV

  - Magazine

  - Direct mail

- Personalized: In this stage, once prospects or potential Leads submitted their information, you can contact them to give further information by

  - WebEx

  - Meeting

  - Phone

  - Email

- Qualify: Once the data in the system suggests that the prospects are a potential fit, sales rep must "work the Lead" (call, email, meeting, etc.) to identify if the Lead is qualified or not. Typically, there are three to five qualification questions companies institutionalize as part of the business development operating procedure. The Sales Development Representative (SDR) team qualifies the prospect by validating (yes to the qualification questions: identify a potential buyer) those qualification questions.

- Convert Lead: Once the Lead is qualified, it now must be converted (See Figure 2-2) to an Account. When converting a Lead, the system automatically generates a contact record by using the contact information already provided (by the person to whom you have spoken).

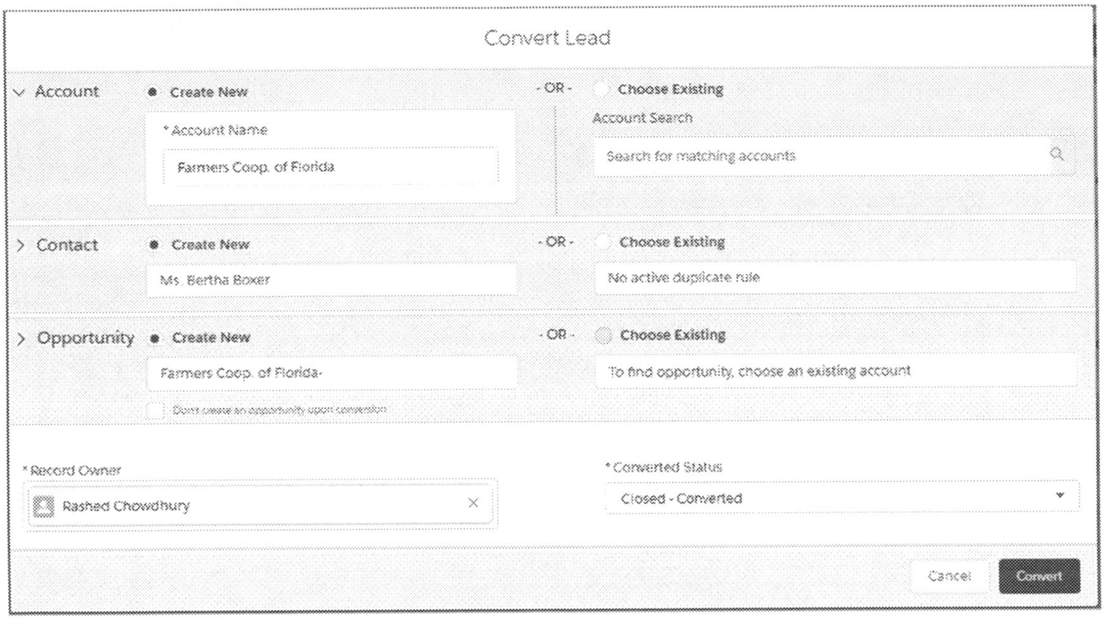

Figure 2-2. *The Lead conversion process in Salesforce*

An account is created as a part of converting the Lead. This gathers all the pertinent business information to apply to the account record. Afterward, an Opportunity record is created to start tracking and finally selling products.

Key fields to populate:

- Record owner: This field should be populated automatically from the Lead owner field. If the owner changes for some reason, you can select the right owner from the lookup field and choose from the list of users.

- Account name: In the event Salesforce finds an account that closely matches the company field from the Lead record, you can select an option from the drop-down list and associate the Lead record to an existing account or create a new account record.

- Opportunity name: Populate this field by entering an opportunity name following the company's opportunity naming convention. In the event without any naming convention, it is a good idea to follow and probably establish a naming convention, for example, Client name + Product/Service + YY/YY for the period covered.

- Converted status: This field is populated automatically by Salesforce with the default value that the selling organization (your company) has selected for the qualified Lead.

Converting Leads into customers requires Marketing and Sales alignment. Pardot provides Sales and Marketing with the intelligence they need to personalize outreach and engage prospects at the right time. Sales users who also use Pardot are more likely to say they target the right deals. This is likely due to Pardot's ability to help sellers effectively qualify and manage prospects, making them more efficient

Marketing sources may be immediately assigned to a sales representative for contact and qualification, or they may be nurtured through a series of marketing touches until the point where the Lead is deemed as having real selling potential. This is usually accomplished through a Lead scoring process.

Lead Process

Leads should be defined as a limited information record that needs to be qualified as a real potential selling prospect before conversion. Leads may be acquired in various ways, such as event attendance, webinar attendance, purchased lists, website visits, web content downloads, referrals from existing customers, or entry by sales.

Before you can begin working on your Leads, you should consider creating a Lead process for your organization. In Salesforce, Lead processes use the **Lead Status** field to identify a Lead within the Lead lifecycle. Depending on the complexity of the organization, you can create and maintain multiple Lead processes (Figure 2-3) for your organization to use.

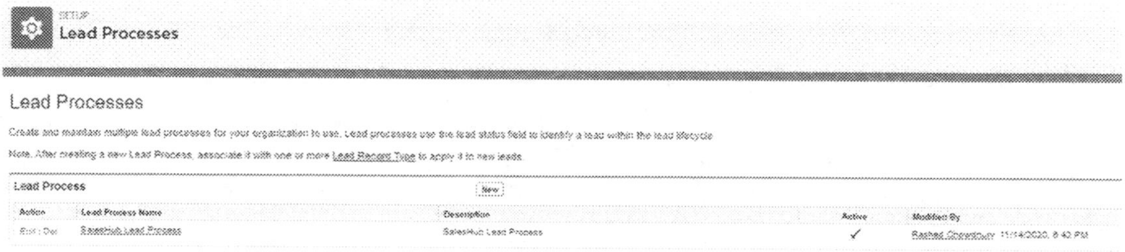

Figure 2-3. *List of Lead Processes in Salesforce*

Note   After creating a new Lead Process in Salesforce, associate it with one or more Lead Record Types to apply it to new Leads.

During the Lead Process (Figure 2-4) setup, you will see that there is a list of available values (derived from the Lead stage picklist field in the Lead object) to choose from to set up your Lead process. Once you select the known values from the list and add them to be included in the Lead process, become your company's Lead process. Note that removing a status from the Lead process will not remove the value from any records already containing the status.

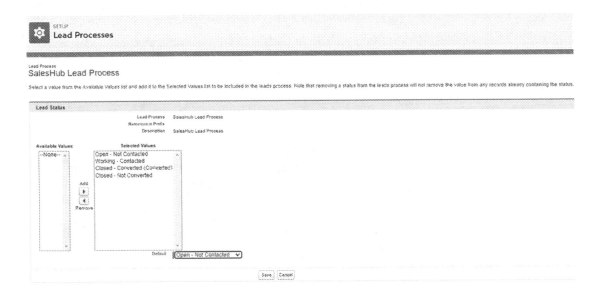

Figure 2-4. *Lead Process definition in Salesforce*

You may have to plan and execute marketing campaigns that generate demands for your products or services. Capturing those Leads via a variety of channels, including the company website, is critical. In Salesforce, the Lead object hosts all the Leads generated from various sources and can be configured to provide a summarized (total number of Leads by a Lead source) view, including a visual representation of the Lead sources as shown in Figure 2-5.

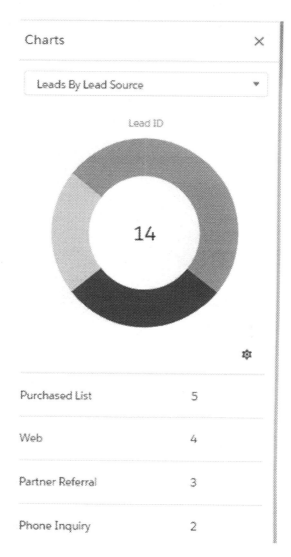

Figure 2-5. *List of Leads grouped by Lead Source in summary view including a chart in Salesforce*

Once the Lead process is established, the Salesforce organization will be ready to accept a new Lead record. One can manually create a Lead record, cloning an existing Lead, or import a list of Lead files into Salesforce.

When adding a new Lead manually in Salesforce, as shown in Figure 2-6, at a minimum, you have to complete the required fields (fields with red * sign). In this example, Last Name, Company, and Lead Status fields are required and must be populated to add the Lead record in Salesforce.

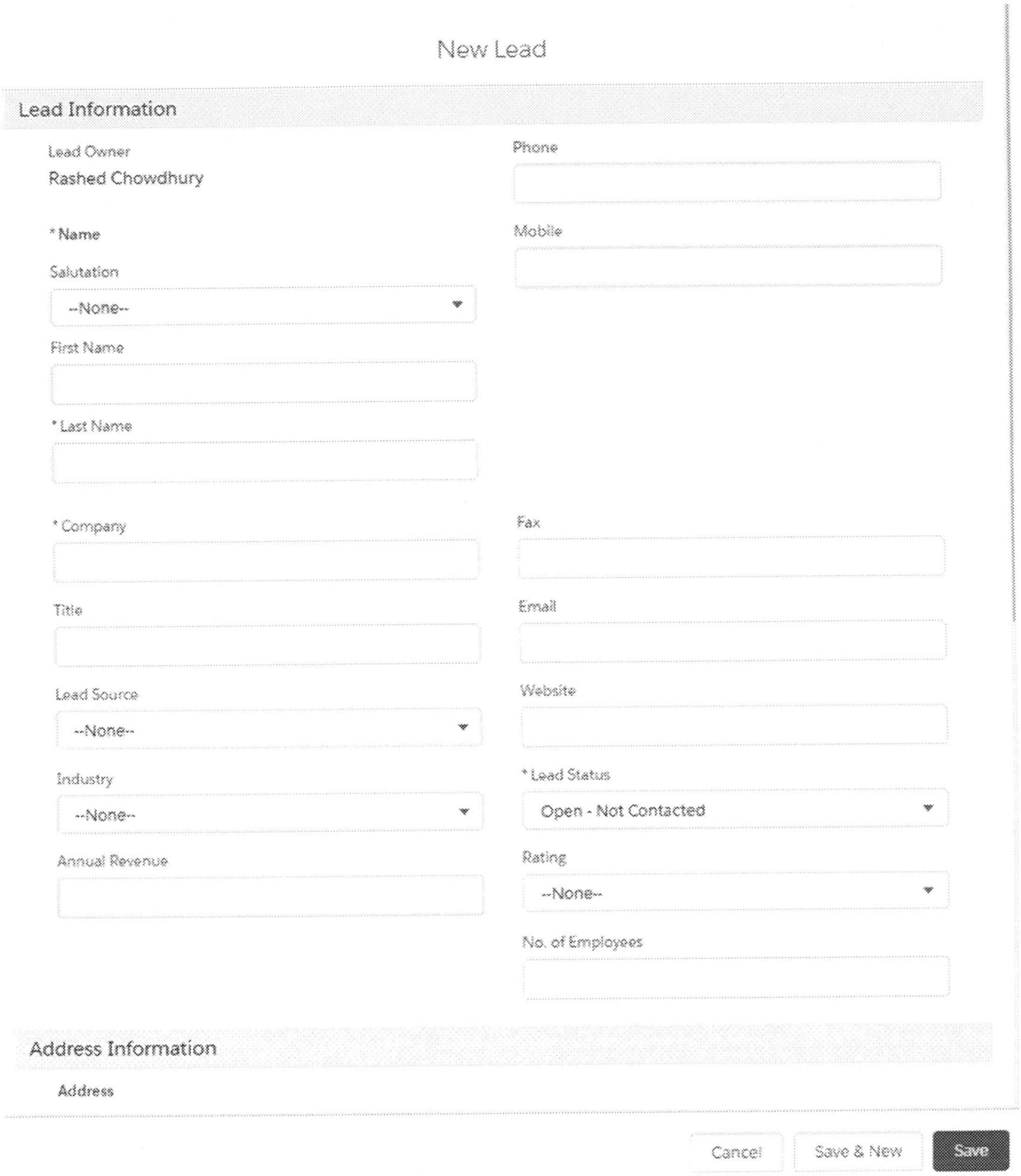

New Lead

Lead Information

Lead Owner
Rashed Chowdhury

* Name

Salutation
--None--

First Name

* Last Name

* Company

Title

Lead Source
--None--

Industry
--None--

Annual Revenue

Phone

Mobile

Fax

Email

Website

* Lead Status
Open - Not Contacted

Rating
--None--

No. of Employees

Address Information

Address

Cancel   Save & New   Save

Figure 2-6. *New Lead data entry screen in Salesforce*

In some cases, you may not have all the accurate and relevant information at hand. Over time, the Lead owner will have to find and populate the rest of the attributes of the Lead so that the sales rep and automatic Lead qualification process can qualify the Lead to convert them into account, contact, and opportunity.

During the Front Office design architecture, you may think what and how to show senior management the effectiveness of the marketing campaign. Being able to calculate the return on investment (ROI) of marketing efforts, identify what effort (marketing campaign) is working, and determine the core market demand are key areas to focus. Typical key performance indicators (KPIs) to consider during the Lead generation process are as follows:

- Campaign ROI

- Top search terms

- Lead by source

- Lead quality

Figure 2-7 shows how a business can generate more Leads and optimize the Lead processes to capture them in a centralized CRM system.

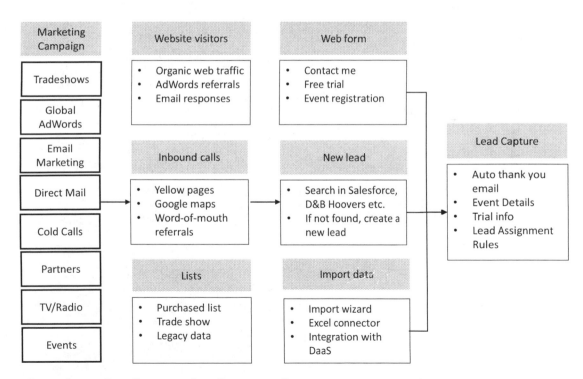

Figure 2-7. *Lead generation framework*

Marketing campaigns come in various forms and shapes that include trade shows, email marketing, direct mail, cold calling, partner marketing, radio/TV commercials, paid media services, and webinars. Generating more Leads in various marketing channels and capturing them in one centralized cloud-based system like Salesforce to prioritize them, assign resources to qualify them, and finally compute the campaign effectiveness are some of the critical goals of today's Salesforce-based Front Office strategy.

Some of the automation considerations when setting up a Lead in Salesforce are (1) automatically send a thank you email to the Lead and (2) assign the Lead to the available rep to follow up using Lead Assignment Rules.

Information on a Lead is usually limited to contact details such as Name, Address, Email Address, and Phone Number. Company-level information may also be discovered in the early stages of the Lead process.

Qualify the Lead – Programmatically

Once marketing has developed Leads, score and grade them so sales can then attempt to convert the most valuable Leads first. Hard data may be used to score Leads, such as their name, location, or contact information. The more you know about the Lead, the better it is. Other data may be derived from behavior activities, such as trade show visits, website visits, or the Lead's downloads. Figure 2-8 shows how to develop Lead scoring and grading mechanism and develop a point-based system to identify them in hot, warm, and cold status, which drives the priority-based culture in terms of working the Leads.

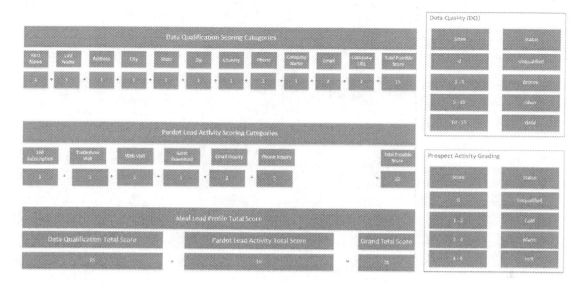

Figure 2-8. *Lead scoring and grading framework*

This data can all be combined to score a Lead to ensure sales follow up with the best Leads first.

Grading of inbound Leads ensures that the Leads being passed from marketing to sales match your company's ideal customer profile. At the same time, Lead scoring is based on a Lead's activity. When using Lead grading, Leads are automatically evaluated based on several implicit factors and assigned a letter grade (A–F). The criteria typically are Industry, title, company size, revenue, and so on and are located within the Pardot section in Salesforce CRM.

Lead Qualification Process

Leads assigned to a sales rep should remain within the Lead object in Salesforce. The sales rep is then responsible for gathering specific data points to determine whether this Lead is truly qualified.

Some general qualifiers usually include whether there is a need that can be met with the company's product, whether the Lead (as shown in Figure 2-9) is in the position of a dealmaker or influencer, whether there is an available budget, and so on. Lead-qualifying questions should be agreed upon by both marketing and sales.

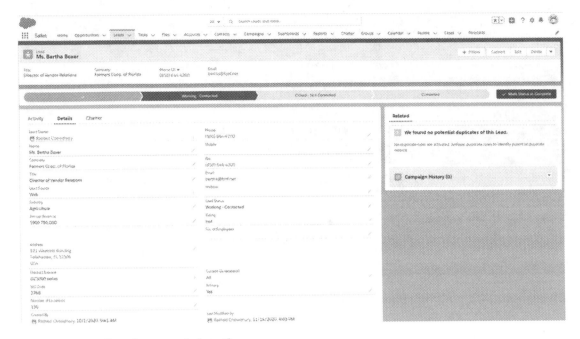

Figure 2-9. *Leads record detail page*

If a Lead does not fall within the markers for qualification, the rep should consider whether this Lead may meet the attributes later. If that is the case, the representative should update the Lead Status to one that will indicate the need for further marketing nurture (Figure 2-10). For instance, let's say that a Lead suggests that they have just made a move to a similar product/service you offer, and they are under contract for several years. Continued effort should be made to keep the brand familiar to the Lead. A Lead that does not meet the qualifier markers should be marked as unqualified or Closed (not covered).

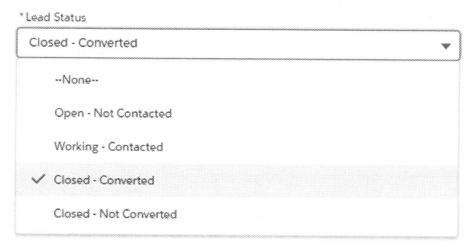

Figure 2-10. *Lead stages*

Unqualified Leads will not be converted into Accounts, Contacts, and Opportunities but will remain within the Lead object. The record and the activity associated with it may be referenced at any time.

Timeline for Lead Qualification Activities

In each stage of the Lead lifecycle process, the organization has to plan out the details, including the list of tasks or activities and qualification process for the Lead to move to the next stage as shown in Table 2-1.

Table 2-1. *Lead action schedule*

Week	Stage	Tasks/Activities	Qualifications Outcome
Week 1	Open	• Phone call • Email • Setting up a meeting • Creating a task	Data-driven outcome and expectation • Lead name • Email • Address • Phone • Company name
Week 2	Contact	• Organization's standard qualification questions (determine if the client has a genuine appetite for change, etc.) • Task • Meeting	Behavior-driven outcome and expectation • Want at least three to five Lead qualification questions to be a yes to qualify • Qualified = Y/N (automation consideration)
Week 3	Qualify	Converting the Lead!	System-driven outcome and expectation • When converting the Lead, it creates a record for each of the following: • Account • Contact • Opportunity

For example, in week 1, when the Lead stage is open, typical tasks and activities are to make contact by making a phone call, sending an email, or meeting the prospect. The overarching goal during this stage is to validate the core data points for contact, including an accurate name, email address, phone, company name, and address. At a minimum, the following data fields are required to make a Lead record in most organizations, which could vary:

- First and last name

- Email address

- Company name or phone number

In week 2, the sales rep needs to determine and qualify the Lead to make sure they are a good fit for both the buying and selling organization. A specific Lead qualification questionnaire should be designed to identify the perfect Lead and possibly create an ideal customer profile and some type of Lead scoring mechanism. Typically, three to five questions should be included in the Lead qualification assessment process. Here are a few Lead qualification questions:

- Does the client have a genuine appetite for change?

- Would they embrace value over price?

- Do they need our value proposition to execute their goals (capacity/capability)?

- Does the client have a clear and transparent decision-making process?

- Are there cross-selling relationships?

- Do we have senior-level relationships?

- Is the client financially stable and responsible?

- Is the commoditization risk low?

- Does the client have a strong brand?

- Would they commit to a long-term contractual partnership?

Most of the answers should be yes for the Lead to qualify. The rep should record these answers, and automation could be put in place so that a field could be set to Qualify = Y/N depending on the answers to the qualification questions.

In week 3, if the qualified field is set to yes, then the rep should converting the Lead in Salesforce. Converting a Lead (Figure 2-11) is a function in Salesforce that converts a qualified Lead into an account, contact, and opportunity via the Convert button on the Lead record within Salesforce.

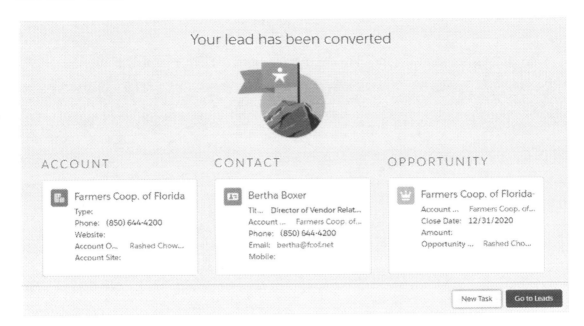

Figure 2-11. *Lead has been converted into account, contact, and opportunity in Salesforce*

Converting the Lead using this method ensures individual connections are made in the database to facilitate reporting. The IDs of the account, contact, and opportunity are populated on the converted Lead record.

Another important note is the creation of the contact role record on the opportunity. This allows for the connection between a marketing campaign effort to contacts and those contacts' influence on opportunity revenue.

Lead Management

You want to organize and manage your Leads in Salesforce to make the best usage and value out of them. Using the Lead list view, as shown in Figure 2-12, you can organize them using a specific set of criteria to limit the total number of records.

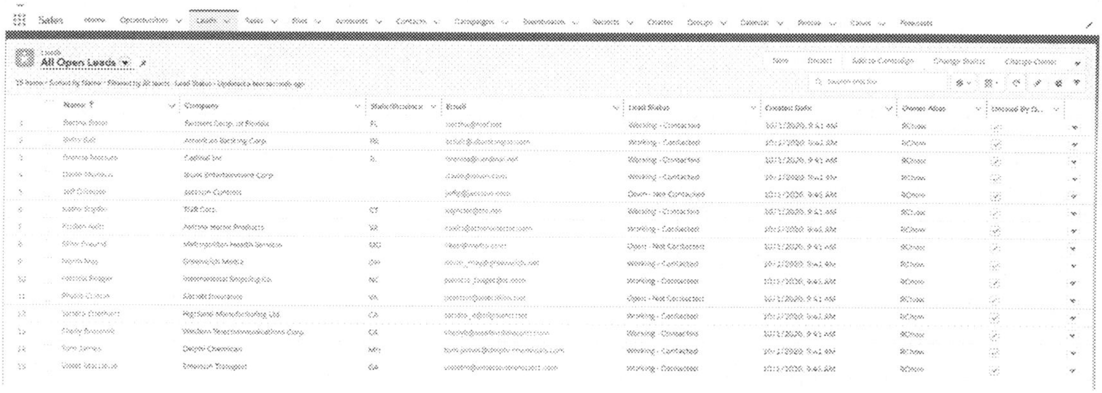

Figure 2-12. *List of Leads in the Leads homepage in Salesforce*

Salesforce comes with four predefined list views that include All Open Leads, My Unread Leads, Today's Leads, and Recently Viewed Leeds.

- All Open Leads: This view provides a list of all the Lead records with an Open Lead status.

- My Unread Leads: This view provides a list of all Lead records that haven't been viewed.

- Today's Leads: A list of Leads that were created today.

- Recently Viewed Leads: A list of Leads that were viewed recently.

Besides these standard list views, you can create a customized list view, as shown in Figure 2-13, to meet a specific set of criteria you may have.

Figure 2-13. *Custom list view*

For example, if you want to view all Lead records from the state of Florida, you will define a new set of criteria where the state is equal to "FL" using the drag-and-drop list view configuration window in Salesforce as shown in Figure 2-13.

Here are some of the Lead management best practices listed for reference. For example, setting up an Account-Based Marketing (ABM) strategy is highly effective for targeted and strategically essential accounts. Lead scoring is a scientific method that unveils the importance, urgency, and priority of the Lead so that the selling organization can follow up based on speed and assigned adequate resources.

- Lead generation: Capture qualified sales Leads through high-quality content and targeted inbound and outbound campaigns such as emails promoting whitepapers, events, trade shows, webinars, and so on.

- Lead segmentation: Capture as much relevant info as necessary for Leads and contacts that will allow for establishing an ABM (Account-Based Marketing) strategy for sending emails that are more targeted and personalized.

- Lead scoring: It is crucial to set up the Lead scoring criteria in the system to update Lead lifecycle stages. Leads accumulate positive scores for behavior and demographics. Also, apply negative scoring for form answers or actions that designate a Lead as a poor fit, for example, competitor company, low budget, or noncompany email address.

- Transfer and assign Lead to the sales team (Pardot forms): For Pardot forms, set up completion actions that directly assign a Lead with a task to specific individuals within each service line or business unit. Additionally, set up email notifications to them as well as to stakeholders deemed necessary to receive these. Once a task is assigned, they can reassign the Lead/contact to the respective Lead owner for follow-up. Setting forms up this way in lieu of a queue eliminates two potential problems:

  - If a new Lead comes in via a form, it will not transfer over to Salesforce without a Lead owner.

  - If these are in a queue, there is a chance they are not followed up promptly. Assigning a task creates a sense of urgency vs. using a queue.

- Utilize Salesforce campaigns in conjunction with Pardot forms: Set up completion actions to add these Leads/contacts to their respective campaigns once a form is completed to track responses.

Lead Assignment Rules

Lead assignment rules enable an organization to automatically assign Leads to users or queues based on the criteria you define (as shown in Figure 2-14). You can create multiple rules with different conditions, but only one rule can be active at a time.

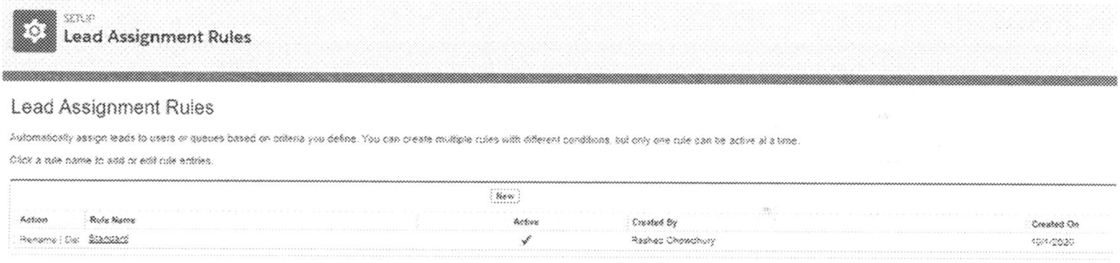

Figure 2-14. *Lead Assignment Rules in Salesforce*

You can add rule entries that specify the criteria used to route your Leads (as shown in Figure 2-15). You can reorder rule entries on this page after you create them.

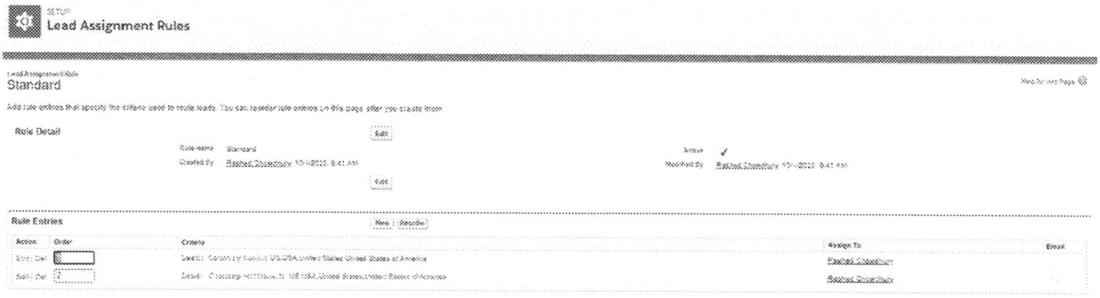

Figure 2-15. *List of Lead assignment rules that automatically route Leads based on predefined criteria in Salesforce*

In this example, our first entries are set as Lead: Country EQUALS US, USA, United States, United States of America) AND (Lead: City CONTAINS St. Cloud); the system will automatically assign the Lead to Rashed Chowdhury if the condition becomes true. The order in Lead Assignment Rules determines which rules to execute first.

Lead Settings

To specify the default Lead behavior for your organization, you have to configure the Lead Settings, found in the standard setup with administrator privilege, as shown in Figure 2-16.

The default Lead owner typically gets set automatically to the default administrator. In a smaller organization, the default Lead owner could be a person; however, creating a queue owned by a group of people (sales operation team) is a good idea so that multiple people can monitor the Leads.

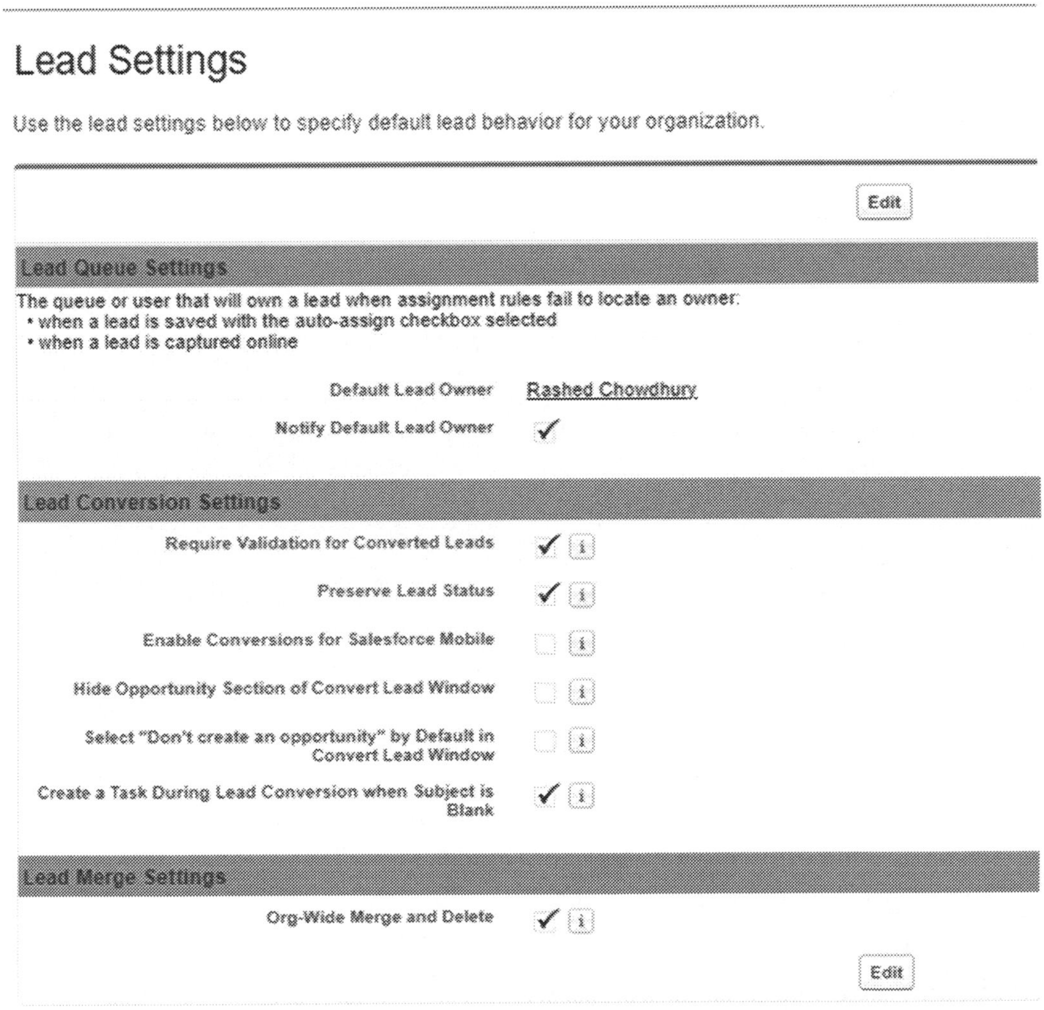

Lead Settings

Use the lead settings below to specify default lead behavior for your organization.

[Edit]

Lead Queue Settings

The queue or user that will own a lead when assignment rules fail to locate an owner:
 • when a lead is saved with the auto-assign checkbox selected
 • when a lead is captured online

Default Lead Owner   Rashed Chowdhury
Notify Default Lead Owner   ✓

Lead Conversion Settings

Require Validation for Converted Leads   ✓ [i]
Preserve Lead Status   ✓ [i]
Enable Conversions for Salesforce Mobile   ☐ [i]
Hide Opportunity Section of Convert Lead Window   ☐ [i]
Select "Don't create an opportunity" by Default in Convert Lead Window   ☐ [i]
Create a Task During Lead Conversion when Subject is Blank   ✓ [i]

Lead Merge Settings

Org-Wide Merge and Delete   ✓ [i]

[Edit]

Figure 2-16. *Lead settings to define the default behavior for an organization in Salesforce*

Require Validation for Converted Leads should be set as checked because when users convert Leads, the system enforces required field settings, field validation rules, workflow actions, and Apex triggers.

Also, Preserve Lead Status should be set as checked because it prevents the Lead status from changing to the new Lead owner's default value during Lead conversion.

Enable Conversions for Salesforce Mobile shouldn't be checked since most organizations don't convert Leads on the mobile app.

Don't create an opportunity upon conversion option is not checked by default under the Convert Lead screen's Opportunity section. However, it would be best to consider turning this option because we want the Lead conversion process to create an opportunity record automatically.

If you are a sales rep and member of a queue in Salesforce, you can access the queue in the list view drop-down list located on the Leads homepage. You can accept the ownership of a Lead from the queue list page, which looks just like the regular list page.

Web to Lead

Using preexisting web pages on your company's website, you can capture contact and user profile information from users and automatically generate new Leads in Salesforce, enabling you to respond in real time to customer requests, as shown in Figure 2-17.

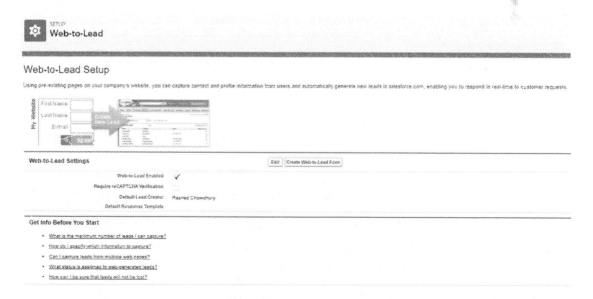

Figure 2-17. *Web-to-Lead setup screen in Salesforce*

The Web-to-Lead setup in Salesforce is straightforward. Once enabled, Salesforce will automatically create the web form and generate the HTML code which your webmaster could easily set up a page on your website to capture new Leads, as shown in Figure 2-18.

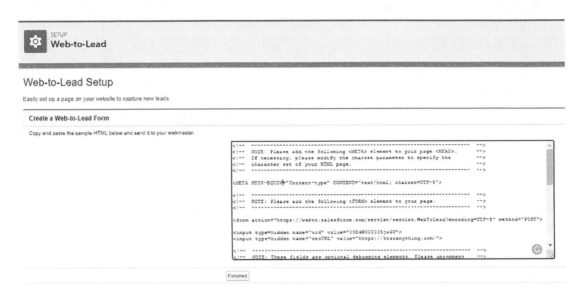

Figure 2-18. *Web-to-Lead code generated automatically from Salesforce to be inserted in the company website*

The following is the Web-to-Lead HTML code for reference:

```
<!--  ----------------------------------------------------------------  -->
<!--  NOTE: Please add the following <META> element to your page <HEAD>.-->
<!--  If necessary, please modify the charset parameter to specify the  -->
<!--  character set of your HTML page.                                  -->
<!--  ----------------------------------------------------------------  -->

<META HTTP-EQUIV="Content-type" CONTENT="text/html; charset=UTF-8">

<!--  ----------------------------------------------------------------  -->
<!--  NOTE: Please add the following <FORM> element to your page.       -->
<!--  ----------------------------------------------------------------  -->

<form action="https://webto.salesforce.com/servlet/servlet.
WebToLead?encoding=UTF-8" method="POST">

<input type=hidden name="oid" value="00D4W000005jw9V">
<input type=hidden name="retURL" value="https://tracanything.com/">
```

```
<!-- ---------------------------------------------------------------- -->
<!-- NOTE: These fields are optional debugging elements. Please uncomment-->
<!-- these lines if you wish to test in debug mode.                    -->
<!-- <input type="hidden" name="debug" value=1>                        -->
<!-- <input type="hidden" name="debugEmail" value="rashed@saleshub.info">-->
<!-- ---------------------------------------------------------------- -->

<label for="first_name">First Name</label><input  id="first_name"
maxlength="40" name="first_name" size="20" type="text" /><br>

<label for="last_name">Last Name</label><input  id="last_name"
maxlength="80" name="last_name" size="20" type="text" /><br>

<label for="email">Email</label><input  id="email" maxlength="80"
name="email" size="20" type="text" /><br>

<label for="company">Company</label><input  id="company" maxlength="40"
name="company" size="20" type="text" /><br>

<label for="city">City</label><input  id="city" maxlength="40" name="city"
size="20" type="text" /><br>

<label for="state">State/Province</label><input  id="state" maxlength="20"
name="state" size="20" type="text" /><br>

<label for="phone">Phone</label><input  id="phone" maxlength="40"
name="phone" size="20" type="text" /><br>

<input type="submit" name="submit">

</form>
```

Social Account and Contact Settings

Enable and configure Social Accounts, Contacts, and Leads so your users can see social profiles for their accounts, contacts, and Leads – directly in Salesforce, as shown in Figure 2-19. You can also choose to turn on the social network like Twitter and YouTube in your org for users to access Twitter feeds and view customer's social data.

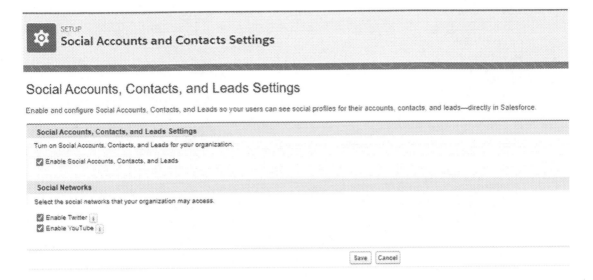

Figure 2-19. *Social account and contact settings enable social profile directly within Salesforce*

This is another specific setting. Once social networks for Twitter are enabled, Salesforce would allow Twitter feeds so users can see their accounts', contacts', and Leads' bios and tweets. In Salesforce Lightning Experience, users can access Twitter only, even if other networks are selected.

Same with YouTube social network setting. Salesforce would allow YouTube feeds so users can see videos related to their accounts, contacts, and Leads. YouTube is available in Salesforce Classic Experience only.

Contact Overview

A contact is a person with whom you do business. Contacts are a critical element of Salesforce. Salesforce allows you to track relationships between contacts and capture the necessary personal drivers of each contact, which is key to your selling success. Always create contacts from within an account. In Salesforce, an organization uses contacts to store information about the people they do business with. Contacts are not independent entities instead of an account, and you can contact other records like opportunities, tasks, events, or email. When you add hierarchy information, link contacts to multiple accounts within the org, you can unleash the contact feature's full potential.

Specific contact information:

- Name: Full name of the contact

- Position title: Contact's title at the company

- Mailing address: Company address (generally)

- Phone: Number at which the contact can be reached

- Fax: Fax number

- Mobile: Cellphone number

- Department: Area in which the contact works

- Account name: Company for which the contact works (Lookup field)

- Reports to: Contact's manager

- Assistant: Assistant's name (if possible)

- Asst. phone: Assistant's telephone number at which to be reached

- Lead/referral source: From where the contact came

- Address/phone/email validation

- Inactive: If checked, the contact is NOT active

- Gender: Male/female

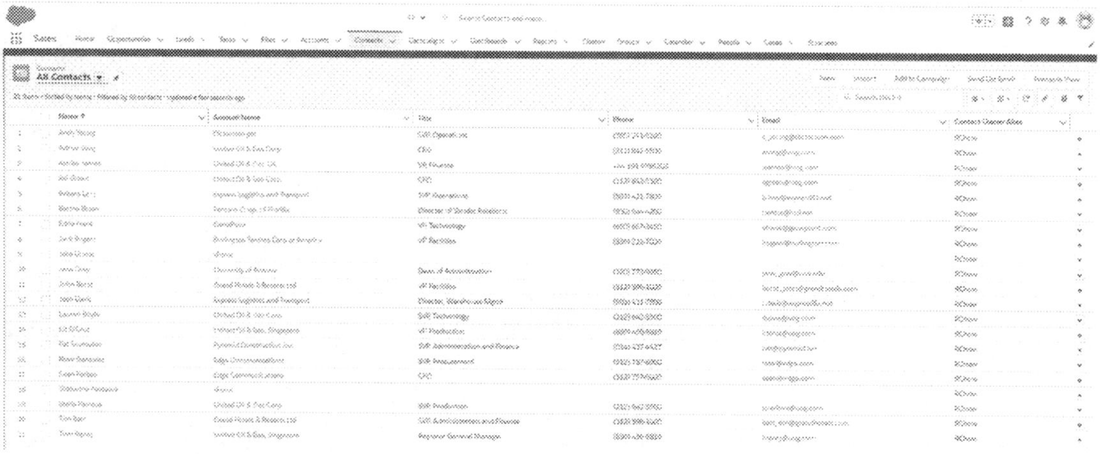

Figure 2-20. *List of contacts in Contacts object home screen in Salesforce*

Salesforce contact database (see Figure 2-20) helps in managing contacts comprehensively by enabling you to create new contacts for accounts (See Figure 2-22), updating their contact information (see Figure 2-21), scheduling meetings, and sending training and event invitations. It also provides facilities like sending email, logging calls, maintaining notes, and sending requests to update contact details. Another critical concept to understand is the contact role in Salesforce. Contact roles specify each Contact's responsibility in an account, case, contract, or opportunity. When you use contact roles in your Salesforce org, your team always knows who to contact and when. The typical contact role consists of Decision Maker. Economic Buyer, Evaluator, Executive Sponsor, Influencer, Technical Buyer, and User Buyer. These are familiar roles used in Sales Methodokloguy platforms such as Miller Heiman.

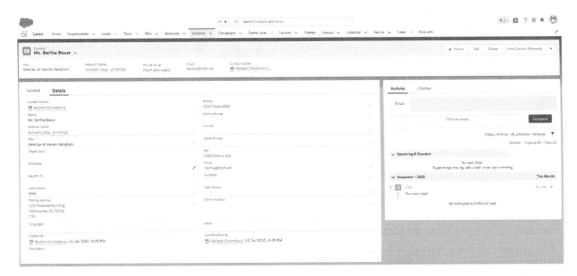

Figure 2-21. *Record details of a contact in Salesforce*

Figure 2-22. *Contact hierarchy in Salesforce*

Contact Organization

Whether you are selling for a long time or just staring out, you probably have a big list of contacts. Where do you keep all the information about your contacts, business details, and professional and personal interactions over the year? A diary, scrap paper, or personal notebook may work for a few weeks, but if you want to plan, manage, and intelligently capture future interaction and be able to excel in your selling game, the Salesforce contact database can be a great solution where you can store all of your contact data in a secured, centralized cloud-hosted system. Not to mention being able to link your account and opportunity data with your contact record will help close more deals and improve the overall view of your business performance.

Summary

In this chapter, we reviewed Leads, the Lead process, and how to qualify the Lead and convert them to create an account, contact, and opportunity from Salesforce's point of view. We also covered what action to take during each stage of the prospect journey in the Lead object. In the next chapter, we will discuss the concept of opportunity, opportunity pipeline management, sales stages, and entry and exit criteria of the opportunity stages.

CHAPTER 3

Opportunity

In the previous chapter, we had an overview of Leads, the Lead process, how to convert them to create an account, contact, and opportunity. We also covered Lead stages, how to qualify a Lead, and what action to take during each Lead stage. The following topics will be covered in this chapter:

- Opportunity definition

- Building an opportunity pipeline

- Sales stages

- Sales stage example

- Challenges and trends

- Leverage technology

What Is an Opportunity?

Within Salesforce, an Opportunity is an object representing a business transaction (or potential transaction). It is a business deal that is in progress. An Opportunity is automatically created when a Lead is converted to an Account. It has fields for data such as a closing date, projected revenue, or competitors.

Salesforce comes standard with two different types of Opportunities. These types, which are fields a user can set for each Opportunity, are new business and existing business.

A new business is an opportunity (See Figure 3-1) for a company with which you have not yet done business. An existing business is one with which you have already done business, but you are selling them something different this time. Setting an opportunity's type is useful to categorize opportunities and see how much business is done with new clients vs. existing ones.

© Rashed A. Chowdhury 2021
R. A. Chowdhury, *Building a Salesforce-Powered Front Office*, https://doi.org/10.1007/978-1-4842-6676-2_3

Salesforce is an increasingly important tool for companies around the globe for both recording and managing the sales activity. As a segment or business unit within the corporation, you will be increasingly asked to provide both qualitative and quantitative updates on the sales activity.

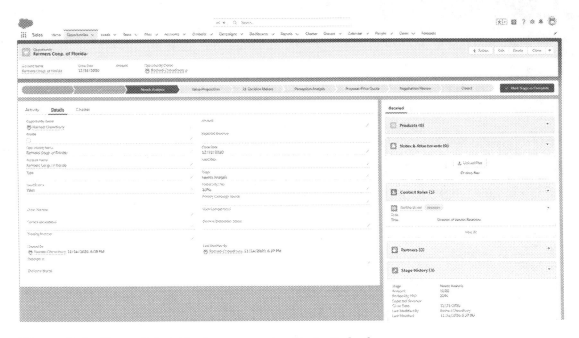

Figure 3-1. *Record detail of an opportunity in Salesforce*

Custom types can also be created by the user, which is useful for categorizing opportunities according to a company's needs. Once a type is designed, it will show up in the picklist for the type field of an opportunity. Being able to tailor Salesforce to fit your company with all the features you need to run your business is one of its major strengths.

An Opportunity object is a management aid to nurture and align accounts. Opportunities are tracked in detail in stages. This module helps manage the funnel effectively as well as manage all related tasks and activities for an opportunity, making this an effective single window for opportunity management. A 360-degree view of the opportunity is maintained as the application provides for maintaining all relevant information including products and competitive threats. You navigate the opportunity page to browse and update existing opportunities as well as create new ones.

Standard Opportunity Record

A collection of fields that make up the data on your business deal is an opportunity record in Salesforce. Details and related are the two main areas of opportunity. Details hold the opportunity summary data, and related contains all the details level related opportunity data. The key goal of this object is to manage a potential business deal and keep track of all the transaction level details. Typically, Salesforce loaded these standard fields in an opportunity record. Here are the standard fields in an opportunity object:

- Account name: The name of the account is the legal name of the entity. The account name is the entity that is paying the invoice to you.

- Close date: The close date is when the negotiation of a new opportunity is expected to be finalized or an existing business opportunity to be renewed. The date the opportunity is expected to close or the actual date the business was closed.

- Amount: The value of the opportunity over some time (12 months, 24 months, etc.). This is calculated based on the product information related to this opportunity.

- Opportunity owner: The person who owns the opportunity within the selling organization is the opportunity owner.

- Opportunity name: Describe the products or services you are selling in this opportunity. Following a naming convention is a good practice, especially if you have a large organization. The name of the account concatenated with the product or service name and annual term tied to it could become a naming convention, Account name + Product/Service + Annual period (yy-yy).

- Stage: The Opportunity Stages are the typical categorization of how an Opportunity – New, Enhanced, and Existing – moves from potential business through closing. A sales stage is one of a series of measurable steps in the sales process – the status of the opportunity in the selling cycle.

- Type: The Opportunity type can be New or Enhanced business (new revenue), Renewal or Existing business (recurring revenue), or Marketed Renewal (at recurring risk revenue).

- Probability: Your best estimate of the company successfully closing this sale. The percentage is automatically entered when you select the stage, but you can override the percentage. Use the following to help you estimate:

  - 20%: Long shot.

  - 50%: One in two possibilities.

  - 75%: One in two possibilities with positive buy signals.

  - 90%: Vendor choice through verbal commitment.

  - Update this percentage as the selling cycle progresses.

We are often asked to provide information to senior management on our sales activity. Through the effective use of the opportunity description field, we can minimize the need to cascade unnecessary questions. Every opportunity description should contain

- A brief description of the specifics of what the opportunity is and the stakeholders involved (imagine you were being asked to explain what the opportunity is) – a couple of lines is sufficient.

- A brief explanation of how you have calculated the opportunity value should be part of the opportunity description.

Adding Product to Opportunity

You may have to add products (See Figure 3-2) as your opportunity advances toward the proposal stage. Attaching notes, contract information, and customer meeting recap not only helps keep the customer informed but the members of the selling team as well.

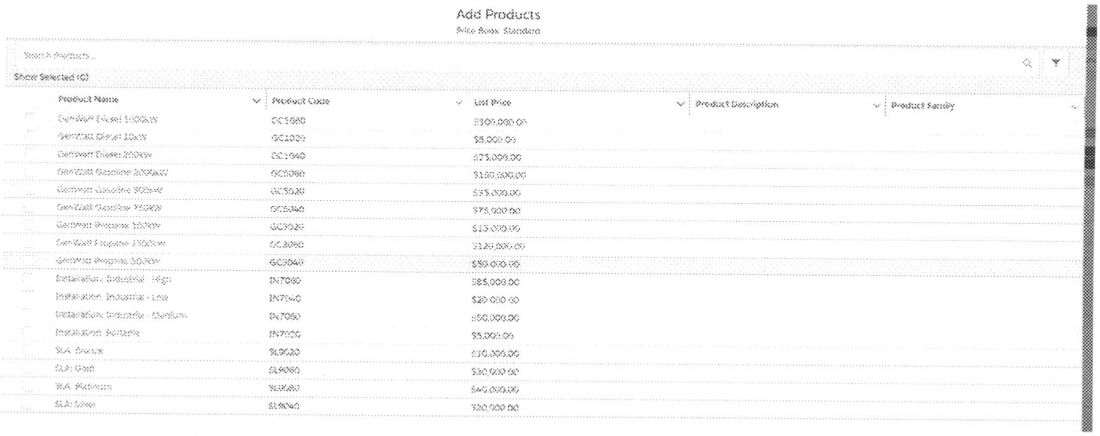

Figure 3-2. *Add products to an opportunity*

Once you select the product (See Figure 3-3) from the product list, you will immediately be presented with a product selection guided screen to populate quantity, sales price, date, and so on. The cost from the product will automatically update the opportunity amount and expected revenue.

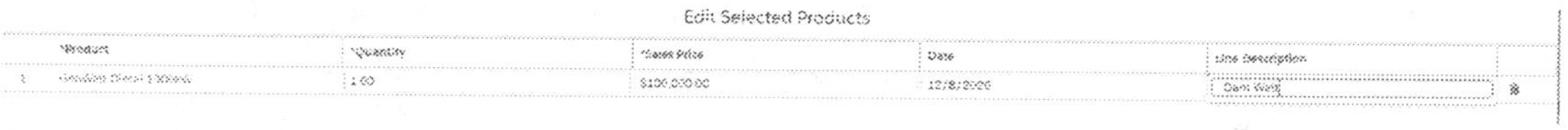

Figure 3-3. *Editing selected products*

Once the product is added (See Figure 3-4) to the opportunity record, the amount and expected revenue fields get populated directly from the price of the product in the price book.

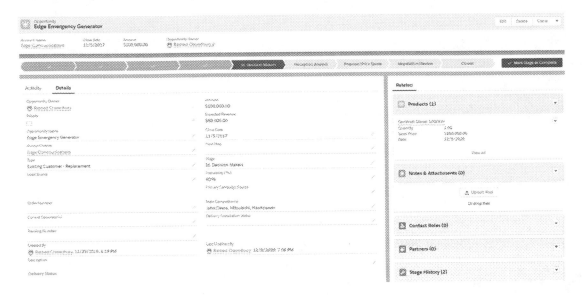

Figure 3-4. *Opportunity details with newly added product*

From the best practices and user adoption perspective, you want to make sure not to bog down the system with too many custom fields and complex opportunity management process because you will have to make sure that the users are using Salesforce and not make it overly complicated.

Creating a New Opportunity

Whenever you receive a genuine sales opportunity, of any value, from an existing client/prospect (should originate from the Lead journey), you should create an opportunity as shown in Figure 3-5. Any existing managed business which is not currently entered into Salesforce should also be added to Salesforce.

Who	Account Name	Client or service receiver
What	Description	Product or service
How much	Opportunity Amount	Value of the sales
When	Close Date	When the deal will be final

Figure 3-5. *Minimum data point of an opportunity*

An opportunity should be created for each transaction, which is the result of a single decision from the client. This concept applies to both new businesses that you are attempting to secure and account for the incumbent. Let's take an insurance claim management company as an example:

- If a client is seeking to appoint both liability and property loss adjusters and you know that the client will be awarded the combined business, you will be awarded either both lines of business or neither, and you should create one opportunity.

- If a client is seeking to appoint both liability and property loss adjusters but will be making their decision on each line of business, you may win the property but not the liability, then each line of business should be treated as a separate opportunity. This is also the case for where you are creating renewal business opportunities.

Opportunity Organization

Now, let's discuss the opportunity organization.

Calculating an Annual Opportunity Amount

The annual opportunity amount should always represent what you can reasonably expect to receive in revenue from the sale in the 12 months following the business being fully implemented. Here are a few guidelines to consider for a service organization:

- The amount should always be entered into Salesforce in US dollars.

- This figure should not be calculated on the amount of revenue expected between the close date and the end of the financial/calendar year. This figure should exclude applicable local taxes.

- It is recognized that there are "ramp-up periods" when setting up accounts. The annual opportunity should be based on 12 months of revenue once the program is fully implemented.

- The annual opportunity amount should be reviewed regularly when the opportunity is in the pipeline and when it is won or a renewal opportunity to ensure it reflects reality as closely as possible.

Types of Opportunity

When creating an opportunity in Salesforce, the user is asked to select the type of opportunity that the sale is. Salesforce has five kinds of opportunities, which are divided into two general groups:

- New customer
  - New business: This should be selected when the opportunity is for a completely new client which you do not do any business with or a new line of business for an existing client (cross-selling).
- Existing customer
  - Upgrade: This field is equivalent to upsell and should be selected for a client you already do business with where you are:
    - We are increasing product volumes.
    - We are adding additional territories to programs.
  - Replacement
  - Downgrade

Stale Opportunity

An opportunity is stale once its close date is in the past. Stagnant opportunities are corrected by amending the opportunity with a close date, which is in the future, or amending the close date to today and closing of the opportunity as either won or lost.

- Any new business opportunity which is stale by more than 30 days should not be included in your new business pipeline at a global level.

- Stale renewal business opportunities should be included in your reporting.

Building a Business Pipeline

Sales Pipeline should represent all open opportunities, both new and renewal, where you are yet to receive a yes/no decision from the prospect/client.

When a new/enhanced business opportunity enters the business, the first action should be to create an opportunity in Salesforce to reflect it. Once an opportunity has been entered into Salesforce, the system will automatically include it in the relevant pipeline.

Once an opportunity, either new or renewal, has been closed as won, the user should click the "Renew Opportunity" button at the top of the opportunity page. This will create a renewal opportunity for the same date the following year, which will appear in our pipeline reports. If an opportunity is lost, it should not be renewed.

- The user should ensure that the percentage probability of the opportunity renewing in the following year is reviewed once the opportunity has been renewed.

- Where you enter into a multiyear contract, the user should ensure that ONLY the next open year of the contract is in the pipeline, not all years in the contract. This is because there is still a chance that you could lose the business over the term of the contract.

- Where an enhanced business win is the upsell of existing product lines, you should merge the revenue of the improved business win into a renewal opportunity for the renewal.

- For example, if we win the enhanced business of an extra $1m on an existing account, it should be recorded as an enhanced business win. Instead of renewing this once it is won, you should add the additional revenue from the enhanced win to the renewal opportunity for the existing renewal opportunity.

- Year 1: Renewal business for RSA subsidence = $3m and enhanced RSA subsidence win = $1m

- Year 2: Renewal business for RSA subsidence = $4m

Opportunity Qualification Questionnaire

The following questions should be asked:

- Is the key to buying influencers in growth or trouble mode?

- Are there proven coaches?

- Do we have a clearly defined economic buyer and know the mode?

- Can we keep ourselves out of vendor jail?

- Is the financial framework acceptable to us?

- Is the revenue potential worth the effort?

- Does the opportunity fit?

- Does the opportunity have a transparent process and time scale?

- Is there an opportunity to increase revenue through the provision of additional services?

- Does our solution align with the client/prospect strategic plan?

Building an Opportunity Pipeline

An opportunity pipeline (See Figure 3-6) represents open opportunities, including new and renewal businesses. An open opportunity is one where a yes or no decision has not yet been made by the prospect or client. An opportunity pipeline can be measured by the financial year and gross. When measured by the financial year, all opportunities are grouped by close date for a specified year. When calculating by gross, all open opportunities are included.

When a new opportunity has been created, it should immediately be entered into Salesforce. If it isn't in Salesforce, it didn't happen. After the opportunity has been entered, Salesforce will automatically include it in the relevant pipeline.

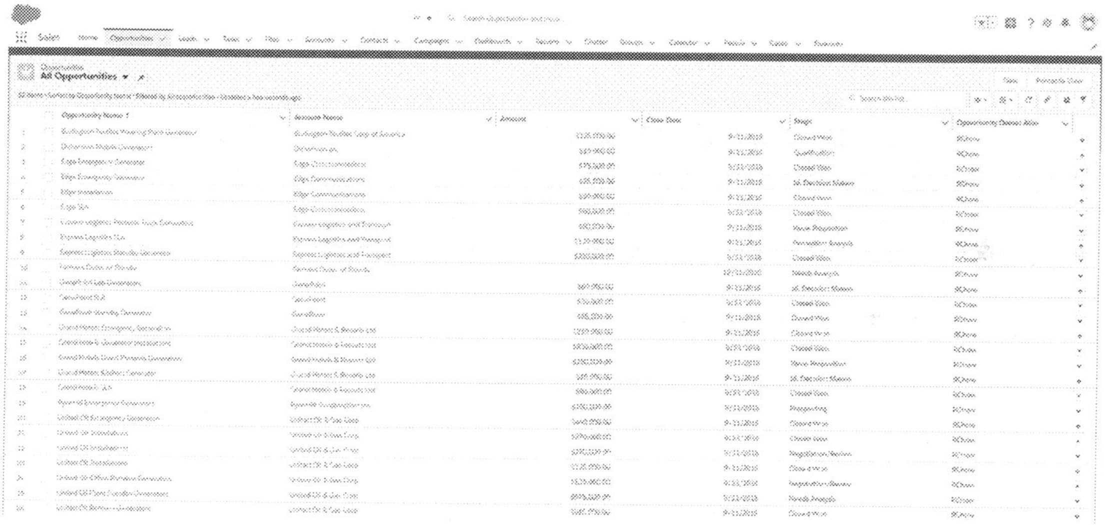

Figure 3-6. *List of opportunities in opportunity object home screen*

When a renewed business opportunity has been won, it should be entered as a Renew Opportunity at the top of the opportunity's page. This creates a renewal opportunity for the same date but for the following year and will appear in pipeline reports. If an opportunity has been lost, the user should not renew it in Salesforce.

Sales Stages

As an opportunity progresses through the sales pipeline, it will go through several sales stages. Some typical primary stages you may find in Salesforce are Prospecting, Qualification, Need Analysis, Value Proposition, ID Decision Makes, Perception Analysis, Proposal Price/Quote, Negotiation, Closing, Closed Won, and Closed Lost.

Each of these sales stages generates an automatic sales success probability percent, and this can be manually edited to reflect reality. This probability reflects the confidence we have that we will win the opportunity.

- The % probability is multiplied by the annual opportunity amount to calculate the expected revenue. For example, $100,000 at 10% would have an expected revenue of $10,000. Through utilizing this across all of our opportunities, we can use the balance of probabilities to gain an understanding of the dollar value of what we can expect to win.

- Globally, typical pipeline reports both on the annual opportunity amount and on the expected revenue. For example, if there are ten opportunities with a yearly opportunity amount of $100,000 and all have a 10% probability, then the company's annual opportunity pipeline will show as $1,000,000 with an expected revenue of $100,000.

- It is paramount that users regularly, at least once per month, review the sales stage of their opportunities and % confidence rating of their opportunities and amend so that our reporting is as accurate as possible. For example, create a task with a due date and follow up. Call the prospect and log the call. Create an event (meeting) with the prospect and capture the meeting itself and the outcome, and create a follow-up task, including notes and attachments.

In the Prospecting stage, your business is still reaching out to the potential customer for the first time, done in hopes of establishing a relationship and eventually creating a sale. It is usually the first step in the sales pipeline.

The Developing stage comes directly after Prospecting. After you have first contacted a prospect, you continue to communicate with them and get closer to a sale. Hopefully, this stage will lead to the Negotiation stage, where your business and the prospect negotiate on the price for the products/services rendered.

The final two stages are Closed Won and Closed Lost. A sale would be Closed Won if the sale were successful following negotiations. If it was not successful and business between your company and the prospect will not be happening, the sale is Closed Lost.

Each of these stages is assigned probabilities in Salesforce. The stages specifically used and their probabilities are up to the salesperson and can be custom created and assigned. The probability represents the likelihood that the opportunity will end up as a sale by the end of the sales pipeline. It generally trends upward throughout the stages, with an opportunity in the Prospecting stage having the lowest probability, while an opportunity in the Negotiating stage is having the highest probability of becoming a closed sale.

Users should ensure they keep Salesforce up to date with the latest information on opportunities. They should be created where necessary and kept current on what stage they are in and other information relevant to the sale. This is important to ensure accurate reporting within Salesforce.

Sales Stage Example with Exit Criteria

Table 3-1 represents an example set of sales stages. There are a few different stages than the basic ones described earlier. This table shows a sample set of probabilities for each stage and shows how a sale is more likely the deeper into the sales pipeline a prospect move.

Table 3-1. Entry and exit criteria in opportunity stages

Stage	Probability (%)	Entrance Criteria	Exit Criteria	Who's Involved?
Target/ Prospect	10%	• Converted lead	• First meeting held • Presented product	Sales Pre-sales
Qualify	20%	• First meeting held • List of requirements generated	• Reviewed requirements with the prospect • Identified decision-makers at the prospect • Identified how to meet requirements • Entered in the estimated amount • Entered in an estimated close date	Sales Pre-sales

(*continued*)

Table 3-1. (*continued*)

Stage	Probability (%)	Entrance Criteria	Exit Criteria	Who's Involved?
Requirements	40%	• Requirements and solution determined	• Three proposals are created • Proposals are approved by Ops • Manager (VP 20% discount) • The updated amount and close date • Scheduled meeting to review the proposal with decision-makers	Sales Pre-sales Sales Ops Sales Manager Sales VP
Presentation	60%	• Scheduled meeting	• Presented all three options • Prospect verbally commits to a deal or signs a letter of intent	Sales Pre-sales
Acquisition	80%	• Prospect agrees to the proposal	• The contract is drawn up (by legal if nonstandard) • Prospect signed contract • Prospect issues PO	Legal Sales Ops Sales
Closing	90%	• PO is approved	• PO is set up for invoicing • Product is shipped	Sales Ops
Closed Won	100%	• Product is shipped		Sales Ops
Closed Lost	0%	• Prospect ends sales cycle		Sales Ops Pre-sales Consultants

The entrance criteria for a given stage are specific events that have occurred for a prospect to be considered as a part of that stage. The exit criteria are the last events that must occur for the prospect to move onto the next stage. Oftentimes, you will see the exit criteria are the entrance criteria for the following stage.

In the table, the Developing stage is instead referred to as Qualify. This is where you qualify the Lead and start to dig deeper into their business needs. Negotiation is split among multiple stages here to Requirements, Presentation, and Acquisition (See Figure 3-7). From Requirements to Acquisition, the Lead is moving further into negotiations. First is creating proposals, followed by presenting them and finally making the contract.

Figure 3-7. Opportunity stages

Closed Won and Closed Lost are also given one additional stage here – Closing. The closing comes right before Closed Won. The prospect has already signed the contract, and the order has been approved, but sometimes things may come up, and the contract does not always progress to Closed Won. Closed Won is when the product has been shipped, and the sale has been 100% made. The Closed Lost stage may occur at any stage, simply when the prospect has ended the sales cycle and has no interest in continuing.

Summary

In this chapter, we discussed the concept of opportunity, opportunity pipeline management, sales stages, entry criteria, and exit criteria of the opportunity stages. We also covered the definition of opportunity from Salesforce's perspective, building an opportunity pipeline, what to do during sales stages, examples of sales stages, challenges and trends of modern sales, and how to leverage technology to address them. In the next chapter, we will review what the definition of the customer is, how Salesforce defines account, personal account, and consideration for measuring customer satisfaction survey.

CHAPTER 4

Accounts

In the previous chapter, we had an overview of the opportunity, opportunity stages, sample sales stages, and how to build an opportunity pipeline. We also reviewed the definition of opportunity from Salesforce's perspective, what to do during sales stages, challenges and trends of modern sales, and how to leverage technology to address them. The following topics will be covered in this chapter:

- Account object

- Person account

- Account settings

- Account team

- Account data organization

What Is the Account Object?

The Account Object in Salesforce is used to track and store information about the customers with whom you do business. This includes entities such as companies, schools, government agencies, or even individuals. List View is an excellent tool in the Salesforce platform where you can quickly view your data segment using predefined criteria and data conditions. You can use listview to any standard Salesforce object, including Accounts, Opportunities, Leads, and Cases, to find the data points you're looking for. For example, the all accounts list view (See Figure 4-1) in Account Home would enable you to list all accounts in your database.

© Rashed A. Chowdhury 2021
R. A. Chowdhury, *Building a Salesforce-Powered Front Office*, https://doi.org/10.1007/978-1-4842-6676-2_4

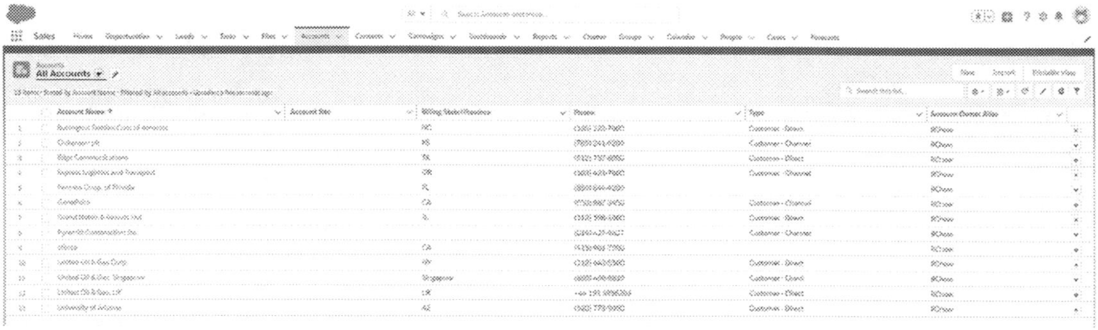

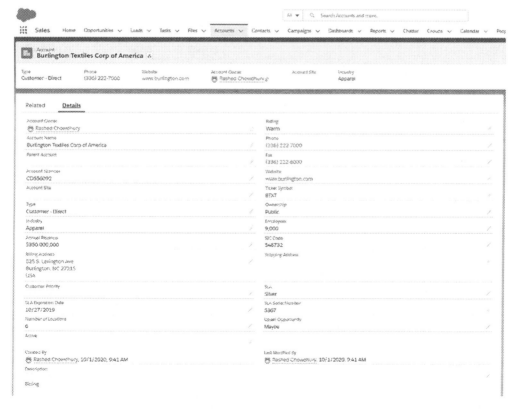

Figure 4-1. *All accounts list view in Account Home*

An account (See Figure 4-2) is like a folder where all of your customer's information is stored. An account has fields such as the company's name, its location, a contact person for that company, and orders. Logs may also be kept of phone calls with the account or service requests. This is a shortlist of the fields included standard with Salesforce. Custom fields may be made as well.

Figure 4-2. *Account details of a given account record*

Adding New Accounts

Within Salesforce, information about a company is stored as an Account Record. This includes information such as its name, location, website, and so on. Reports including contact person, notes, and orders are stored in other types of records instead. Salesforce makes it easy to find all of an account's related records (See Figure 4-3) through the Account Record's homepage. Here, related records will be listed out. You can also locate, create, delete, sort, and filter accounts from the Accounts tab. Once you've selected an account, you can view its record homepage, edit it, and access other related records.

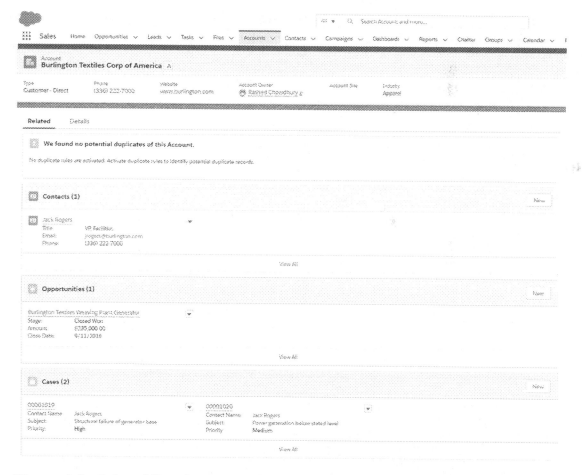

Figure 4-3. *Related list of an account*

Salesforce includes two types of accounts – business accounts and personal accounts. A business account is the default account and is used to store information about companies. Personal accounts are used to store information about individuals.

Account Data Organization and Maintenance

In Salesforce, an Account is a business entity, such as an organization or a company that you work with or negotiate for new business. Accounts are always companies, organizations, or entities, not individuals.

To improve the overall data quality in Salesforce, you can introduce improved processes (See Figure 4-4) and automate them using a nightly job that could validate, standardize, and enrich address, email, and phone records for accounts, contacts, and Leads.

With a tool like Data.com or Informatica Data as a Service (DaaS), you will be able to quickly and easily validate and enrich customer data. Your team will be equipped to confidently connect with customers knowing that you have the most accurate and up-to-date contact and profile data for each customer throughout your Salesforce platform.

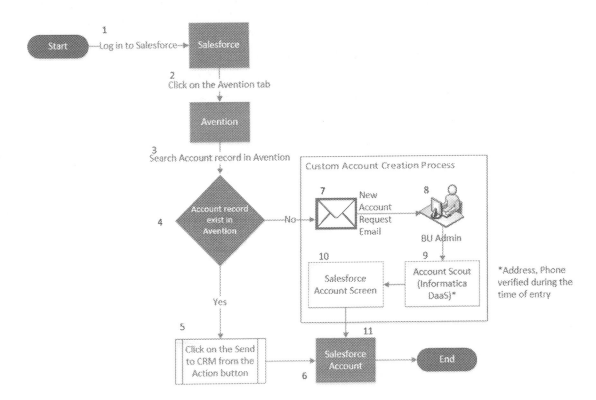

Figure 4-4. *The custom account creation process*

Automated Nightly Verification Job

Every night, data quality (Informatica DaaS, Data.com, etc.) job could run in the background and look for a new account. The nightly job will standardize (convert the mailing address to uppercase, abbreviate St. to Street, complete the mailing address by filling in the blanks, update with the ISO style country code and name), validate (check if the address is valid and registered with the local postal authority: US Postal Service as an example), and make the necessary adjustment to the mailing address and phone.

Another Way to Create or Update Account Data

Informatica's Cloud Customer 360 (CC360) could be installed and integrated into Salesforce so that when a user tries to create a brand-new account from scratch, CC360's account scout (as shown in Figure 4-5) will guide the user entering the account record in Salesforce. When your user starts to type the address, the **type ahead** (Google suggestions of addresses) will suggest a list of fully qualified addresses. Users could pick from the list of proposed addresses or keep typing to enter new address information.

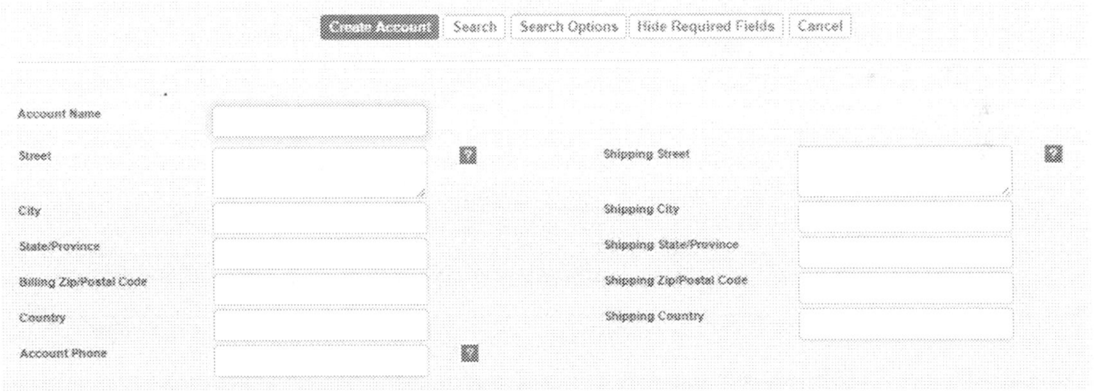

Figure 4-5. *Informatica Cloud Customer 360 – account scout*

The core capability of the Account creation screen will enable address validation in real time, plus the type ahead (Google-like experience during search) will suggest users to pick an address and thus improve data quality before the account even become active in Salesforce. This is one secret source of preventing insufficient data from entering your Salesforce organization.

Once account data is entered (as shown in Figure 4-6), the user will have to press the "?" (click to verify). This will confirm the address and phone data in real time (as shown in Figure 4-7).

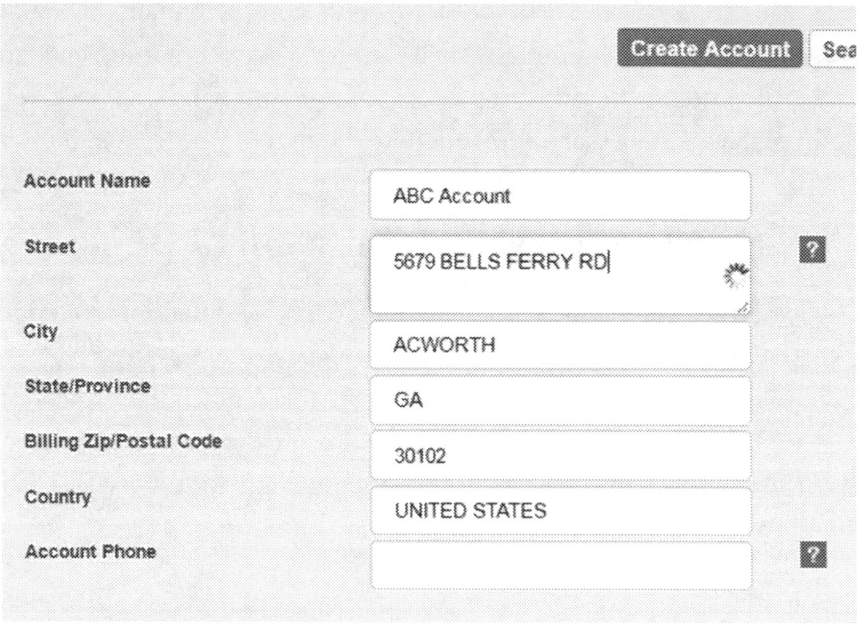

	Create Account Sea
Account Name	ABC Account
Street	5679 BELLS FERRY RD [?]
City	ACWORTH
State/Province	GA
Billing Zip/Postal Code	30102
Country	UNITED STATES
Account Phone	[?]

Figure 4-6. *Account data entered in Informatica Cloud Customer 360*

Account Name	ABC Account
Street	5679 BELLS FERRY RD [✓]
City	ACWORTH
State/Province	GA
Billing Zip/Postal Code	30102-2517
Country	UNITED STATES
Account Phone	678 7614635 [✓]

Figure 4-7. *Account data validated (green checkmark) in Informatica Cloud Customer 360*

The user has to press the Search button before Create Account to make sure no account already exists in Salesforce with the same address that was entered.

If no duplicate account is found, the user will be proceeding with the Account creation process by clicking the **Create Account**. You will be presented with the native Salesforce account screen following the Informatica account scout custom page. Complete entering the required fields (account status, business type, etc.) and other related information. You will be on your way to complete entering your account record. An account will be created in Salesforce with a valid mailing address from the beginning.

If a duplicate account is found, the user will be presented with an error message stating one potential duplicate(s) found, as shown in Figure 4-8.

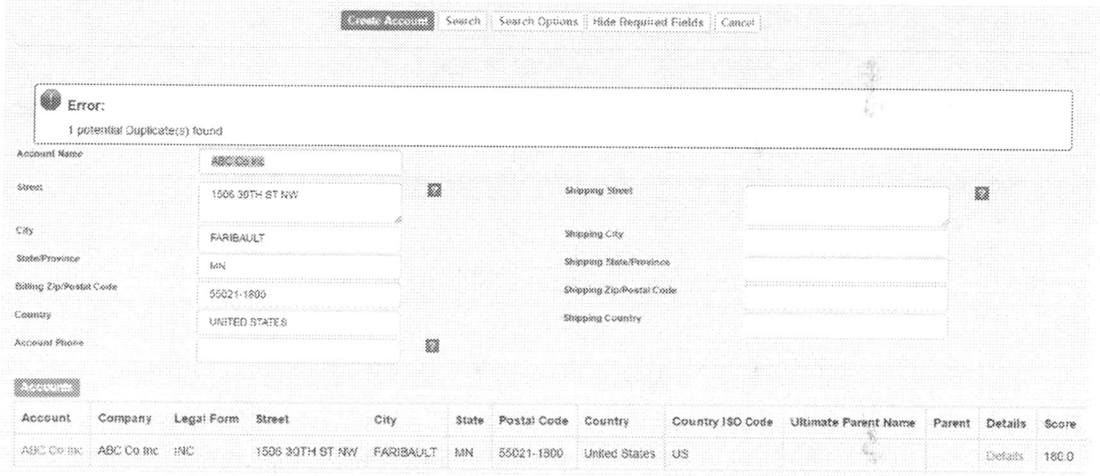

Figure 4-8. *Account data validated (duplicate detected) in Informatica Cloud Customer 360*

The user will have to click the **Detail** link of the result sets, which will bring the View Consolidated Information screen (Figure 4-9).

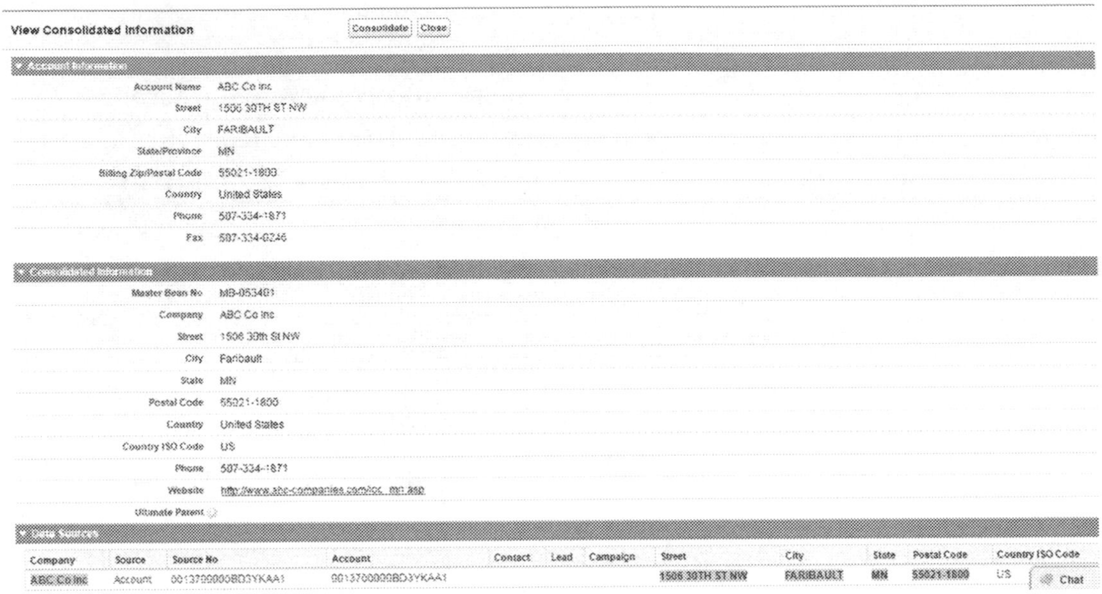

Figure 4-9. *Account data validated (view consolidated) in Informatica Cloud Customer 360*

Finally, the user will have to click the **Consolidate** button to consolidate the accounts.

If you wish not to auto-update the newly created (account record created from D&B Hoovers or manual entry by a user) account address, phone, and email, your administrator user can add a Check (Y/N) custom data field, which could control if the record should be updated automatically or not. This flag could exclude the account from the nightly auto-update procedure.

From my experience, I have seen a lot of organizations move the default account owner (John Doe) to the Account Team as a member and replace the account ownership to a company's (ABC Inc.) name to improve reporting and as part of the account organization effort.

Account Settings

The very first option under general settings of Account Settings (Figure 4-10) in Salesforce is the Show View Hierarchy link on account pages. Go ahead and select this option for your org which will show the user relationships between parent accounts. This account hierarchy (Figure 4-11) relationship is typically the corporate legal hierarchy.

You can always have your Salesforce admin customize hierarchy columns based on your specific data requirements and organization strategy. Data.com, D&B Hoovers, and other companies provide data as a service, and having a service like that ensures continuous data accuracy and a single version of the truth.

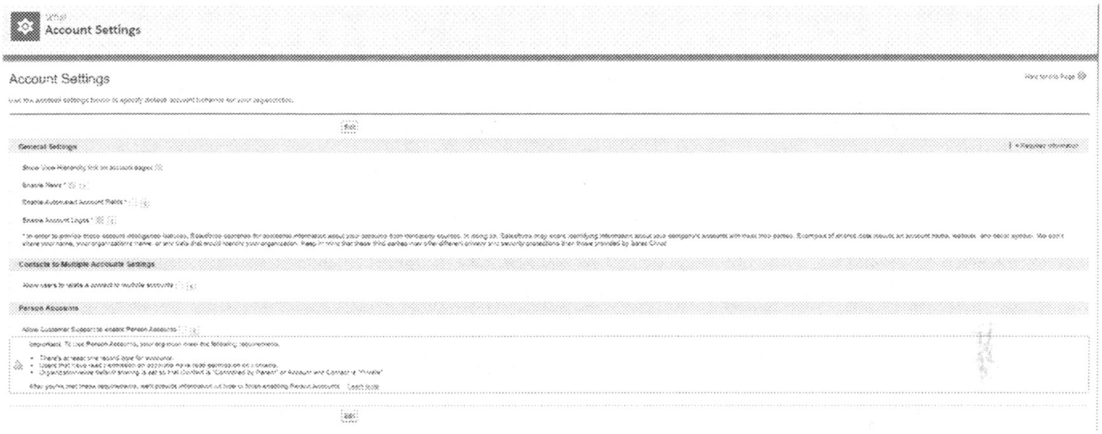

Figure 4-10. Account Settings page in Salesforce

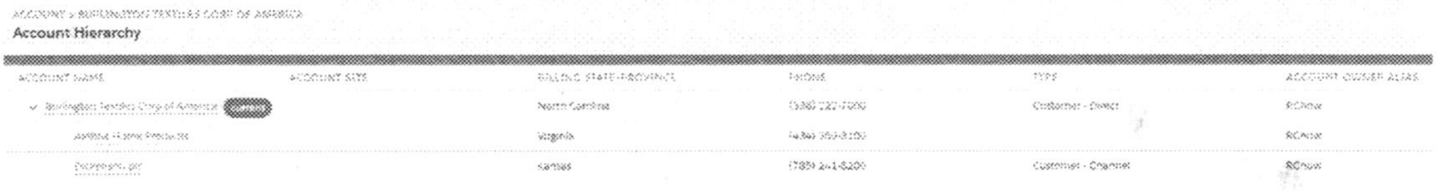

Figure 4-11. Account hierarchy example in Salesforce

Turning on logo for the accounts and enabling automated account fields are the two self-explanatory options that should be checked. You will get a list of US-based companies in the Account Name field as user types. The user can simply select the record and populate the CRM system within the sales prospecting database.

The checked Account Logos option makes the system displays company logos, when available, on US-based accounts. When you turn on these features, Salesforce had to share some of your account data (name, website, stock symbol, etc.) with third-party data aggregator vendor.

There is an option called contacts to multiple accounts under Account Settings, and turning this option on would enable users to relate a contact to multiple accounts.

It is recommended that you adjust your activity settings so that activities (create a task, set up an event, send an email, etc.) don't rack up to the primary account when a contact is allowed to relate to multiple accounts. We should not let users from deleting an account when users delete an account with direct contacts that are having a relationship with other accounts.

Under the person accounts section of the account settings, there is an option called allow Customer Support to enable Person Accounts, consider turning this on if your organization requires to use a person account. Person accounts store information about individual people by combining certain account and contact fields into a single record. Your organization has to meet all the requirements before Salesforce can enable this option.

Your org must meet the following requirements to use the Person Accounts:

- There's at least one record type for accounts.

- Users that have read permission on accounts have read permission on contacts.

- Organization-wide default (OWD) sharing is set so that Contact is "Controlled by Parent" or Account and Contact are "Private."

Once all of these requirements are met, Salesforce will look to enable the person accounts.

Person Account

Salesforce allows you to create an account as a person rather than a business. This lets you store information about an individual consumer. If you're doing business with a particular client instead of a company, "person" accounts are the way to go.

There are differences between a "person" account and a business account. In the most basic terms, a "person" account is essentially a contact in account form. One such difference is that a "person" account cannot have a direct relationship with another account or contact. A person's account will also appear in the contact list view as well as contact searches. Person accounts cannot be in an account hierarchy as well. These are just a few of several other differences between the two types of accounts.

Deleting an Account

If you ever need to delete an account in Salesforce, there are a few things to know. For the most part, it is as easy as pressing Delete from the account's detail page or its row in an account list.

Before deleting an account, you must have a permission to do so. The option will not show up in detail or list view of an account without it. Salesforce administrators may grant this permission. You will also not be able to delete accounts of which you are not the owner unless you are above the account's owner in the organizational hierarchy. If you are an administrator, you can bypass this requirement. You will not be able to delete a partner account if associated records are owned by other users.

Once an account has been deleted, items associated with it are also deleted. All deleted items are placed in Salesforce's Recycle Bin. The system will automatically remove contacts, opportunities, activities, and more alongside the Account object itself. If you choose to restore the account, the system will repair these associated items as well.

As with other record types, accounts can be mass deleted.

Account Team

Accounts sometimes need to have multiple users working with them at once within Salesforce. This is where the Account Team feature comes in. It allows users within an organization to collaborate on a single account. Setting a default team also makes it easy to add regular teams to new accounts as you create them.

For the Account Team to work in Salesforce, you have to enable the Account Teams feature in the account team setup (Figure 4-12). Once the account team is enabled, you have to identify what account page layout (Figure 4-13) you want to introduce these capabilities to. Without exclusively identify, the account team-related list screen won't show up in each page layout.

Figure 4-12. *Account Teams*

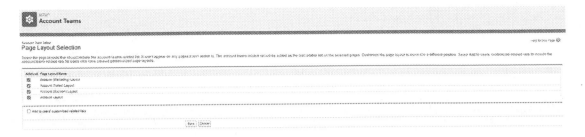

Figure 4-13. *Account Settings page layout*

If you need to move the account team–related list to a different section, you have to consider customizing the page layout. Once the account team page layout setup is completed, you have to finalize the account team role. Salesforce is preloaded with popular team roles like Account Manager, Channel Manager, Executive Sponsor, Lead Qualifier, Pre-sales Consultant, Sales Manager, and Sales Rep (Figure 4-14). You have the option to customize the team role if you have unique requirements.

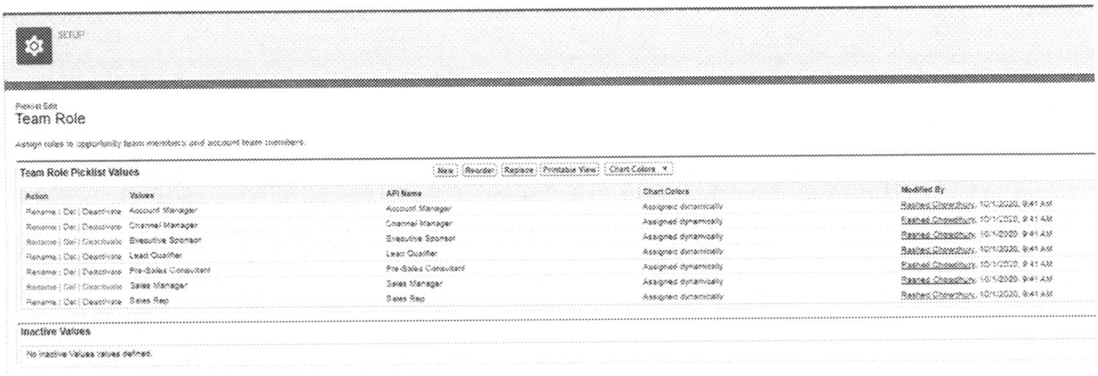

Figure 4-14. *Account Team Role*

Account teams may be used for all accounts in Salesforce. If you own the account, you can assign team members to it. You are also able to give each member varying levels of access to the account and its associated items. For example, the project manager may require full access, while a low-level member of the organization may need read-only access to the account.

Summary

In this chapter, we discussed the concept of the customer, company, account, person account, account team, and how to measure the customer satisfaction survey. In the next chapter, we will review concepts of meeting, email, task, and phone in terms of Salesforce activity.

CHAPTER 5

Activities

In the previous chapter, we discussed the concept of the customer, company, account, person account, account team, and how to streamline account organization processes using technology like Informatica Cloud. In Salesforce, activities are the events and tasks that your users manage. Salesforce enables users to be prepared for any meeting and helps identify the highest priority task at hand. In this chapter, we will be discussing the following topics related to activities:

- Meeting, Email, Tasks, and Phone Calls

- Creating Events

- Tracking Events

- Task

- Creating Tasks

- Tracking and Viewing Tasks

- Repeating Tasks

- Assigning Tasks

- Setting Task Notifications

An activity in Salesforce helps you track and carry out the completion of activities and tasks. It integrates with workflows and approval processes. It provides for the creation and tracking of accounts, contacts, Leads, opportunities, and case-specific tasks and events. There is provision for automated alerts and emails. It integrates with all the different capability areas so that tasks and events are traceable to a single specific business requirement or capability area ensuring end-to-end management from a capability area perspective.

© Rashed A. Chowdhury 2021
R. A. Chowdhury, *Building a Salesforce-Powered Front Office*, https://doi.org/10.1007/978-1-4842-6676-2_5

Activity Settings

Your administrator can choose to keep track of current and past tasks and events of the users in the Open Activities and Activity History related lists or the Activity timeline in Salesforce. Activity Settings (Figure 5-1) is a feature settings page where your admin can modify the following activity settings for the entire organization:

- Enable Group Tasks: This option improves group collaboration and teamwork.

- Roll up activities to a contact's primary account: When an activity is associated to a contact, also display the activity under the primary account for the contact. It is recommended that you don't select this option if you allow users to relate contacts to multiple accounts.

- Enable Creation of Recurring Tasks: This option enables team members to create repeat task and set recurrence start and end date.

- Enable Activity Reminders: This option enables activity reminders for the users before the activity. Users will be able to set 15 mins, 30 mins, 1 hour, 24 hours, and other reminders.

- Enable User Control over Task Assignment Notifications: Enabling this feature lets individual users control whether and how they're notified when someone assigns them a task.

- Enable Email Tracking: This option will let the end users track email that they send from Salesforce.

- Show Event Details on Multi-User Calendar View: When this option is enabled, the mobile app displays a New Task form with key task fields first.

- Add user lists to calendar views in Lightning Experience: Users can add user list views to their calendar instead of adding them one by one. Users with access can create custom list views from the Users Setup menu.

- Allow Users to Relate Multiple Contacts to Tasks and Events: Enabling this feature lets users relate up to 50 contacts to a task or event (except a recurring task or event).

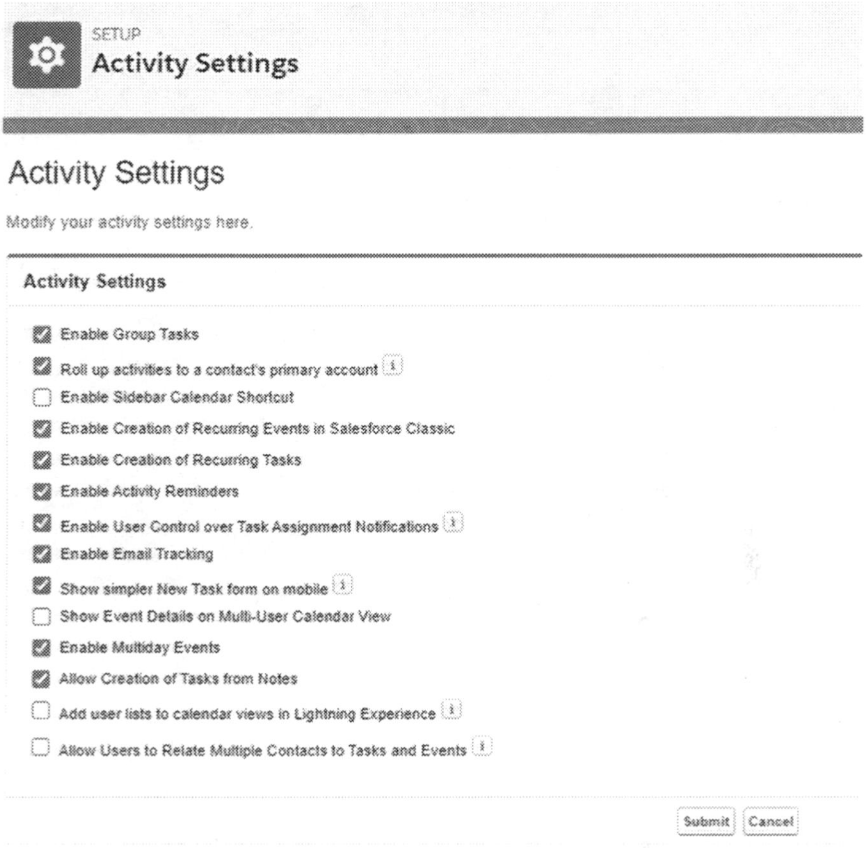

Figure 5-1. *Activity settings in Salesforce*

Record Page Settings

You can choose the way you view activities on record pages (Figure 5-2). There are two ways you can organize and display your activities in Salesforce:

- Related Lists: You can select the Related Lists to show the Open Activities and Activity History related lists as your default activity view. This view shows details for each task, event, and email in the Open Activities and Activity History related lists.

- Activity Timeline: You can select Activity Timeline for a timeline view where you can manage your current and past activities as your default activity view. This view shows details for each task, event, and email in an expandable timeline view.

Related Lists

Select Related Lists to show the Open
Activities and Activity History related
lists.

Activity Timeline

Select Activity Timeline for a timeline
view where you can manage your current
and past activities.

Figure 5-2. *Record Page Settings in Salesforce*

In my opinion, I recommend the Activity Timeline view (including next step and past activities) because it provides a visual image of the timeline with date and time.

Meeting/Events

Within Salesforce, an Event is a meeting or appointment with a scheduled time. These can be tracked within your Salesforce calendar (See Figure 5-3). An event may also be tied to other objects, such as opportunities or accounts. Besides, reports can be generated and used to track upcoming or past events.

Figure 5-3. *Event calendar in Salesforce*

Because events are being tracked in Salesforce, it is easy for your relevant colleagues to stay informed. Your manager or coworkers may use the calendar to keep up to date on what meetings are taking place, as well as information related to the meeting, such as which contact it is with or which Lead.

Creating an Event in Salesforce

There are several ways to create an event in Salesforce. From the calendar view, it is as simple as clicking New Event (See Figure 5-4) or New Meeting Request. You can also click a time or time slot within the calendar to begin creating a new event.

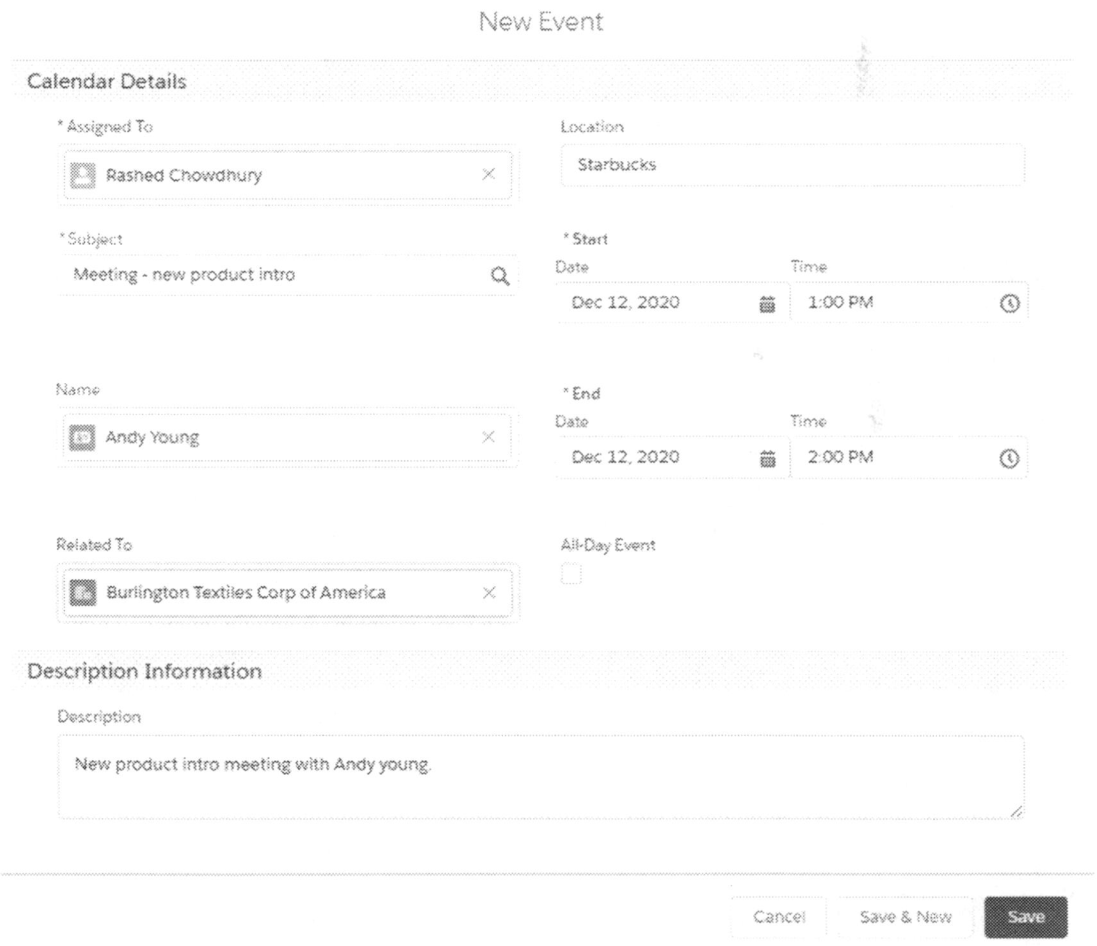

Figure 5-4. *New event (meeting) data entry screen in Salesforce*

Also, you can easily create an event from the homepage in the calendar section (Figure 5-5).

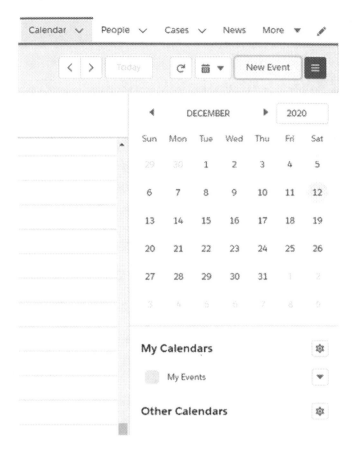

Figure 5-5. *Scheduled meetings and requested meetings from Salesforce event calendar*

The sidebar also allows you to create a new event by using the Create New drop-down list. The Chatter feed likewise enables you to create events. You can even create an event while looking at the detail page for another record. Salesforce will automatically relate that event to the record.

You can update an existing event from nearly anywhere you can view it (other than when it is in a report). Events may be rescheduled simply by dragging the event in your calendar to a new time slot.

Tracking Events

In Salesforce, your calendar makes it easy to view and keep track of events related to yourself. From the Home tab in Salesforce, you can view your Calendar. Here you can see events you own, upcoming events, or past events. By hovering over the event's subject or clicking it, you can also view additional details of the event.

Events may also be seen in different list views across Salesforce. For example, in the My Delegated Activities list view, you can see events you have assigned to other members of your organization. In My Team's Activities list view, you can view events that are owned by people below you in your company's hierarchy. The My Activities, Upcoming Events, and Activities List view will show you past events, upcoming events, and events you own, respectively.

Tasks

A Task, like an event, is another form of activity within Salesforce. It is an action that needs to be completed either by you or the person to whom you assign the task. Rather than have a set time on the calendar in which a task happens, it is instead given a due date. A task is essentially an item on a to-do list.

Creating a Task

Creating a task is easy. You may do it from the Salesforce homepage in the My Tasks (See Figure 5-6) section, or you can use the Create New drop-down box. You can be able to create a task from a record's page. This task will be automatically assigned to that record.

Figure 5-6. *My Tasks screen in Salesforce*

Table 5-1 describes the fields on the New Task screen.

Table 5-1. *Data fields of a new task screen*

Field	Description
Buttons	• Save: Save the event. • Save and New Task: Save the new event and display the New Task screen to create another task. • Save and New Event: Save the event and display the New Event screen to create an event. • Cancel: Exit without saving.
Assigned To	The person is responsible for the task.
Subject	The subject of the task. The subject displays on your Salesforce.com Homepage.
Due Date	The due date is the deadline for completing the task.
Phone	The phone is the telephone number of the contact. This field is displayed only.
Priority	The priority of completing the task. Normal is the default priority.
Status	The status of the task. It is critical to keep the status up to date.

(continued)

Table 5-1. (*continued*)

Field	Description
Contact/Lead	The contact or Lead is to which you want to link the task. This field is automatically populated if you clicked the Open Activities New Task button on the Contact screen.
Account/Opportunity	The account or opportunity is to which you want to link the task. This field is automatically populated if you clicked the Open Activities New Task button on the Account screen.
Email	The email is the electronic mail address of the contact. This field is displayed only.
Description	The description field holds additional information on the task, such as the results of the task. This is a free form field.
Send Notification Email	Send an email to the person to whom you assigned the task.

Tracking and Viewing Tasks

Tracking a task is as easy as creating them. The My Tasks section of the homepage will show you your tasks, as well as the My Activities list view. Also, in that view are completed tasks. Other lists will show you different kinds of tasks, such as the My Delegated Activities list view, which shows you tasks you have assigned to others, and My Team's Activities list view, which shows tasks assigned to those lower in the hierarchy of your organization.

Anywhere you can see a task, you are also able to view details of it. Hovering over the task's subject or clicking the subject itself will both do the trick.

Repeating a Task

Sometimes, a task needs to be repeated either across multiple days or after specific triggers occur. Salesforce makes setting this up simple. A repeated task is also different from a recurring task in that it only is created after the current task is due or completed.

When viewing a task's information, you will see two fields: Repeat This Task and Recurrence Interval. To create a repeatable task, set Repeat This Task to be After a due date or After date completed. Then set Recurrence Interval to be the number of days after the task completion or due date you want the next task to be due.

If the Repeat This Task field is set to Task Closed, that means the task, while closed, was part of a repeating series. This is important, as it serves as a distinction between a repeating task and other kinds of tasks when using reports.

If Repeat This Task on an existing task is set to Task Closed, it indicates that the task was closed as part of a repeating series. You can use this information to distinguish repeating tasks from other tasks for reporting purposes.

Tasks in a repeating series are automatically synced when created if they are made through Salesforce for Outlook.

Assigning Tasks to Multiple Users

Multiple users in Salesforce can be assigned to a single task. Up to 100 users may be assigned in this way. When adding multiple users to a task, it must be done at the time of task creation and cannot be done later while editing a task.

While on the New Task (See Figure 5-7) page, click the lookup icon found in the Assigned To field. In the lookup window that appears, choose the Multiple Users tab. From here, you're able to assign up to 100 members. Clicking will be done when you are finished.

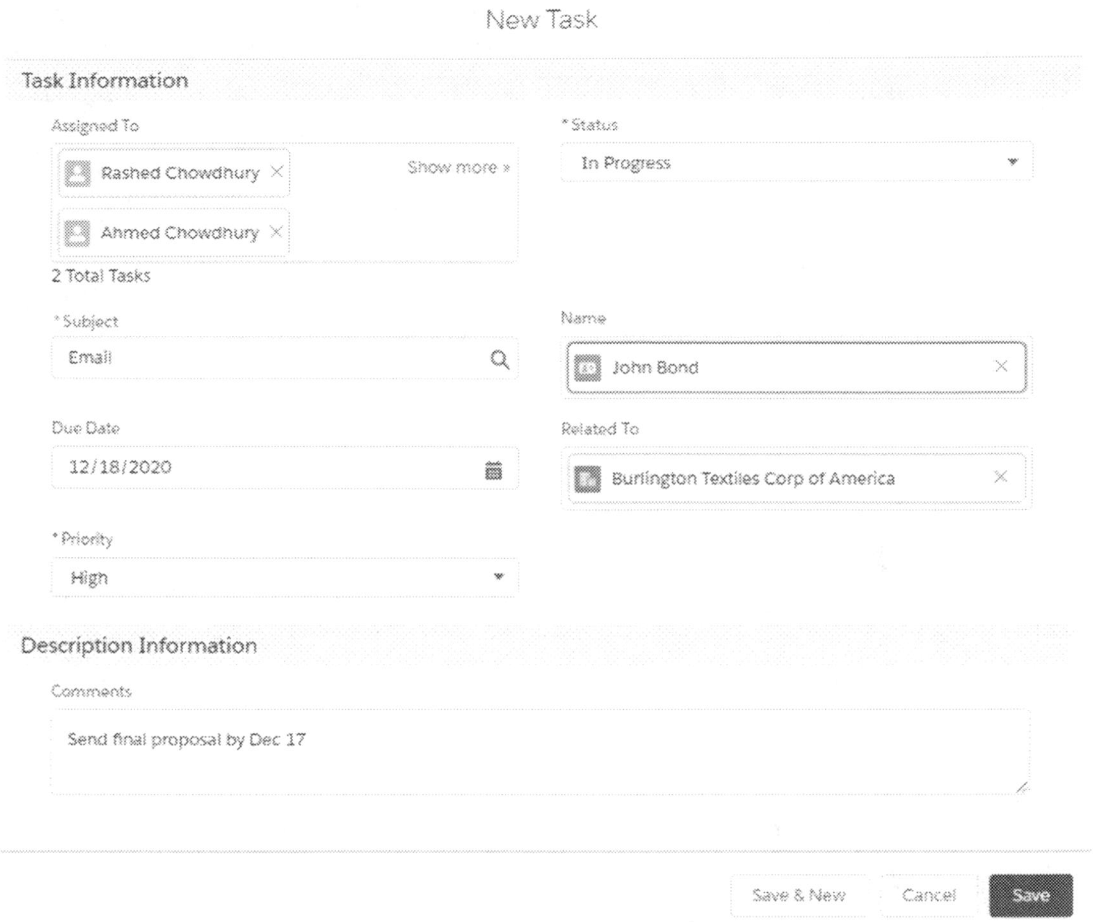

New Task

Task Information

Assigned To

| Rashed Chowdhury ✕ | Show more »

| Ahmed Chowdhury ✕ |

2 Total Tasks

* Subject

Email   🔍

Due Date

12/18/2020   📅

* Priority

High   ▾

* Status

In Progress   ▾

Name

| John Bond   ✕ |

Related To

| Burlington Textiles Corp of America   ✕ |

Description Information

Comments

Send final proposal by Dec 17

Save & New   Cancel   **Save**

Figure 5-7. *Assigning a task to multiple users' screen in Salesforce*

After you assign members to the task, ensure you save the task as well.

Setting Task Notifications

Whenever a task is created, Salesforce can automatically send an email notification. It can also do this when a task gets assigned. An administrator may set up task notifications to work in a few different ways, depending on the needs of your organization.

The first way is that each user in the organization chooses whether they want to receive email notifications upon being assigned a task. If the Salesforce administrator has selected this option, then by default users will receive task assignment notification emails. To disable this function, a user can go to their settings ➤ Calendar & Reminders ➤ Activity Reminders. From there, they can disable the option Email me when someone assigns me a task.

Another option for task notifications is to have the task creator determine whether an email notification is sent, rather than the individual people to whom a task is assigned. With this option set, when somebody assigns you a task, they choose whether you will get an email notification alongside it, rather than it being a personal setting.

The last option is to disable email notifications for tasks simply. You will be unable to receive email notifications whenever tasks are assigned.

Summary

In this chapter, we discussed the concept of activities like creating tasks and events, logging calls, assigning a task to multiple team members, and keeping track of enterprise Front Office activities in an integrated system like Salesforce. In the next chapter, we will review some of the challenges, constraints, and opportunities in the digital marketing space and how to use a Salesforce-based platform to respond to those challenges following industry best practices like Lead scoring, Lead grading, and marketing journey to develop engaging customer experience across all channels.

CHAPTER 6

Digital Marketing

In the previous chapter, we reviewed the concept of activities like creating tasks, setting up meetings, logging phone calls, sending emails, and keeping track of Front Office activities in Salesforce. In this chapter, we will discuss digital marketing, current trends, industry challenges, and how to use a Salesforce-based platform to tackle these challenges. The following key topics will be covered in this chapter:

- Challenges and strategies

- Digital marketing strategies

- Marketing strategy: Process and ownership

- Product go-to-market (GTM) investment approach

- Building effective and measurable campaigns

- Lead scoring and grading

- Targeted nurture program

- Create engaging emails

- Webinar and event marketing

- Engage the audience over social media

- Reporting on marketing initiatives

Challenges and Strategies

Business-to-Business (B2B) marketing faces many challenges in the digital age of marketing. Marketers are strapped for time, and they must focus on the right things. Today's marketers mainly deal with new business development, Lead quality, and Lead generation. New business development involves creating new business opportunities.

© Rashed A. Chowdhury 2021
R. A. Chowdhury, *Building a Salesforce-Powered Front Office*, https://doi.org/10.1007/978-1-4842-6676-2_6

Lead quality is ensuring you are not just creating as many Leads as you can for the sales department, but rather finding good ones who are more likely to convert. Of course, Lead generation is creating the Leads in the first place through processes such as forms or other calls to action (CTAs).

In the digital age, marketers have even more of a role in the Lead-to-revenue cycle than ever before. They are working with the buyer throughout the entire process and, because of that, have more considerations. It is necessary to nurture the Lead throughout the sales cycle, or they may just find another product to purchase instead. Some nurturing can be automated, as well, to save time for a busy marketer.

Buyers today are usually far into the process of deciding on a purchase before they will ever get in contact with your company. On a consumer level, you probably do this as well. If there is a product you want, you will independently research the different options online, read reviews, and eventually decide on what's best for you. Often, if you walk into a store and an employee asks you if you need help deciding on something, you have already done so.

Because of this, marketers need to be more personal regarding the selling process. This may be made easier by segmenting your audience to allow for greater personalization. Some items which may be personalized are mail, email content, and online interactions, to name a few.

Another challenge marketers face is showing executives the return on investment their strategies have brought to the company. With technology, it is easier than ever to attribute revenue to a marketing campaign. Tracking a visitor's activities and linking their points of contact when they eventually become customers allow marketers to show precisely how a customer was obtained.

Finally, marketers must be able to manage several different platforms effectively. All contacts might not be in Salesforce – they might be in an email list, for example. Landing pages and emails require their content. Marketing assets may not be a one-size-fits-all for all the different technology platforms out there today.

Digital Marketing Strategies

So, with all these challenges which marketers face in the digital age, how do they go about combating them? While a few strategies were briefly covered, let us take some time to go more in depth.

Marketing Strategy: Process and Ownership

Creating a marketing plan and strategy has multiple tasks and stakeholders. Only a subset of activities is critical to producing MVP journey and campaign requirements. See Table 6-1.

Table 6-1. *Marketing strategy, process, and ownership*

Strategy	Strategy Development Process Steps
Goal setting	• Mission • Business objectives
Situation analysis	• Audit/new opportunities • Analysis: SWOT, 5Cs, PEST
Marketing mix	• Product dev and price • Promotion and place
Marketing strategy	• Mkt objectives and success • Define targets • Develop budget
Implement and measure	• Deploy campaigns and journeys • Measure, test, learn, adjust

Product Go-to-Market Investment Approach

Figure 6-1 illustrates a go-to-market investment approach.

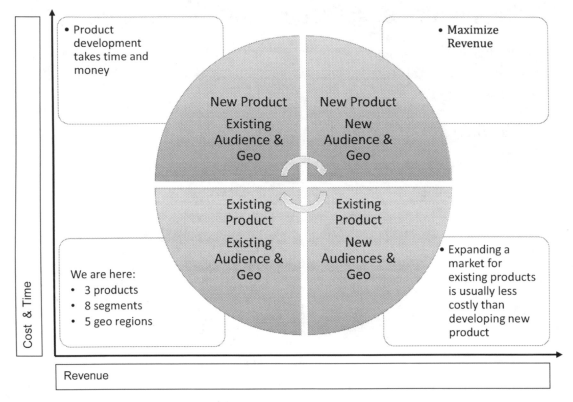

Figure 6-1. *Go-to-market (GTM) investment approach*

Marketing Strategy: New Products

New products do not have historical data from which to build a plan around marketing strategy (See Figure 6-2). Deploying "best guess" journeys in the market for three months will generate enough performance data to create a baseline.

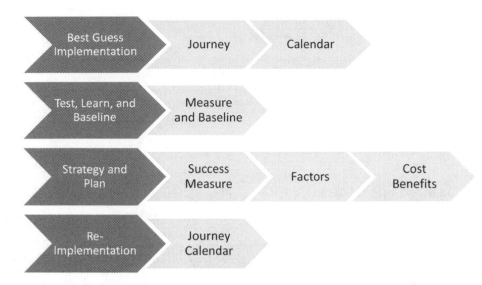

Figure 6-2. *Marketing strategy: new product*

With baseline metrics, a marketing plan can be created for the remainder of the fiscal year.

Building Effective and Measurable Campaigns

When creating a Lead generation campaign, design it from the ground up to be measurable and effective. Your landing pages should draw the readers' eyes into the CTA, and the value you are providing them should be exact. A user wants to immediately see the benefits they will receive if they follow your CTA, whether that be filling out a form, subscribing to an email list, or downloading a brochure.

Ensure you are collecting data and measuring the success of your Lead generation campaigns. Use AB testing to compare different versions of campaigns and find the one which works the best for your company. Track user visits and see how often a user completes your CTA. Do specific images work better on your landing page? Once a user has made it past your CTA, continue to track their progress. Do they eventually make it to a sale? Use this data to see what campaigns not only lead to more Leads but also more converted Leads.

Lead Scoring and Grading

The idea of passing as many Leads as possible along to your sales team and hoping enough will convert is outdated. This wastes your sales team's time as they try to convert a wrong Lead. To combat this, marketers should be qualifying and nurturing Leads before they ever get passed along to sales.

A Lead score is essentially a value placed on prospects that indicates how likely they are to purchase your product. These scores can be automatically calculated based on several factors, including website activity, interaction with your CTAs, and other responses to your marketing campaigns. With automatic scoring, it is easy to track your best Leads and set thresholds for Leads to be passed to sales. This allows the sales team to trust marketing with the Leads they get and build internal morale while also improving Lead quality.

The second half of qualifying a Lead is grading them. A score will determine how interested a Lead is in your company or product. This is useful but doesn't tell you everything. Grading a Lead indicates how interested you are in the Lead. This is measured by a letter A to F. Some of the criteria you can use to grade a Lead are the size of their company, the purchasing authority the Lead has within their company, and their company's industry. For example, you are in the business of selling paper. An executive from a newspaper company who seems interested in your product is going to be graded higher than someone equally interested but who is an intern at an electronics store.

Like Lead scoring, the process of Lead grading can be automated as well. This saves your marketing team time and still lets your sales team handle the best Leads. Get input from your sales team on what makes a good Lead and customize your scoring and grading system accordingly. Set thresholds to automatically send Leads to the sales team who are well qualified and have a good grade.

Targeted Nurturing Programs

Nurturing a Lead throughout the sales cycle is essential to sales conversion. Your nurturing campaign (See Figure 6-3) needs to have the right content at the right time to be successful. It should be personalized to your prospects and feel like a one-on-one engagement. Automating this can save your marketing and sales team time and let you reach out to more qualified Leads. Like Lead scoring and grading, get input from your sales team on the sales cycle and what problems prospects usually have which need to be solved.

Start nurturing prospects from the beginning by sending welcome emails. This is easily automatable and makes a prospect feel more appreciated by your company at a time in which they're comfortable. If they just completed a form, then getting a welcome email from you will not feel unexpected or obtrusive.

Do not let Leads forget about your company and its products either. Send emails at regular intervals to keep your products fresh on their minds. If a Lead has gone cold, these emails may help reengage them and get them back into your sales cycle.

Nurture Program Name	Key Criteria	Program Manager	Opportunity Goals	Timing
National Nurture Program				
Accelerated Pipeline				
Stage 3 Nurture Program				
Cold Lead Nurture Program				
60 Day Nurture Program				
90 Day Nurture Program				
120 Day Nurture Program				
Accelerated Pipeline – SMB				
Accelerated Pipeline – Mid Market				
Accelerated Pipeline – Strategic				

Figure 6-3. *The Lead nurture program framework*

Once a Lead is further into your sales cycle, you can shift gears on how you nurture them. Narrow down the content you send to Leads to be more product focused. Show them what makes your product unique and how it is a better purchasing decision than your competition. The content should clarify how your product will give customers an advantage, as well as the disadvantages they'll receive from not using it. Include data from the industry, such as reports or press articles, which help give your company authority.

Near the end of a sales cycle, when a Lead is close to making a purchase, offering a particular discount or other promotional offers may help them pull the trigger. After a Lead has been converted, there are still tasks that can be automated, such as sending helpful introductory resources such as Frequently Asked Questions.

Create Engaging Emails

Emails are a tried-and-true marketing method with a good ROI and a broad reach. Craft your emails to be engaging and target the correct segmented audience. Consumers respond well to more personal-feeling emails. This can quickly be done through automation and segmentation.

There are several other things to keep in mind when designing your emails. Keep your emails clean and uncluttered with an obvious Call to Action. Distinguish it with its color or overall placement relevant to the other content in the email. Additional information should be easy to read and well organized with bullet points and clear sections.

Images may be used to break up the monotony of a straight, text-filled email. They breathe more life into the email and are also useful to help set apart your CTA. Even videos are being used more in marketing emails nowadays and can help make your email stand out from the crowd. Whether you use images, videos, text, or a combination of all three, ensure it is readable on a mobile device.

Not only should your emails be well designed, but they also need to make it to an inbox. It does not matter how nice or engaging the email is if nobody ever reads it. Forms from landing pages are an excellent way to gather emails. There is a strong chance an email gained from a form is valid and has its inbox contents read by someone. Just make sure users are made aware they will be receiving emails when submitting the form. The last thing you want is for them to mark your email as spam if they were not expecting it.

Getting your emails sent to a good inbox is one half of the equation. The other half is avoiding spam filters or being marked as spam. In the worst-case scenario, if your domain is marked as spam enough times by an email provider or ISP, they may blacklist you. This could severely hamper your ability to perform email marketing.

The content design of your emails should be crafted to avoid spam filters. Using too many images as compared to text content will trip spam filters. Additionally, it makes your email size larger. As obvious as it sounds, always perform spelling and grammar checks on any emails you send out. Bad spelling and grammar are both signs of spam, and emails containing either are more likely to be marked by users as spam. Ensure your subject line does not have common spam phrases or vocabulary such as cash, rates, or be your boss, to name a few examples.

Outside of content, respecting the user is key to not getting marked as spam. Always let your user opt in to receiving emails from you. If the user receives an email from you, it should not be a surprise to them. An even better practice is to have your user opt in through something such as a form and then send a follow-up email, which is the real opt-in. This will help avoid your email being marked as spam and also ensure your email list is full of users who are interested in your marketing.

Keeping an up-to-date and clean email list is useful for knowing your emails and avoiding spam filters. If too many of your emails are going to an invalid address or one which has not been used in a long time (dormant), then ISPs may mark you as a spammer. Never buy email lists. For one, there are legal issues with it, and two, it violates the privacy of the users to whom you would be sending emails. Many of the emails in the list might be invalid, dormant, or spam traps set by an ISP as well.

Whenever you do hit an email address that bounces, remove it from your mailing lists. If some emails never get opened, either try to use a reengagement campaign or remove them from your list. This is to ensure your list is up to date with users who want to (or are even able to) receive your emails.

Webinar and Event Marketing

While webinars may not be the best B2C marketing tool, they do work well for B2B marketing. It is much easier to gather people together for a virtual webinar or conference than an in-person meeting, and it is an easy way to show interested buyers what makes your product so unique. People who sign up and attend your webinars are good Leads. Their information is already on hand, plus they have already been nurtured.

Not only are webinars an easier way to gather people than in-person, but it is also more affordable. Rather than renting out space and ensuring everyone can travel to that location, you only need an Internet connection and some webinar software to get started. While at a webinar, it is a lot easier to engage more personally with potential Leads than other forms of marketing. If you send out a marketing email, it is a one-way line of communication. A webinar may open a dialogue and allow you to be more personal with your Leads.

Show to those attending your events or webinars that you are at the top of your industry. Unlike marketing material such as printed ads, a webinar or event allows you to give live demonstrations of your products or services. Webinars allow you to show, not tell, your audience your product is excellent, and your company is the industry authority.

So, with these benefits in mind, it is vital to run the webinar and event correctly. From the beginning, make sure it is well promoted. It's no good having a great, well-planned event if nobody watches or shows up. Get the word out and promote the event across whatever channels you can. Share it on your social media leading up to the webinar/event and even as it starts to try and procure some last-minute attendees. If your event is in-person, consider streaming it to broaden its reach and allow more people to attend.

Prepare all your material beforehand and practice it. If there are multiple speakers, ensure they have all rehearsed their parts and that you have practiced transitioning between them. Not only should speakers practice going over their content, but you should also ensure those involved know how to use the webinar software and that technical issues are figured out before the event.

During the event, stand out and make it worth attending. This goes without saying, but don't let your event be just another booth at a show or a forgettable webinar. Make your event polished and deliver quality content to those attending. Be different – have games or interactive elements at your event to help engage attendees.

After the event or webinar, be sure to follow up on every Lead. Gathering all of those Leads and then doing nothing with them is a waste. It is vital to clearly identify which Leads were obtained from your webinar or event, so your ROI (return on investment) can be more easily tracked and calculated. This is an easy task to automate. Additionally, if a business signed up to attend but then was not able to show up, this is an excellent opportunity to try and reach out to them.

Finally, do not let all the content created for your event or webinar be one and done. After the event is over, consider using material from the webinar to create blog posts or other content-driven marketing. Record your webinars or other demonstrations so you can put them on your website and create quality content.

Engage the Audience over Social Media

Social media is a great way to connect and engage with your target audience. It feels more authentic than other ads and has a broad reach. There are a variety of platforms available for you to choose from, and you should decide beforehand which ones to target. If you're a smaller company or have fewer resources to devote to social media, consider only using a couple of forms of social media rather than spreading yourself too thin across all of them.

Do some research before making your posts. See what your competitors are posting and what keywords come up a lot in searches related to your field. Also, you can see where your competitors are posting and which form of social media works best for them. Then, of course, strive to do it better.

When developing content, it is good to have a mix of gated and non-gated posts. Non-gated content is good for getting new followers to see that your company produces quality products. After you've proven yourself, sharing gated content is an excellent way to gather interested Leads. If you have a blog, then social media is a great way to boost its popularity.

The content you create should always be on-brand. Develop guidelines for your social media managers so posts can align with company values and uphold a particular image. Make sure that across all your social media channels, your brand is aligned for a consistent company image. Make sure you have disaster response plans in place in case there's a major social media blunder or crisis as well.

Build your social media presence by linking to your social media pages on your website or blog. Of course, you should also be active on social media itself. Set up regular posts through social media automation tools so that even if your social media manager is unavailable, you are still active. People will be more likely to see your posts if they're regular and frequent. In addition to bars, be involved in communities related to your industry. It's an excellent way to gather Leads, as people who participate in those communities are interested in those subjects.

Use analytics to figure.out what is working and what isn't. See which posts are more popular and receive more favorites and which posts drive more views to your company pages. Track how many Leads are generated through your various platforms to have a more meaningful metric for the effectiveness of social media. Gather demographic information from your followers, as well, to gain insight into what your target audience should be.

Reporting on Marketing Initiatives

You have created all these marketing campaigns and strategies and followed through with them – now, how do you measure their success? Some obvious metrics to observe are Lead generation and conversions as Leads are created from different marketing initiatives, the track which initiative created what Lead. Tracking this data is easier than ever with marketing automation software.

Find which metrics are most important to your company and use them to glean important information about the ROI of your marketing initiatives. Here is an easy one: How much revenue has been generated due to your specific marketing initiatives? As you should have been tracking which Leads and opportunities were created from those particular marketing campaigns, this data is then readily available. From this data, it's easy to discover how many customers come from specific marketing initiatives out of the whole.

When choosing which metrics to report, consider which ones sound the most important to executives. Measuring follower growth rates, social media impressions, and favorites all may sound good, but they aren't directly about the bottom line. You need to answer why. Why are these things important? How have these new followers impacted revenue? Is there a correlation? Have you seen growth in social media impressions as well as increased conversions originating from social media?

The cost of gaining a new customer from one of your marketing initiatives is an excellent example of a metric about which executives care. Measure this metric over the long term to see trends. If the cost to acquire a new customer is trending upward, it's essential to recognize that's happening to figure out its cause.

Sometimes, marketing doesn't always lead to a new customer for every prospect it reaches. But that doesn't mean it's worthless. Later on down the road, those marketing efforts may influence that prospect into becoming a Lead. If your marketing initiative has reached several prospects, but they have not yet become customers, perhaps a future marketing initiative will be the push they need to convert.

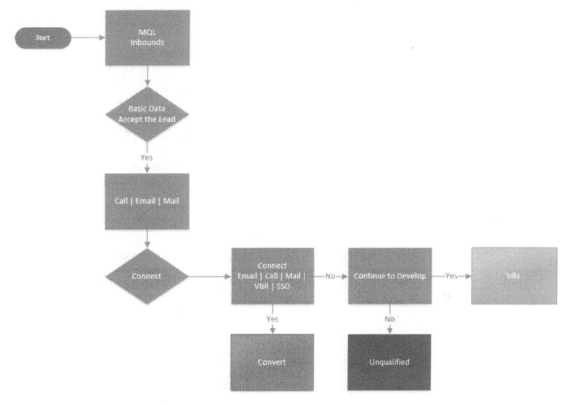

Figure 6-4. *Sales Development Representative (SDR) work processes*

Send prospects to your Sales Development Representatives (SDRs), so they can further qualify (See Figure 6-4) them together with your marketing campaigns. After the SDRs have created qualified Leads from prospects, they can send them to the sales team directly. This helps not to waste your sales team's time with cold or unqualified Leads.

Summary

In this chapter, we reviewed digital marketing, current trends, industry challenges, and how to use a Salesforce-based platform to tackle these challenges. We also discussed key concepts of digital marketing strategy, marketing processes, Lead nurture program, engaging audiences over social media and webinars, investment approach for the product go-to-market, and Lead scoring and grading. In the next chapter, we will learn marketing campaigns, setting up actual campaigns in Salesforce and configuring the audience, identify key performance indicators, and measure campaign effectiveness. We will also review and unleash the power of the Marketing Cloud by Salesforce.

CHAPTER 7

Marketing Campaigns

In the previous chapter, we covered digital marketing, current trends, industry challenges, and how to use a Salesforce-based platform to tackle these challenges.

In this chapter, we will learn marketing campaigns, setting up actual campaigns in Salesforce and configuring audience, identify key performance indicators, and measure campaign return on investment (ROI). We will also discuss the core offering of Marketing Cloud by Salesforce and its use cases in the Front Office environment following innovation that unlocks the power of machine learning and artificial intelligence to optimize customer experience and transform the way we do business globally. The following topics will be covered in this chapter:

- People, process, brand, messaging, and ROI

- Measuring campaign data

- Creating a campaign in Salesforce

- Creating a target list in Salesforce

- List uploads: Pre-event and for general email purposes

- Post-show: Conference list uploads

- Routing

- Contact list

- Planning a marketing campaign

- The power of Marketing Cloud

Marketing campaign makes managing prospects and customers a breeze, and in today's business environment, you need all the help you can get with CRM (Customer Relationship Management).

© Rashed A. Chowdhury 2021
R. A. Chowdhury, *Building a Salesforce-Powered Front Office*, https://doi.org/10.1007/978-1-4842-6676-2_7

Why Marketing Campaigns

Marketing campaigns are how you raise awareness of your products, services, and your brand. They lead to sales and are an essential part of your business. Salesforce allows you to create marketing campaigns within its Marketing Cloud platform, ensuring your information stays connected from marketing to Lead generation to sales.

Figure 7-1. *Form-based messaging approach*

Salesforce helps marketing campaigns in a variety of ways. A marketing campaign's core goal is to create awareness or Leads, and there are several tactics to achieve that goal. Salesforce can track email lists, website ads, trade show attendance, social media postings, press releases, phone calls, and more (See Figure 7-1). While Salesforce itself cannot execute most of these campaigns, it can be used to track essential data related to them. Marketing campaign is a series of marketing tactics and programs that are all designed to achieve a specific business goal (increase revenue, Leads, customer adoption, etc.).

Measuring Campaign Data

Every marketing tactic you use is going to have different criteria for its effectiveness. To ensure your campaign is working well and to discover which parts of it are performing the best or worst, it's essential to track these criteria. Here is an example set of standards:

- Email: How many emails were sent? Of those sent, how many were opened? Did your targets click through any URLs in the email? How many emails bounced and never made it to a target? How many emails resulted in an unsubscribe from the target?

- Postal mail: How many letters sent out were returned to the sender? How many people responded to the mail's call to action?

- Event: How many people RSVP'd to the invitation? How many people attended the event? What was the ratio of invites to attendance?

- Website: How many users on your website click through to view your products or services? How many page views does your site receive? How many page views do more important pages receive?

- Social media: How many likes/favorites did your social media post receive? How many comments did the post receive? How many people followed your post? How many page follows were gained after your post? How many people shared your post?

- Phone calls: How many phone calls were made to how many targets? How many of these phone calls resulted in meetings? What were the follow-up tasks created for the phone call? How many targets responded to your phone call's Call to Action?

Creating a Campaign in Salesforce

Now that you have an idea of what criteria you can track, here is how to create your marketing campaign within Salesforce. There are four high-level steps/processes to create a marketing campaign in Salesforce: (1) create a new campaign, (2) search and update a campaign, (3) add campaign members, and (4) add opportunity.

First, navigate to the Marketing App. Click Campaigns and then click New (Figure 7-2).

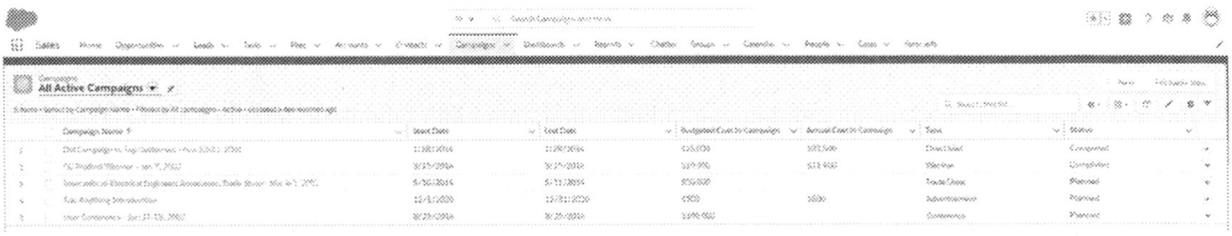

Figure 7-2. *Campaigns home screenshot from Salesforce*

Then, enter all information that applies to the campaign (Figure 7-3).

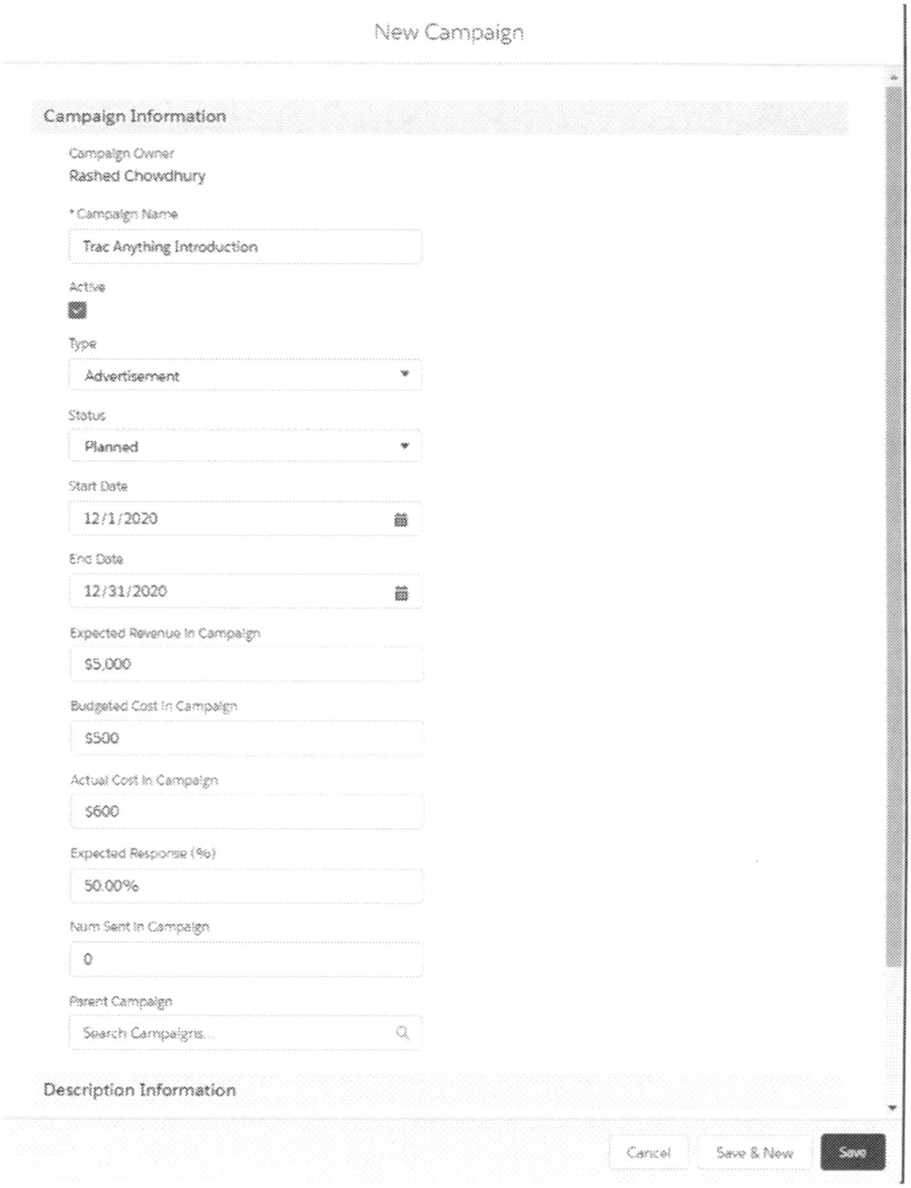

Figure 7-3. *New Campaign data entry screenshot from Salesforce*

Click Save, and your new campaign (See Figure 7-4) will be created.

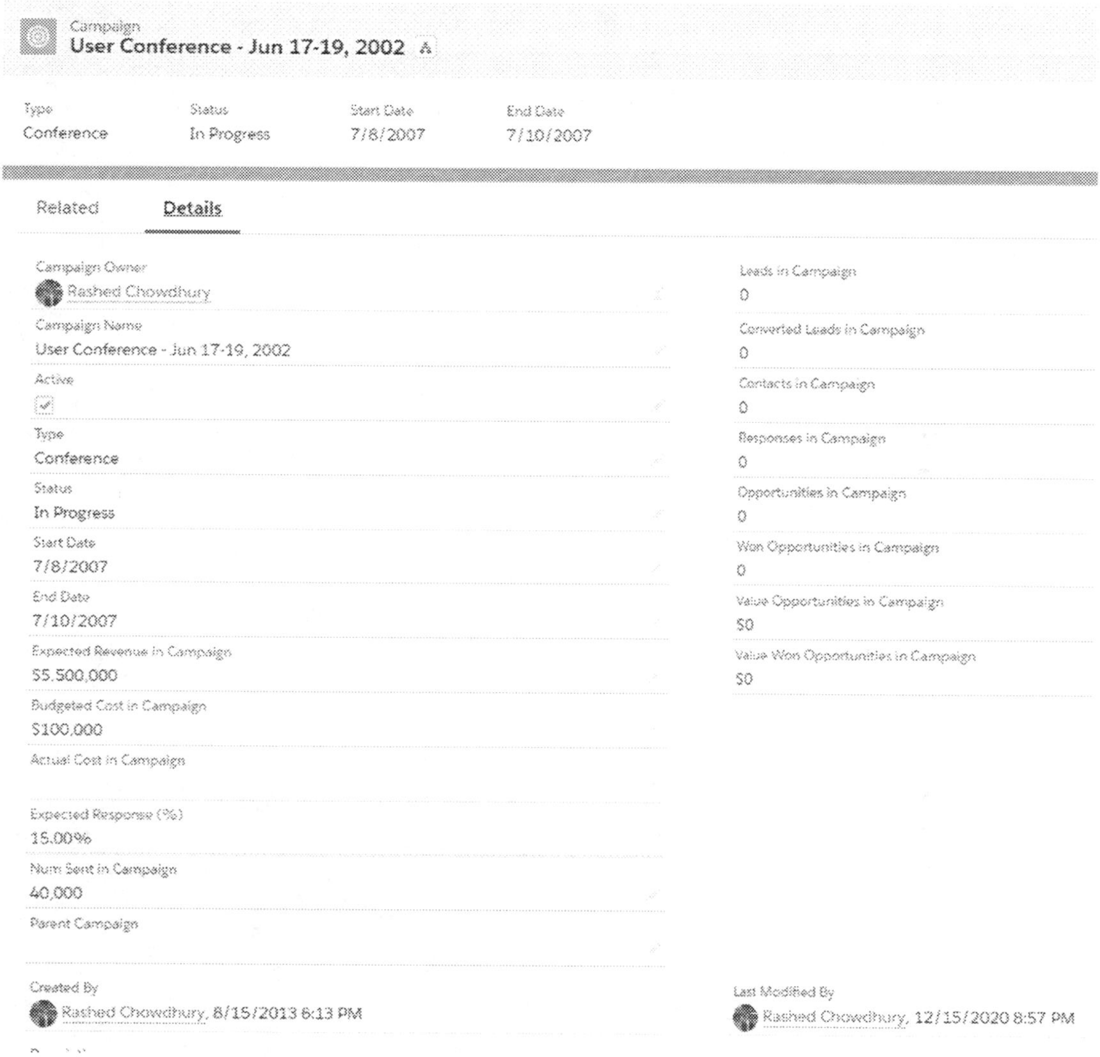

Figure 7-4. *Campaigns details screenshot from Salesforce*

Creating a Target List in Salesforce

A Salesforce target list (See Figure 7-5) defines who should be targeted for the campaign. To do this, first, navigate to one of your campaigns. At either the top or bottom of this campaign, click Manage Members and then click Add Members – Search.

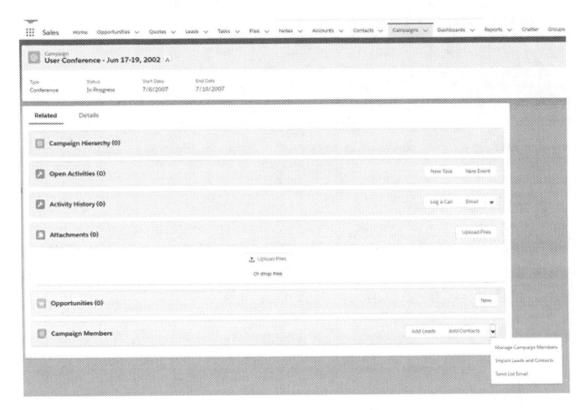

Figure 7-5. *Creating a target list screenshot in Salesforce*

Next, choose whether the campaign members (See Figure 7-6) you will be adding are Leads or Contacts. Then use the fields to enter additional search criteria before clicking Go.

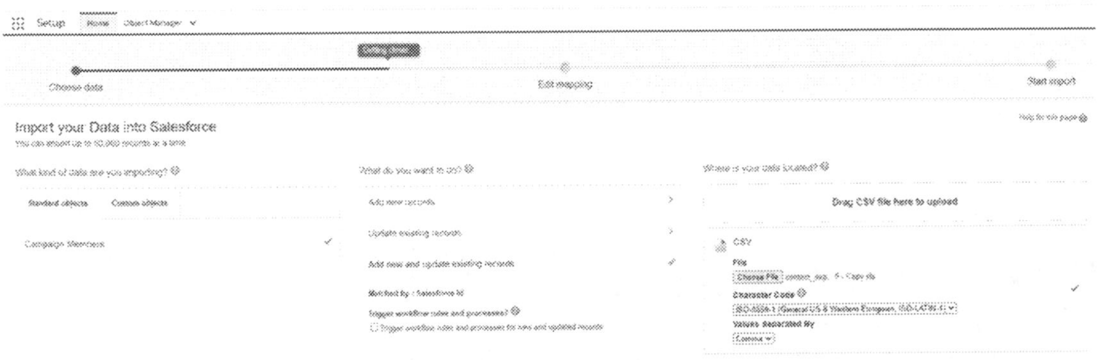

Figure 7-6. *Manage campaign members screenshot in Salesforce*

Finally, check the box next to the people you would like to add to the campaign. Then click Add with Status and select the members' statuses.

Contact List

Keep the following in mind regarding the contact list:

- With all lists for upload, it is unknown how many of these accounts and contacts are currently in Salesforce. The list will have to be segmented first, identifying all contacts where the account is new. The accounts will have to be created before loading the new contacts. Once all the accounts are in Salesforce, you can link them to their corresponding accounts.

- The contact list itself will need to be cleaned and enriched to support the new contact record requirements. Once the data file is prepared, it should be loaded into Salesforce.

- File upload is dependent on the list data itself and takes time to prepare; therefore, you should allow a minimum of one week for upload to Salesforce to take place.

List Uploads: Pre-event and for General Email Purposes

Lists that need to be uploaded into Salesforce should be sent to the Front Office technology team (the team that is responsible for digital marketing and technology enablement). Typically, the list should be from a report created within Salesforce and easily be added to a Salesforce campaign for an email. However, if it does not contain all the necessary Salesforce fields, the Front Office technology team will review the list for the required fields and append as needed, then verify the email addresses, dedupe the list, and upload to the campaign. You should give the team a heads-up and please allow a minimum of one week for the list to be fully developed and vetted.

The following fields are required when importing a list to Salesforce for an email campaign:

- First name
- Last name

- Email address

- Company

- The Lead owner (verify before uploading)

Any additional fields such as Address 1, City, State, Postal, and Notes can also be added if that information is available.

Post-Show: Conference List Uploads

Lists for upload, whether from trade shows, webinars, and so on, that need to be uploaded into Salesforce should be sent to the Front Office technology team. Once received, the Front Office technology team should review the list to make sure all the required fields are included and append as necessary. The list will then be examined to verify the email addresses, dedupe the list, and upload the document. You should probably give the team a heads-up and allow a minimum of one to three days for the post-show list to be fully developed and vetted.

The following fields are required when importing a trade show list into Salesforce:

- First name

- Last name

- Email address

- Company

- Lead referral source (typically added manually)

- Lead source name (typically added manually)

- Lead owner

Any additional fields such as Address 1, City, State, Postal, and Notes can also be added, so there is no need to remove these.

Lead Assignment Rules

All contacts should be loaded in as Leads, and they should be assigned a contact owner (either an Account Executive or Sales Rep). The sales development team should follow the standard operating procedure and working the Lead to begin the Lead qualification process. Having ownership (even manual assignment) for all Leads, especially new Leads, would ensure a proper follow-up conversation with the potential prospect and not being ignored.

Planning a Marketing Campaign

Before you start a marketing campaign, there are several vital components to which you should give thought and research to ensure maximum effectiveness:

- Define audience roles: When selling to another company, it is vital to consider the role of the Lead you are trying to convert within their business. Depending on the position they hold within their company, they are going to have different concerns. These additional concerns mean your marketing approach needs to be tailored to fit their needs. Likewise, the general target audience is vital to consider. Nail down exactly to whom you are intending to sell when designing a marketing campaign.

- Understand timing: How you market to your Leads is dependent on how long your sales cycle typically takes or if the sale is limited on time. After your first contact, how often are you able to contact prospects? Is the holiday season coming up, and sales need to be made before then before people start taking vacations? Keep your sales cycle time in mind when making these decisions. For example, if it typically takes one month from the first contact to a Lead won, plan so your marketing campaign generates those Leads a month before the sale needs to happen.

- Define your KPIs: Key performance indicators are a must when measuring your campaign's effectiveness. Some examples of which to keep track are measuring revenue generated from the campaign vs. the cost of the campaign and breaking down which part of the campaign is bringing in the most converted Leads. Use KPIs to find what works and does not work for your campaign, so you do not waste time and money.

- Have a library of content: Marketing for your business may be bolstered by having a good set of content available. More and more often, consumers are doing their research about where to do business. Having quality blog posts, social media posts, and information about your company online will, in turn, enhance your brand and encourage prospects to choose you.

- Determine responsibilities: Figure out who is going to oversee managing your campaign. Will they manage the creation of it? Will they monitor it and update it, as well? Or will different people specialize in each task and be separately assigned?

- Map content to sales cycles: Where you are with a prospect in terms of the stage of the sales cycle is essential for delivering to them the most compelling content. The content you want to send to a Lead you have almost won will be very different from the content you send to a Lead with whom you have not had the first contact.

- Test, test, test: Your campaign is not going to be perfect from the get-go. Analyze your KPIs and use that analysis to adjust your campaign. Add new content or edit existing content when necessary, adjust the timing of your campaign tactics, change your audience, and so on. Use the data you have gained to make intelligent decisions going forward.

More on Key Performance Indicators

Calculating the return on investment (ROI) of a marketing campaign and quantifying opportunity influence from campaign activities to understand marketing effectiveness are a couple of the essential key performance indicators (KPIs). It is also necessary to track the conversion rate of the Marketing Qualified Lead (MQL) to Sales Qualified Lead (SQL) and then benchmark them against the industry vertical to outline improvement opportunities.

Call to Action (CTA)

A Call to Action in marketing refers to some part of the advertising or marketing material asking the customer to respond or make a purchase immediately. Here are some important ideas to keep in mind when designing your call to action:

- Keep it short: Call to action should be concise and to the point. They are the simple action you want the potential customer to take. For example, Call now, Share on social media, and Subscribe to our newsletter are all less than five words and let the customer know what you want them to do.

- Do not be bossy: Do not demand your customer to take any action or do something for you. Instead, it should encourage the customer. Make the message sound more personal. For example, instead of just saying subscribe on an email list submission field, you could try saying "Let us do this".

- Convey value: Do not make the user feel as if you are the one benefitting from the action; you are having them take. Ensure they know what they are getting out of it with your call to action message. As an example, if you have an advertisement trying to get users to click through to your cooking recipes site, discover 1000+ New Recipes to Try entices the user and make their click feel powerful.

- Make the call to action obvious: If your call to action in your marketing email or homepage is hard to find, then its value is significantly decreased. Make sure the call to action stands out and has a clear purpose. It should not blend in with the background and should be readily noticeable.

- Indicate urgency: If your CTA makes the user feel as if they have a limited amount of time to act or that there is a limited quantity of something they want, they will naturally feel more compelled to follow through. Limited time offers help drive users to commit when they might otherwise sit on the fence or do nothing.

- Test: Keep track of how well your chosen CTA is working for you. Use A/B testing to compare different CTAs and see how well they perform against each other. Even if a clear winner is found from doing this, find a new CTA and A/B test it against your previous winner. Continue to improve your CTAs throughout your marketing process.

Creating a Good Landing Page

A landing page is the first page a user sees when they click through an ad or link to your product or service. A landing page is created for a marketing or advertising campaign. The objective of a landing page is to get the user to perform your call to action.

Keep the design of your landing page simple and focused. Since the goal of the landing page is for a user to convert, the CTA should be the focal point of the site. Content on the page should all be built around this CTA and should not be too distracting. Try to limit scrolling or eliminate it. Ensure that the value you are providing to the user is clear and persuasive.

If your landing page has sign-up forms or other forms of some kind, keep the number of fields limited to four or less if possible. Too many fields will lead the user to think it is too much effort or that you want too much information from them, and they will leave. After they have completed and submitted the form, send an immediate automated email response to provide feedback that the process was completed successfully.

Users may feel disinclined to share their personal information with you when filling out forms. To combat this, consider displaying testimonials on your landing page. Showing other people who have converted and are happy with your company will help ease your users' minds and make it easier for them to convert.

Use images and videos rather than lots of text. This plays back into the need to keep your landing page simple. Keep your content comfortable to view and absorb. Consider having the images or videos be a free item from the content to which your CTA serves as a gate. If the user is signing up to receive your "12 Tips to Success," sharing one tip is an excellent way to prove your value.

After the user has converted with your call to action, such as submitting a form or signing up for something, send them to a thank you page (or use a thank you pop-up). Not only does this let the user feel appreciated, but it is an excellent opportunity to lead them to other portions of your site and to sell additional products or services. Thank them for completing your CTA and provide links to other areas of your site.

Email Campaign Planning

When planning an email campaign (See Figure 7-7), consider using an email campaign blueprint. This is a comprehensive, complete plan for building out your email campaign. The following are topics covered in the blueprint:

- Campaign ownership:

  - Who should the campaign be assigned? Typically, this should be the person who is responsible for the campaign.

  - Who are the final reviewer and approver of the campaign? The reviewer and approver have the last word on the list, campaign content, and graphics.

- Campaign objectives and plan:

  - Who should be involved in the Object and Plan for the campaign? The campaign owner is responsible for putting together a team of individuals who will help drive the campaign.

  - Who is your target audience: enterprise, mid-market, SMB (small business)?

  - What is the expected outcome of your campaign? Here is where you should discuss why the campaign is essential and the outcome of the result.

- Campaign content development:

  - Who is responsible for developing the content for your campaign? Does your campaign require the assistance of marketing or sales?

  - What is the expected date for having your content developed for your campaign? You may want to discuss a timeline with the content development team, including a hard stop when the content needs to be delivered.

- Campaign content approval:

  - It should take no longer than one week to receive approvals for your content. Approvals should come from the following subject experts:

- • Head of the business unit

- • Legal (if applicable)

- • Marketing communications

- Campaign timeline:

  - What is the timeline for having your campaign reviewed and approved?

  - What are the target start and end dates for your campaign? Timelines change; these are targeted dates and not finalized dates.

- Campaign final approval:

  - The approximate time for campaign approval should take about 1–2 business days.

  - The final campaign approval is specific for the business unit and no other departments:

    - Campaign owner

    - Head of the business unit

- High-level discovery: Essentially a "heads-up" to both the content marketing team and the Front Office technology team (digital marketing tech team) that an email will be needed and a short description of use cases. Typically, the Front Office technology team sends the brand manager the email blueprint requirement document to start completing at this point. The brand and product management team should always complete the blueprint! This will reduce the time it takes to complete the build.

Figure 7-7. *Steps of email campaign*

- Strategy meeting: All the stakeholders should have a meeting with the Front Office technology team to complete the email blueprint and discuss key requirements of the campaign, including

  - Type of email

  - Email schedule and number of emails

  - Campaign flow (Pardot Engagement Studio or Journey Builder) if needed

  - Call to Action/CTA (what step do you want the prospect to take?)

  - Copy, including subject line and preheader

  - Form requirements

  - Suggested completion actions (Lead routing)

  - List requirements

  - Landing page requirements (if needed)

- Collect assets: During this time, the Front Office technology team will start to collect the assets for the email, such as

  - List

  - Copy

- Graphics

- Gated assets and content (whitepaper, brochure, etc.)

- Build and test: MarTech team will spend this time building the email, completion actions, and Salesforce CRM campaigns, then test and refine.

- Stakeholder review: Once the build is complete and tested, email samples will be sent to the stakeholder for review and approval.

- Marketing approval: Once the stakeholder approves, the campaign will route to the marketing head for final approval.

- Deploy: Campaigns are now ready for launch.

- Reporting: Initial reporting is sent to stakeholders for review 72 hours after the email launch.

Pardot Use Cases for Developing an Email Campaign

The purpose of email marketing is to nurture Leads and educate the segments about products or services and get them to click a Call to Action (CTA) and engage by downloading a piece of content such as a whitepaper, register to attend an event, or fill out a form to be contacted by a member of the sales team. Then the salesperson will qualify them and engage.

Let us take how B2B insurance companies typically leverage Pardot (See Figure 7-8) for an email campaign:

- Storm alerts

- Trade shows/events

- Webinars

- Downloadable content (could be a whitepaper, video, or brochure)

- General awareness

- Post-event (thank you) emails

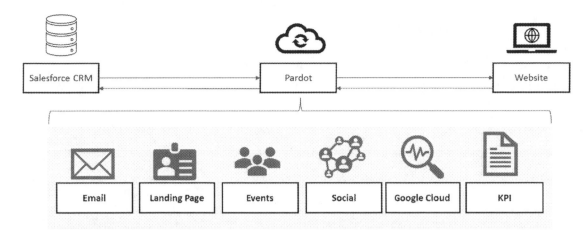

Figure 7-8. *Pardot processes*

Many companies typically send one email; however, a fantastic option within Pardot is called Engagement Studio, where a series of emails can be built and automated to dispatch depending on the action taken (or not) by the Lead over a specified period. This would be considered a good nurture program and highly recommended to adhere to email best practices.

In Table 7-1, we listed a set of critical criteria and an opportunity goal with timing for Cold Leads as an example of a nurture campaign.

Table 7-1. *Nurture example outlining key criteria, opportunity goal, and timing*

Name	Key Criteria	Opportunity Goal	Timing
Cold Leads	• These are the people who were not quite sure about it. • They lack contact information and interest. • This campaign will help you gather the information you need. • Send an initial email, and you will determine the next steps based on the client's actions.	Grow the business.	• Leverage Pardot Engagement Studio with three emails. • Send an initial email followed by resending to non-opens 72 hours after launch. • Every two weeks, send an additional piece of content to email openers until they fill out a form to be contacted by a representative.

Build a Successful Email

So far, we have discussed how to plan and generate an email campaign. Let's review what makes an email itself. Typically, four key items should be covered in a good marketing email as follows:

- Subject line: Keep the subject line short and to the point. Give them a reason to open the email!

- Preheader: The preheader is the summary text that follows the subject line when an email is viewed in the inbox. Consider this another way to present your subject line. Give them an additional reason to open the email.

- Copy: Keep it to a minimum. If you need to tell more about a product/service, put it on the landing page with the form. In the email, you want to entice them to click the CTA. Don't say it all in the email. I found a paragraph and three bullet points as a good standard.

- Call to action: The client clicks the call to action; now what? *(A call to action is what you want your customers to do once they receive your email, i.e., select a link or image within the email.)*

Build Your List: Salesforce Components

Spend some time analyzing the needs and campaign objective before defining the email body and create the prospect list (See Figure 7-9). This is the algorithm (set of rules and criteria definition) that pulls the contact and Lead record from the database.

- Campaign involvement for lists should be limited to

  - Client development team (the sales and account team that owns and knows the relationship)

  - Service line, brand, or business unit as the campaign owner

  - MarTech team

- Pull together your target lists using internal and external databases as needed.

  - Notify the Front Office technology team of the target criteria to pull lists from Salesforce CRM or third-party database marketing platforms like D&B Hoovers, Data.com, and so on.

  - The campaign organizer may also provide the list, collected via other means.

- Create a campaign in Salesforce.

  - Naming convention consideration: Service Line/Business Unit, Year, Quarter, and name of the event.

    - BSI 2020 Q1 RIMS

    - CCS 2020 Q1 PLRB

  - The number of campaigns you wish to create should be dependent on the number of different activities you plan to track. The idea is to create one parent campaign and add in additional "child" campaigns under the parent campaign.

- All list members should be added to their appropriate campaign. Brand managers and marketing activity owners should coordinate this with the Front Office technology team.

  - Campaign owner–provided lists should be consulted with the client development team for vetting. The MarTech team should load the list to the Salesforce campaign and Pardot list.

  - Salesforce CRM and Pardot or Marketing Cloud should be configured to establish real-time synchronization so that email communication bounces, campaign data, journey builder data, opt-outs, and so on can automatically sync with Salesforce CRM.

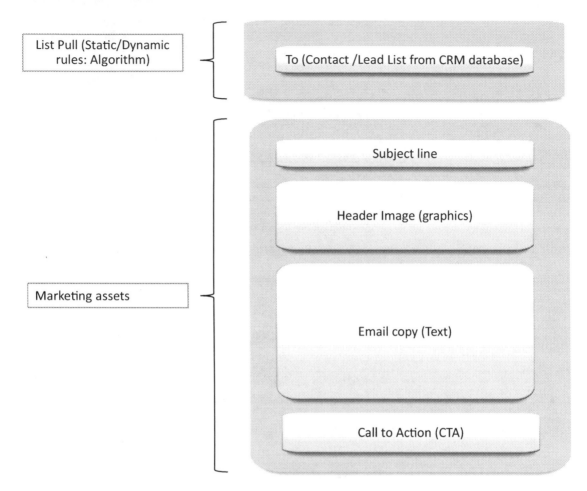

Figure 7-9. *The email body and prospect list illustration*

Build Your List: Additional List Options

If you do not have enough members in your campaign or want to expand your prospect reach, you can build a list with D&B Hoovers and integrate them into Salesforce CRM.

Basic integration activities of D&B Hoovers are as follows:

- Search for a company and verify company details. Send the company record to your Salesforce CRM ORG.

- D&B Hoovers' integration interface can be downloaded in your Salesforce CRM ORG and then configured to look for duplicates. If it finds a match, you can

- Choose to update the existing Lead or add a new one. This action oftentimes refers to "upsert" in Salesforce language. Always update the current Lead so that the latest information (name, address, contact details, etc.) can be readily available in your CRM ORG.

- If no match is found, you could set up a new Lead to be created following a confirmation message.

If you are building an extensive list for email, this should typically need to be scrubbed with existing records to eliminate hard bounces. It is a good idea to keep track of hard bounces and record them in your CRM system so that you don't add them back to your prospect list.

You should also consider the following method when building your prospect or watch list:

- View existing opportunities/accounts/Leads in Salesforce.

  - There are ways you can configure the D&B Hoovers system for a "CRM Watchlist" in your D&B Hoovers subscription. This option would enable you to view any new updates from your existing CRM contacts in D&B Hoovers.

- Create a prospect list.

  - You could consider searching for a concept or keyword like "insurance."

  - Advanced filter options would enable us to filter out an exact target prospect list. These lists in D&B Hoovers are smart list – criteria (i.e., your filter settings) are saved, and the list will auto-update with whatever companies match that criteria at the given time.

Email Form Completion and File Download

When a Lead fills out the web form in a campaign or landing page, be sure to have Pardot Completion Actions set up. These will ensure that the Lead status is set correctly in the Salesforce campaign, alerts are sent out, an owner is assigned, a task is assigned to the Lead owner, and so on. The following is a sample of how you could set up completion actions.

For a service line or business unit, the following completion rules could be standardized in addition to other completion rules:

- Send auto notification to the sales leader.

- Send auto notification to the sales operation.

- Send auto notification to the Front Office technology team.

- Assign Leads to a sales operation until an available rep could be found.

- Assign the task to a sales operation until an available rep could be found.

- The sales operation will then reassign to the proper Lead owner for follow-up.

Campaign Reporting

The approximate timeframe for reporting on a campaign is 1–2 weeks after the campaign ends. The following questionnaires and exercises will enable you to frame up the baseline reporting for the campaign:

- Team involvement for reporting and matrix

  - Client development: Provide Lead status, contact activity, and email statistic reports to the business unit leadership

- Lead influence

  - How many Leads came in from your campaign?

  - How many of these Leads converted?

- Contact influence

  - How many existing contacts responded to your campaign?

  - What is the value of the Company/Account (Value of Open Opportunities, if existing)?

- What is the current status of the Company/Account (i.e., Client, Prospect, Other)?

- What is the current relationship score with the Company/Account?

- Opportunity influence

  - Did your contact or Lead take your "call to action" or respond to your communication?

  - How many opportunities were generated from your campaign?

  - What was the total value of your opportunities?

  - The business unit and client development team will effectively work together to assist each other with campaign follow-up communication.

The Power of Marketing Cloud

We have seen the technology shift from mainframes to client-server and into the cloud where everything is connected – from friends on social networks to mobile phones and even the products in your house (See Figure 7-10). We are seeing this incredible shift where these devices and apps are getting smarter with artificial intelligence. Most of us have already come to expect intelligent experiences in our daily, personal lives. As a result, your customers are only getting more and more informed.

Figure 7-10. *We are living in a smarter world where technology is continually evolving*

So, we can question why can't both consumer and business applications be as smart as Amazon.com? We are in a new world where customers' expectations are different, and to be successful, companies need to meet these new expectations, wherever and however they connect.

Customer Experience Is Imperative

Imagine, if we can deliver a personalized solution in a connected platform and respond to customers at the moment they need and want in real time, would not that be a fantastic customer experience? How can one platform connect all customer data in a single view of the customer that allows marketers to orchestrate experience across all touchpoints? Also, how is it possible for all marketers to use the same tool across all channels? In my decade of IT and Front Office building experience, I concluded that Salesforce is "that platform" that unifies marketing, sales, customer service organization (See Figure 7-11), and operation to provide a consistent 1:1 personalized and on-time Front Office experience.

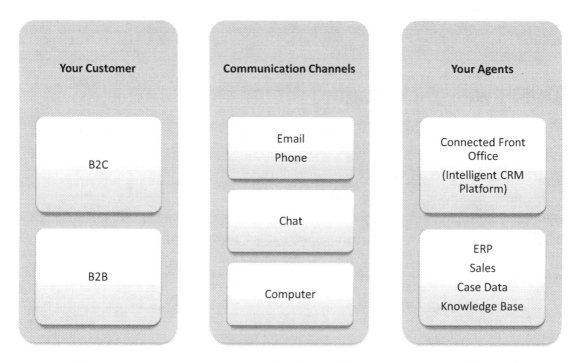

Figure 7-11. *Customer support organization and customer service channels*

From awareness to acquisition to onboarding and engagement all the way to retention and advocacy, the Salesforce platform is providing the marketing capabilities as shown in Table 7-2.

Table 7-2. *B2C and B2B marketing capabilities by Salesforce*

B2C	B2B
Advertising	Advertising
Digital commerce	B2B marketing automation
Email and mobile messaging	Guided selling
Custom mobile app	B2B marketing analytics
Connected products	Mobile apps for marketers
Social media integration	Budget and event management apps
Communities – online portal services	Collaboration and file sharing
Customer service	Customer support

Connect the B2C Customer Experience

So, what exactly are the customer experiences, and how do you connect them? Let's follow along a typical path of connected B2C customer experience:

- Outbound targeted ad activated by a scheduled job.

- The consumer clicks a targeted ad powered by Salesforce Data Management Platform, DMP.

- The consumer is directed to a commerce experience powered by Commerce Cloud.

- The consumer receives a special offer after abandoning the shopping cart (abandon car journey automation by Marketing Cloud).

- The consumer buys a product.

- The consumer is suppressed from the ad campaign via Salesforce DMP (Salesforce Marketing Cloud, SFMC).

- The consumer puts on a cross-sell journey through Journey Builder.

- The consumer downloads the loyalty app powered by Heroku (formerly named as App Cloud).

- The consumer joins the Customer Community and finds fellow friends and enthusiasts.

- The consumer contacts Customer Support via live message and gets an issue addressed.

- The consumer evangelizes experience on social media platforms (Instagram and Facebook).

Connect the B2B Customer Experience

Here is your B2B connect customer experience:

- The Lead fills out a form on a Facebook campaign.

- The Lead gets pushed into Pardot + Sales Cloud.

- The Lead becomes scored, graded, and nurtured until sales-ready.

- The prospect is not yet ready to buy; the Rep places them into nurture.

- The Sales Rep sees a prospect marketing activity.

- The Sales Rep gets a real-time notification of a hot prospect.

- A personalized marketing content is sent to the prospect over time.

- The Rep closes the deal in the following quarter.

- The support keeps the customer for life.

Marketing Cloud: Email Studio

Salesforce is a leader in email. Salesforce allows customers to execute intelligent campaigns faster, across any device, and at a massive scale. The platform is sophisticated enough to perform highly personalized campaigns at an enormous scale for the largest B2C marketers in the world while being intuitive enough for every marketer to create personalized campaigns, using predictive and dynamic content blocks for useful emails, all without the need to code.

Marketing Cloud: Mobile Studio

Mobile marketing delivers a unique touchpoint with your customers and complements other channels like email, the Web, and social. Here are the core capabilities:

- The mobile studio delivers time-sensitive messages such as reminders and alerts, keeping your brand top of mind of customers.

- Salesforce powers mobile marketing to drive app engagement to keep customers coming back. Target customers with location-based marketing to surprise and delight.

- The mobile studio is delivering real-time alerts using personalized data stored on the customer success platform to have a single view of the customer.

Note   Mobile marketing is the closest customer touchpoint to have 100% reach.

Marketing Cloud: Advertising Studio

Advertising studio securely uses your customer data to drive all your Google and Facebook and display advertising at scale.

Here are the core capabilities:

- Audience and campaign management.

- Connected to the journey: Use Journey Builder to connect your advertising to the rest of your marketing, sales, and customer service.

- Integrated Lead generation: Drive powerful Lead generation campaigns across Facebook's network and automate Leads directly into Salesforce.

- Bring CRM to AdTech: Connect CRM and Salesforce DMP and other ad tech partners to reach customers in the display.

Marketing Cloud: Journey Builder

Journey Builder is a cross-channel consumer engagement solution. There are four core components (See Figure 7-12) to delivering relevant, personalized customer journeys in the Salesforce platform.

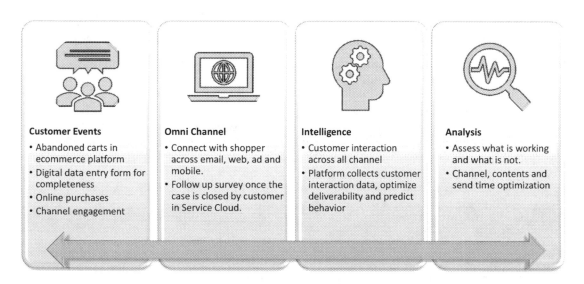

Customer Events
- Abandoned carts in ecommerce platform
- Digital data entry form for completeness
- Online purchases
- Channel engagement

Omni Channel
- Connect with shopper across email, web, ad and mobile.
- Follow up survey once the case is closed by customer in Service Cloud.

Intelligence
- Customer interaction across all channel
- Platform collects customer interaction data, optimize deliverability and predict behavior

Analysis
- Assess what is working and what is not.
- Channel, contents and send time optimization

Figure 7-12. *Four core components of Journey Builder*

- First, let us consider placing the shopper in the middle of everything a selling organization is doing by standardization into what they are telling us by their behavior. In the digital world, here are a few key customer events: abandoned carts in an ecommerce platform, digital data entry form for completeness, online purchases, and channel engagement – Journey Builder is capable of listening to all of these customer events and then enables the technologist and marketing to react to these events in real time.

- Second, let's connect all the experiences. With Journey Builder, marketers can present the shopper with the information they need in the channel they prefer. They can join the experiences across email, the Web, ad, and mobile. Also, with natively integrated Sales and Service Cloud activities, selling organizations or brands can incorporate interactions across their business into the journey.

For example, selling organizations or brands can listen for a case being closed in the Service Cloud and send a follow-up survey. If the response to the survey is negative, Journey Builder can automatically reopen the case, so the customer receives a follow-up phone call.

- The third is the channel type. Listening to how customers are interacting with your brand and offering these connected experiences across channels is the ideal state – and it needs to be done at a massive scale for every single customer. With Journey Builder, brands create these interactions, and then the platform does the heavy lifting. Marketers can react to customer engagement or lack of attention, test to see which channels perform the best, and route customers down different paths in the journey based on their data – automatically.

- The fourth is analysis. Marketers must always be assessing what is working and then can change their strategy to meet customer needs. Journey Builder allows marketers to set a goal and monitor how customers are progressing toward that goal and see inline engagement metrics to understand what channels and content are performing best.

Social Studio

Social Studio is a complete social marketing platform, powerful enough for social listening, analytics, publishing, and engagement. Here are the core capabilities:

- Connected social: Connect social to Marketing, Service, and Sales and trigger one-to-one journeys based on social insights.

- Mobile-first social: Manage social campaigns on the go with the Social Studio Mobile App.

- Create alignment with the command center: Display and analyze all of your digital interactions across email, social, customer care, and more.

Salesforce DMP

Salesforce DMP can capture data from any source and device, which unify, segment, and activate audiences to increase customer engagement. Core capabilities follow:

- Leverage AI to discover new audiences: Use Salesforce Einstein to analyze billions of profiles and trillions of events to find new high-value segments.

- One-to-one ad targeting on any device: Drive more relevant and valuable customer experiences.

- Bring CRM to the Salesforce DMP: Bring customer data securely across marketing, sales, and service using Advertising Studio to Salesforce DMP to enhance digital identity and increase ROI.

Weekly Journey Monitoring Support Activity – Sample Time for Ten Journey

For any medium- to large-sized marketing organization, there are people, process, and technology that are in place and dedicated to carry out the group agenda which essentially support the overall organizational mission. In digital marketing space, when you build specific journey by focus areas (strategy, knowledge, project management, operation etc.), you have to consider planning adequate support resources and time to monitor, research, decide, and adjust.

In Table 7-3, I outlined the activities for each of these focus areas with estimated time to accomplish them and tally up the total time in hours per week for planning purposes.

Table 7-3. Journey monitoring framework

Focus	Monitor	Research	Results and Decision	Change and Adjust	Total Time
Strategy	• Journey goals check • Goals forecast check • Communication plan check • 3 hours	• Identify issues • Questions to team • 1 hour	• Receive answers • Input on hypothesis • Drive decisions • 1 hour	• Final approval on changes • 1 hour	6 hours per week
Knowledge and insights	• Journey component • Journey tests • Baseline and forecasts • 3 hours	• Identify issues • Answer questions • Hypothesize results • 8 hours	• Receive questions • Identify questions • Input on hypothesis • Input on decisions • 3 hours	• Make analytics/test changes as needed • 1 hour	15 hours per week
Project management	• Monitor conversations • 1 hour	• Monitor conversations • 1 hour	• Coordinate conversations for the weekly meeting • 1 hour	• Document and send change requests • Monitor and report on change status • 2 hours	5 hours per week
Market ops	• Marketing schedule • Channel ops • 3 hours	• Identify issues • Answer questions • Hypothesize results • 3 hours	• Receive questions • Identify questions • Input on hypothesis • Input on decisions • 3 hours	• Make journey campaign and ops changes as needed • 3 hours	12 hours per week

(continued)

Table 7-3. (*continued*)

Focus	Monitor	Research	Results and Decision	Change and Adjust	Total Time
Creative	• Creative performance • 2 hours	• Identify issues • Answer questions • Hypothesize results • 2 hours	• Receive questions • Identify questions • Input on hypothesis • Input on decisions • 2 hours	• Make creative changes as needed • 2 hours	8 hours per week
Tech and data	• Platform and data perf. • 2 hours	• Identify issues • Answer questions • Hypothesize results • 2 hours	• Receive questions • Identify questions • Input on hypothesis • Input on decisions • 2 hours	• Make data and tech changes as needed • 2 hours	8 hours per week

I hope these activities listed in the framework provide you with a perspective when you build your marketing organization.

Artificial Intelligence and Machine Learning

A machine task that solves a problem based on a set of rules (algorithms) is typically defined as artificial intelligence (AI). For example, a user in audience segment A is sent a personalized email message based on three key predictive digital behaviors.

A method of training algorithms so that an artificial intelligence (AI)–powered machine can learn how to make a decision is called Machine Learning (ML). For example, the machine automatically analyzes a user behavior over time and determines audience segment A has four key predictive behaviors.

"Predictive Models" and "Model Training" are traditional marketing terms with similar meanings to AI/ML. A key difference between Models/Training and AI/ML is that AI/ML typically is integrated into a MarTech (marketing technology) platform to automatically perform tasks vs. loading human-created model results into a MarTech platform to drive tasks.

Summary

In this chapter, we learned a great deal about the marketing campaign, setting up an actual campaign in Salesforce and configuring audience, identified key performance indicators, and measured campaign return on investment (ROI). We also covered the core offering of Marketing Cloud by Salesforce and its use cases in the Front Office environment following innovation that unlocks the power of machine learning and artificial intelligence to optimize customer experience and transform the way we do business globally. In the next chapter, we will introduce you to a few concepts and frameworks, including customer segmentation, executive scorecard, and framework for business development owners.

CHAPTER 8

Front Office Concepts

In the previous chapter, we learned more about marketing role, process, brand, marketing messaging, marketing ROI, creating a Salesforce campaign, managing prospect database and the power of Salesforce Marketing Cloud, identifying key performance indicators, and measuring campaign return on investment (ROI). We also discussed, core offering of Salesforce Marketing Cloud and its use cases in the Front Office environment following innovation that unlocks the power of machine learning, artificial intelligence to optimize customer experience and transform the way we do business globally. Marketing campaign makes managing prospects and customers a breeze, and in today's business environment, you need all the help you can get with CRM (customer relationship management). This chapter will review a few concepts and frameworks, including customer segmentation, executive scorecard, and framework for business development owners. We will cover the following topics in this chapter:

- Customer Segmentation/Categories of Customers

- Framework for Your Business

- Why Measuring Customer Satisfaction Is Important

- Net Promoter Score (NPS) Process

- Dashboard Design: Business Performance, Profitability, and Scorecard

- Using and Understanding Top Line Revenue Growth Dashboards – A Real-World Perspective

- CRM Planning Questionnaires

- Decision-Making Framework

© Rashed A. Chowdhury 2021
R. A. Chowdhury, *Building a Salesforce-Powered Front Office*, https://doi.org/10.1007/978-1-4842-6676-2_8

Customer Segmentation/Categories of Customers

Knowing how to engage with your customers is key to building brand loyalty and helping them to feel good about your business or product. Using a variety of effective customer touchpoint methods (Figure 8-1) is, therefore, necessary to improve the perception of your company, its products, and its brands.

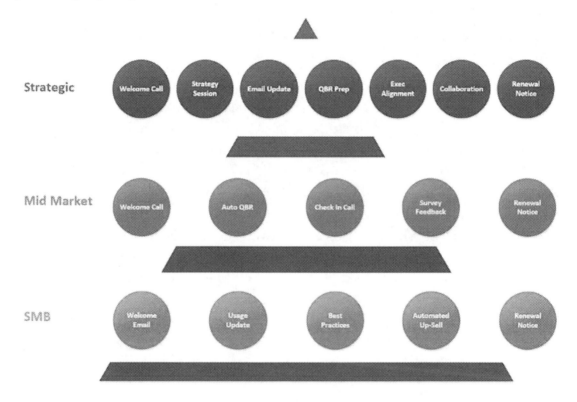

Figure 8-1. *Customer touchpoint framework, use technology to scale*

Small to Medium Businesses

Small to medium businesses are usually defined as having from 1 to 100 employees, $5 to $10 million in annual revenue, and are typically less widespread geographically. Connecting with them as a market segment is going to work differently than with mid-market or enterprise-level businesses.

A typical early touchpoint is a welcome email. They are usually sent after some sort of first interaction has been made, whether that is signing up through a form or purchasing a product. These welcome emails are a great way to start building a relationship with your new customer. Ensure that you include links to your company's website and social media profiles to give the customer more ways to connect with your company.

If you offer your customer any SaaS (Software as a Service) subscriptions, ensure you track usage of the service by the user. Using this data, you can give the customer a report of their usage summary during their subscription. It is an easy update throughout the year to maintain a useful touchpoint.

Use technology to automate upsells for existing customers. Together with that, use the 360-degree customer view which Salesforce provides to find and execute the best upsell opportunities. It is easy to automatically send an email in response to a purchase made by a customer with an upsell opportunity in it.

If a customer has created a contract with your business, renewal notices are an easy touchpoint on which to execute. You can send them out at different intervals (e.g., three months before renewal, one month, or one week) to reach out to your customer multiple times. It allows them to make another purchase with you and get your company on their mind.

Mid-market

A mid-market business is more extensive than an SMB but still smaller than enterprise. They will have over 100 employees and up to about 1000. Their annual revenue ranges from $10 million up to $1 billion. They will often have multiple office locations and be more spread out geographically.

Mid-market accounts are more extensive than SMBs and deserve a little more attention from your company to get the sale. Rather than (or in addition to) a welcome email, consider sending a welcome call. A sales rep's time is better used to call a mid-market business than a small business, considering the higher revenue a mid-market business may bring. That human touch can make all the difference in a sale here.

Another call you can make to your mid-market accounts is the check-in call. This serves as an excellent opportunity to connect and see how well they're implementing your product, as well as what steps they can next take to ensure they're getting what they want from the product. The call should be used to make sure goals are being met with your customer and to find new plans on which to move forward.

Quarterly Business Reviews (QBRs) are critical with larger clients. Technology can be used to speed up this process for your mid-market accounts. Use predefined templates and data from Salesforce to populate relevant fields. Some field examples include ROI from your product, license renewals, and support tickets. Before the due date of each quarter, your client's QBR should be automatically created from Salesforce and be ready to send. Have your system send out a reminder to your business leaders when the report is about to go out.

Gathering survey feedback from your accounts at different touchpoints is a great way to see what is working and what is not. Use survey information to improve your customer journey and therefore build up customer loyalty. Of course, sending a survey is a touchpoint, and some considerations should be made. Make sure the survey feels as if it is worth their time to fill out. Do not make it too long!

Just like SMBs, renewal notices should be given to your mid-market accounts. Getting these accounts renewed is even more critical, so make sure this is a touchpoint on which you execute well. Consider sending notices through sales representatives instead of just automated emails if the account holds enough value.

Enterprise/Strategic

An enterprise business is even larger than mid-markets. They have over 1000 employees, and their annual revenue is $1 billion and up. An enterprise will have several offices, usually located in several countries, and do business around the world. They are precious customers because of their size.

A welcome call is even more worth it for an enterprise business than for a mid-market. They'll typically have a much higher sales volume, so that extra effort of human touch is worth it. Retaining an enterprise business as a customer is extremely valuable and worth spending the additional resources and workforce.

A strategy session where you meet with key stakeholders from an enterprise with whom you wish to do business may help ensure the enterprise's priorities are being seen and their needs are being met. Use these sessions to create a plan and a timeline of your objectives that align with your customer's goals.

Sending out email updates is an easy way to utilize technology to keep your business information up to date and on your customers' minds. Email updates may promote news about your company, information related to your industry, or any events that will be going on soon, such as conference booths or panels your company will be hosting/attending.

Quarterly Business Reviews (QBRs) are essential to demonstrate the value your company is bringing to your customer. With enterprise clients, QBRs are face-to-face meetings with your customer, where you go over what you can do next to continue to support them and how well your products or services have worked for them. Since QBRs are high-touch events that require lots of time and staff, they should be saved for your top segments of customers – enterprises.

Doing business with larger companies means your own business needs to have executive alignment. Your executives all need to follow the same vision and work toward realizing the same goals. Selling to enterprises is often going to require more resources and staff to work together toward the original sale and in customer retention. Executives in different departments moving in different directions will not help make that sale.

Depending on the product or service you're offering, a collaboration with your enterprise client may be a great way to ensure you're delivering what the customer wants. Use joint application development to keep your customer involved throughout the entire process of creating an application for them. This means while you develop the systems, consistently interview and have workshops with the client to make sure you're meeting all their objectives. At these workshops, your client provides their subject matter expertise to your team.

Renewal notices should be made with enterprises as well and are perhaps the most important for the enterprise client as, again, they'll typically have the highest sales volume out of all your different customer segments. Thus, they must renew contracts or orders. Sending them reminders through human representatives is worth it to ensure renewal is made.

Framework for Your Business

As an executive, you have goals and strategies you require to be met and followed. Measuring the performance of these goals and strategies may be achieved using an executive scorecard (Figure 8-2). First, split your goals into different areas of focus, such as improving your company's brand or tracking how well the company uses its budget or how it uses opportunities.

Focus Area	Description	Goal	2017	2018	Grade
Client Meeting	• Product Level Meetings • Executive Level Meetings	10 2	8 0	12 1	B
Brand	• Social Media • Brand Awareness • NPS (Net Promoter Score) *	125 30 8.5	125 30 8	155 35 8.9	A-
Budget	• Event • Meals & Entertainments • Travel & Living	$100K $25K $15K	$100K $22K $12K	$150K $35K $18K	C
Opportunities	• Leads Captured • Qualified Leads • Qualified Visits • Opportunities • Revenue ($)	100 35 55 3.5M 1M	87 30 44 2.8M 750K	137 20 52 XXX XXXX	B-

*The Net Promoter Score is an index ranging from -100 to 100 that measures the willingness of customers to recommend a company's products or services to others.

Figure 8-2. *Executive scorecard framework*

In each area of focus, mark which goals or strategies were implemented in that area. For example, in the Opportunities focus area, your goal was to capture 100 Leads and generate $1M in revenue. Then, compare the actual results of each year to your goal. Using these results for each goal, create a grade for a focus area. These grades broadly show how well the company meets its goals and follows through on its strategies.

As a business development owner (Figure 8-3), you are tasked with identifying new business prospects, developing Leads, contacting Leads, and winning over new customers.

Activity Categories	Activity Description	Percentage Allocated
Daily BDO Login	Each BDO will login once per business weekday from desktop, iPhone, iPad or Blackberry (Company holidays are excluded)	10%
5 Hot Prospects Identified With 4 Activities Per Prospect	20 activities total (activity type is not important)	15%
10 Warm Prospects Identified with 2 Activities Per Prospect	20 activities total (activity type is not important)	15%
15 Cold Prospects Identified With 1 Activity Per Prospect	15 activities total (activity type is not important)	15%
Prospect Activities	All prospects will have at least 1 recorded activity per month	
	If the BDO has more prospects than the minimal amount, each of those prospects will have at least 1 recorded activity per month	15%
	Note: If the BDO only has the minimal amount of Hot / Warm / Cold prospects, this requirement has already been met	
New Customers Won	2 new customers per month, each new customer MUST have moved from a hot, warm or cold status type to new customer status type during the month	10%
Overall Activity Tracking	100 total activities recorded to contacts owned by BDO (activity type is not important)	15%
Add-In Tools	The BDO has logged in 1X with any of the following: Salesforce for Outlook, Salesforce 1, Desktop Chatter, Salesforce Mobile App	5%

* BDO = Business Development Owner / Sales Rep

Figure 8-3. *Guideline for business development owner*

Generate prospects and group them as hot, warm, or cold, depending on how close the customer is to needing your business. A hot prospect will be in clear need of the service or product your company provides, such as having visited your website. A cold prospect will not have had any contact with your company.

Next, get in contact with those prospects and try to win them over as customers. Record all activities used to contact and win over customers and log your new customers in a tool such as the Salesforce mobile app.

Why Measuring Customer Satisfaction Is Important

Reaching out to your customers and ensuring they are satisfied is key to finding acceptable business practices and increasing profits. There are a variety of methods when it comes to reaching out to customers and gathering feedback (Figure 8-4). Customer Satisfaction Surveys (CSAT), Voice of Customer, and Net Promoter Score are just a few. No matter which you choose, it is also essential to act on this feedback; otherwise, it is not a way to grow but simply becomes a data point.

Customer Satisfaction Surveys (CSAT) are done using a survey asking questions similar to measure your satisfaction with our product/service on a scale. Included is a scale with 1 indicating the customer is very dissatisfied and 5 showing the customer is very satisfied. After results have been gathered, customer satisfaction can be measured by summing up the number of 4 and 5 ratings, dividing that number by total respondents, then multiplying by 100 to get the percentage of satisfied customers.

Voice of Customer (VOC) is used to gather customers' expectations and preferences. By collecting this feedback, including a customer's wants and needs, you can ensure your products and services meet demands and the right issues are prioritized.

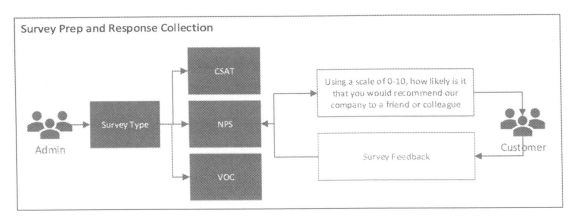

Figure 8-4. *Survey preparation and response collection*

Net Promoter Score (NPS) is another popular customer satisfaction methodology. It is a measure of customer loyalty. The fundamental question is: How likely are you to recommend us to a friend or colleague? On a 0–10 scale. From here, this feedback is assembled into three groups: promoters, passives, and detractors. A promoter (score of 9–10) is a loyal customer who is likely to continue buying your product, as well as telling others about it. A passive customer (score of 7–8) is one who is satisfied with your product but not necessarily loyal. A competitor may quickly gain their purchase instead. Finally, a detractor (score of 0–6) is an unhappy customer. Through negative word of mouth, they can damage your brand and limit sales. From here, calculating the Net Promoter Score is easy. Simply subtract the percentage of detractors from the percentage of promoters. For example, having 60% promoters and 30% detractors gives an NPS of 30.

GetFeedback is a useful tool that hooks into Salesforce and can be used to automatically trigger customer surveys, as well as push responses to relevant organizational personnel.

Net Promoter Score (NPS) Process

Now, let's discuss the rules of the road when it comes to the Net Promoter Score (NPS) process.

Identifying Clients to Survey

Each Global Service Line (GSL) and Tier 1 country (United States, United Kingdom, Canada, Australia) should determine the most appropriate methodology for identifying client accounts that should be surveyed based on their specific book of business. At a minimum, top clients based on revenue to the company should be surveyed. This may be based on a minimum revenue threshold (e.g., accounts generating > $X), percentage of the service line or geography's total revenue (e.g., top X accounts equal 40% of revenue), or some other definable revenue parameter. Though there is no limit to the number of accounts that can be surveyed, the ability to follow up on client feedback within a reasonable timeframe should guide decision-making on the number of accounts to be surveyed within a given period.

Identifying Contacts to Survey

At a minimum, the corporate company's primary contact at the client organization must be surveyed to ensure we understand their perception of the company and obtain feedback regarding the overall health of the client relationship. It is recognized that some service line and Tier 1 countries may have existing processes in place to capture NPS and client satisfaction feedback from other roles within the client organization. Let's not discourage these processes, but they should not be used as a substitute for obtaining feedback directly from the primary contact.

Enterprise vs. Global Service Line (GSL) vs. Product Line Scores

We must understand the client's overall perception and satisfaction with the company. Therefore, NPS scores should be captured at the enterprise level. In those instances where a client identifies explicitly a desire to provide separate scores for individual service line or product line, a score must be captured for each global service line or product line they purchase to offer a full measure of their satisfaction.

153

Follow-Up on Client Feedback

Clients providing an NPS score of 6 or below (detractor) require a follow-up call and meeting to address client concerns more specifically. Call/meeting notes should be documented in Salesforce by creating an activity directly from the relevant NPS form.

Entering Net Promoter Score (NPS) Follow-Up Activity in Salesforce

Calculating the firm's Net Promoter Score will not provide a long-standing value if you do not act on the feedback that is given by your clients. Closing the feedback loop with clients to ensure you fully understand and act upon any concerns they raised during the NPS survey is essential to improving the client experience and turning detractors and passives into promoters. Logging follow-up activity and action plans (See Figure 8-5) in Salesforce will enable the company's account managers and leadership to track the follow-up progress and ensure every client concern is addressed.

NPS Action Plan							
Plan Id	Action Item	Status	Owner	Target Date	% Complete	Type	NPS id
Plan Id	Action Item	Status	Owner	Target Date	% Complete	Type	NPS id
Plan Id	Action Item	Status	Owner	Target Date	% Complete	Type	NPS id
Plan Id	Action Item	Status	Owner	Target Date	% Complete	Type	NPS id

Figure 8-5. *Net Promoter Score (NPS) action plan*

Net Promoter Score measures customer experience based on a client's response to a single question: "Using a scale of 0–10, how likely is it that you would recommend the company to a friend or colleague?" Capturing this client feedback in Salesforce contributes to a better understanding of the overall client relationship while also informing marketing and process improvement efforts.

NPS Categories

The following are NPS categories:

- Promoters (scores 9–10): Loyal enthusiasts who will continue buying and refer others, fueling growth

- Passives (scores 7–8): Satisfied but unenthusiastic customers who are vulnerable to competitive offerings

- Detractors (scores 0–6): Unhappy customers who can damage a brand and impede growth through negative word of mouth

---

Helpful tips   Before completing the NPS form, ensure the contact you surveyed is a contact on the account in Salesforce. If the contact is not on the account, you must create it before creating a new Net Promoter Score form.

Dashboard Design: Business Performance, Profitability, and Scorecard

Dashboards in Salesforce allow you to easily view charts, reports, and graphs all in one place for easy reading. It summarizes data for you and displays it graphically. Dashboards are easy to put together, with components that are simply dragged and dropped into place.

Creating a Dashboard

Creating your dashboard is very easy and only takes a few steps. First, ensure you have some reports created so the dashboard will have data to show. From there, go to the Dashboards tab and click New Dashboard.

Drag components onto your new dashboard from the left-hand side of the screen and customize it how you wish. Populate these components with report data following this click path:

Dashboards tab ➤ New Dashboard ➤ + Component ➤ select report ➤ select chart type.

Finally, click "Save" and give a name to your dashboard. After you close out of this page, you'll be returned to the dashboard page and see your new dashboard.

Designing a Good Dashboard

As you've seen, creating a dashboard is easy. But what about creating a good one? What are some design principles to keep in mind when making your dashboards?

Before you can create a useful dashboard, you should create good reports. Since dashboards only show you report data in a clean, visual way, it makes sense that a useful dashboard requires an excellent report. To start, find out what executives want to know. Use the key performance indicators (KPIs) they give you for your reports. Keep your reports aligned with your company's vision and its business objectives.

The next rule is to keep it simple. Don't try to cram 20 different charts onto your dashboard just because you can. Make sure you are only showing relevant data. Try to have a main KPI displayed on the dashboard, with several other reports supporting that one. Have at least one dashboard which only shows a primary KPI, with other key metrics of the organization shown as well to provide a high-level overview of the organization.

The placement of your charts in a report is essential. Typically, people are going to first look at the upper-left corner of whatever they view. This means your most important data (or whatever it is you want to be seen first) should be placed in the upper-left corner of the dashboard. After placing charts, use headers and footers to label your data and make it more logical and presentable. Lastly, remember charts in rows or columns, but don't do both. Order your more critical information by row or column or categorize information by row or column.

With Salesforce Enterprise Edition, you can automatically email out a dashboard to users. This emailed dashboard will look just like the regular dashboard and can be clicked through to view the report itself. Emails may be scheduled to be sent out on a settable basis, such as daily or weekly. This is an outstanding feature of which to make use if some users are not very active on Salesforce or you want to make sure your team is up to date in an accessible way.

Using and Understanding Top Line Revenue Growth Dashboards – A Real-World Perspective

Top Line Revenue Growth Dashboards provide senior leaders with the ability to monitor sales and client retention performance, insight into the type and timing of opportunities within the pipeline, and a view of upcoming sales and retention opportunities requiring a higher level of oversight. Individual dashboards should be developed for each Global Service Line (GSL) and Tier 1 country (US, UK, Canada and Australia, as well as the enterprise as a whole.

Understanding Dashboard Components

Every Top Line Revenue Growth Dashboard should be composed of at least three columns:

- New business

- Renewal business

- Opportunities requiring a higher level of oversight

The pages that follow outline what information is represented by each component and provide insight into how leaders should utilize the information.

Note   For a large global service company, oftentimes, business units are classified as Global Service Line (GSL). Countries and geographic locations are grouped by tiers. In this case study, Tier 1 country classification consists of the United States, the United Kingdom, Canada, and Australia.

New Business: Current Year (CY) Funnel (by Sales Stage and by GSL or Tier 1)

- Information included: Reflects the current year's pipeline (based on close date) of open New and Enhanced opportunities by Sales Stage and GSL/Tier 1; includes only those opportunities with a close date more significant than today.

157

- Business insights: A low number of opportunities in the early sales stages (Target/Prospect Qualify) signals a risk that there may be too few opportunities to progress through the funnel. However, it is essential to note that the funnel will evolve as the year progresses, with the bulk of opportunities falling in later sales stages. Such a progression indicates your sales team is successfully managing their opportunities and moving them toward closure. By the end of the year, the vast majority of opportunities should be in the latest sales stages (Acquisition or Closing) or pushed forward into the next year.

New Business: CY Conversion (Overall and by GSL or Tier 1)

- Information included: Reflects the Closed Won and Closed Lost New and Enhanced opportunities by GSL/Tier 1; includes only those opportunities with a close date in the current calendar year.

  Understanding your new business conversion rate allows you to determine what level of funnel coverage is needed to meet your annual goal. For example, a 25% conversion rate indicates you need a total funnel of four times your plan to meet the goal, whereas a 50% conversion rate would mean you need two times your goal.

- Business insights: Low conversion rates signal a need to dig deeper into your lost opportunities. Many sales colleagues enter every potential opportunity into Salesforce, then qualify them and ultimately mark them as Closed Lost if it is not a good opportunity. This should not be a cause for concern. However, if several opportunities are marked Closed Lost in the Presentation stage or later, a more in-depth assessment is warranted to understand root causes and trends in lost opportunities.

New Business: CQ Top Wins and CY Top Wins

- Information included: Identifies the top 10 Closed Won opportunities for the current quarter or calendar year based on close date.

- Business insight: Use these components to identify those new clients whose onboarding quickly may warrant a higher level of oversight.

New Business: Next 90 Days Top Opportunities

- Information included: Identifies the top 10 New and Enhanced opportunities that should close within the next 90 days. Top opportunities are based on the annual opportunity amount and a sales stage of Presentation, Acquisition, or Closing.

- Business insight: These high-value opportunities present a higher possibility of closure due to their sales stage and warrant additional oversight by the leadership to ensure the appropriate attention and resources are focused on the opportunity as it progresses through the pipeline and increases the likelihood of success.

Renewal: Next 90 Days at Risk Renewals

- Information included: Identifies those opportunities with a Marketed Renewal opportunity type that should close within the next 90 days.

- Business insights: The Marketed Renewal opportunity type signals that the renewal is At Risk either because the client has issued an RFP or indicated a level of dissatisfaction with our performance.

  Marketed Renewals with large opportunity values require additional leadership oversight and intervention to address client concerns, ensure RFP responses position the company appropriately, and provide appropriate follow-through on at-risk mitigation plans for the client.

Renewal: Next 90 Days Top Renewals

- Information included: Identifies the top 10 renewal opportunities that should close within the next 90 days. Top opportunities are based on the annual opportunity amount and a sales stage of Presentation, Acquisition, or Closing.

- Business insight: These high-value opportunities represent a more significant threat to your business.

  The retention rate should not be successfully closed and therefore warrant additional oversight by leadership to ensure the appropriate attention and resources are focused on the opportunity to increase the likelihood of success. The loss of these opportunities represents a direct impact on your revenue and will require additional new or enhanced business to achieve growth targets.

RFPs Pending Delivery to Client/Prospect

- Information included: Identifies all in progress RFPs, including new, enhanced, and marketed renewals, regardless of the close date.

- Business insight: Use this component to quickly identify those RFP responses that may warrant a higher level of leadership oversight to ensure the appropriate attention and resources are focused on the opportunity and increase the likelihood of success.

New Business/Renewal: Expired Opportunities

- Information included: Identifies those opportunities with an expired Close Date (i.e., a day before today) by GSL or Tier 1 country. The close date represents when the buyer is expected to decide if the company will win the business.

- Business insight: These opportunities represent a significant data quality concern and are leading indicated or outdated information and low Salesforce adoption by individual opportunity owners. All expired opportunities should be reassessed to ensure your team remains in alignment with their buyers' decision-making timelines and updated to Closed Lost or Closed Won or moved to a later Close Date.

CRM Planning Questionnaires

The goal of the interview questionnaire is to understand the company's (organization's) current Customer Relationship Management (CRM) "state." The outcome is an understanding of how the company currently conducts customer management and data governance. This questionnaire is not intended to be answered in its entirety by any one individual. You instead can present the appropriate subsets of this questionnaire to individuals based on their role in the organization.

Project Survey

Business Case

- Has your organization developed a formal business case for a CRM program?

- Are there any specific events that set the creation of a CRM program in motion?

- What are the strategic initiatives of the business that CRM supports?

- Are there any projects that CRM is considered as a critical path?

- What business processes are you targeting to benefit from CRM?

- What are the primary business drivers that necessitate a CRM program? Some examples:

    - Improved analytics

    - A complete view of a customer

    - Streamlined customer service

    - Streamlined business processes

- Macroeconomic or competitive pressures

- Compliance and risk mitigation

- Is CRM an initiative that is intended to support a single critical domain (i.e., customer), or is it intended to be a multidomain platform?

- Are there any known timeframes for specific CRM capabilities to be available to support other initiatives (e.g., CRM integrated with MDM must be rolled out by the end of the year)?

Industry

- Who are your primary competitors?

- Do you view CRM as a potential competitive advantage?

- Are there any legal compliance considerations in your industry?

- Are there any regulatory compliance considerations in your industry?

- Are there any security compliance considerations in your industry?

- Are there industry-specific reference data that you manage or originate?

Sponsorship

- How is the creation of a CRM program being driven in the organization? Is it top-down (an executive mandate) or bottom-up (organically grown from within the organization)?

- Who is the primary owner of your CRM solution? Are they from the technology or business side of the organization?

- Have you established sponsorship for the project? If so, then

  - Is sponsorship established formally (documented and committed) or informally (verbally)?

  - Business sponsors

    - Have you identified business sponsors for the project? If so, who are they?

- Are there additional potential business sponsors who have yet to be engaged? If so, what has kept them from being encountered thus far?

- IT sponsors

  - Have you identified technical ownership for the project? If so, who owns it?

  - Do you have an established CRM implementation team?

  - Will the resources implementing a CRM solution be dedicated to CRM or shared across other initiatives?

Organizational Characteristics

- Is CRM a new concept within your organization?

- Are there existing CRM processes or applications today?

- What level of understanding do you feel your organization has of CRM?

- Is there an overarching need in the organization to educate stakeholders on the concept of CRM?

- Traditionally, how resistant is your organization to change?

- Traditionally, how eager has your organization been to adopt new technologies?

- Overall, how sophisticated are your business users when it comes to technology?

- From the following list of skills commonly needed to implement a CRM solution, please rate your maturity and capacity:

Skillset	Maturity (None, Basic, or Advanced)	Capacity (FTEs)
Project Management		
Business Analysis		
Data Analysis		

Skillset	Maturity (None, Basic, or Advanced)	Capacity (FTEs)
Data Modeling		
ETL Development		
Database Administration		
Data Warehousing/Analytics		
Application Development		
System Administration		
Quality Assurance		
Content Management (Intranet, portals, etc.)		

Project Processes

- Does your organization have a formal Project Management Office (PMO) organization that must be engaged in the CRM program?

- Does your organization have a preferred project management methodology?

- What are your organization's processes for development, testing, quality control, and quality assurance?

- What is the process for deploying solutions to production?

Governance

- Do you have an established CRM governance team/committee?

- Are boundaries of data ownership understood and agreed upon within the organization? Conversely, are there potential conflict areas around data ownership and responsibility?

- Are there disagreements within the organization as to the meaning of critical data (e.g., group A defines a product as X, and group B defines a product as Y)?

- Are employees incented to improve the data quality? If so, how?

Business Survey

Business Overview

- Please describe your role at the company.

- Please describe the business model of the company.

  - Are there multiple lines of business? If so, please describe them and where your role fits within them.

  - How is value created?

  - How is success defined?

  - What are the key performance indicators (KPIs) used to manage performance?

- How does growth typically occur?

  - Organic?

  - Merger?

  - Acquisition?

- How is business performance analyzed?

  - By management

  - By investors

- Do you have available artifacts that would assist with the CRM Assessment?

  - Management reports

    - Finance

    - Sales

    - Marketing

    - Dashboards

  - Investor reports

Current State

- What do the terms "Customer Relationship Management (CRM)" and "Front Office" mean to you?

- Data quality

  - Please describe the issues you've encountered due to low data quality.

  - Would you estimate these issues to be a significant hindrance to your ability to perform your role? If so, how?

  - How are data quality issues currently handled?

  - What efforts have been undertaken previously to improve the data quality?

- Please describe any current or previous CRM solutions you have used.

  - What was the domain(s) managed using that solution?

  - Was it internally developed or built using an underlying CRM platform?

  - Please describe your overall experience with that solution.

  - What functionality did you like and would consider critical to being in any future CRM solution you use?

  - What functionality would you have liked to have, which were critical gaps for you?

- Current data lifecycle

  - How is it initiated – how is data added to the system?

  - When does it end – how is data removed from the system?

  - How quickly do master data move through the lifecycle?

- People
  - Is customer data owned and managed by a single team, or is it owned and operated collaboratively across groups?
    - How many participate?
    - Are they classified?
    - Who participates?
    - Role of participants?
    - The physical location of each participant?
  - Do you feel there are clear ownership and responsibility for master data in the organization?
- Systems
  - Where is data entered in your systems (systems of entry)?
  - What do you consider the most complete and accurate set of customer data (systems of record)?
  - Who are the consumers of customer data (subscribers)?
  - Who manages the data lifecycle?
  - How is the performance of the data lifecycle measured?
- Do you have access to any resources that help define data as well as assist you with locating the data you need (i.e., metadata)?

Future State

- Please describe the key capabilities you feel are necessary for any future CRM program.
- In your opinion, what will be the most significant resulting benefits from implementing a CRM program at the company?
- Who should participate in the data management lifecycle?
- Do you anticipate that stewardship will be a distributed or centralized function?

Domain-Specific Questions

- What are the critical domains of your organization?

Customer

- Who are your customers? Are they businesses or individuals?

- What is the geographic distribution of your customer base?

- How are relationships with your customers formed?

- How is customer information captured?

- How many distinct customers do you estimate exist today?

- How do you interact with customer information?

- Can you describe the lifecycle of a typical customer (e.g., prospect → makes a purchase → ongoing service)?

- What are the common touchpoints and interactions a customer has with the overall organization?

- How hard is it to distinctly identify a customer across all parts of the organization (marketing, sales, finance, service, etc.)?

Product

- What are the products your organization sells?

- How does the company add value to the products it sells?

- Would you estimate that the products the company sells are commoditized?

- Where in the supply chain does the company sit? Does the company manufacture, distribute, or sell to end consumers?

- Product management

  - What is the lifecycle of the product?

  - Does product information originate internally or externally?

- Please describe the current process for defining a new product before it can be sold.

    - How many people participate in this process?

    - How is the process managed?

    - What visibility is there in this process?

- How are product identifiers (SKUs) assigned?

- How is product information managed?

Data Survey

Note   The data survey is performed less as a questionnaire and more through an analysis of sample source data. The following few questions ensure that the CRM consultant has the necessary resources available to perform a rational analysis of existing data.

- Do you have any preexisting data dictionaries or other documentation for each existing system?

- Are there any data models or ER diagrams available?

- For each set of sample data, who is the best resource available to help understand and interpret the data?

- Can we have access to sample data through either direct access to a nonproduction system or a set of files that contain a representative group of sample data?

    - Is it comprehensive, that is, does it contain a complete list of columns to be considered?

Technology Survey

Technology Landscape

- Preferred software technologies – please list the existing technologies in use in your IT landscape for the following types of technologies:

Category	Preferred Software in Use	Notes
SaaS systems		
Server OS		
RDBMS		
OLAP databases		
ETL		
Reporting and Analytics		
Intranet portal(s)		
Extranet portal(s)		
Enterprise Service Bus (ESB)		
Enterprise Resource Planning (ERP)		
Customer Relationship Management (CRM)		
Other LOB applications		

- Does your organization employ an ERP solution, and if so, does it include CRM functionality for one or more domains?

- What is your organization's standard for user authentication and authorization?

- Hardware standards

  - Does your organization have a preference for virtualization? If so, please share any virtualization standards you have defined.

  - Does your organization have a standard for data storage? If so, please share any storage standards that are defined.

- Data archiving

    - Does your organization have a policy for archiving data?

    - If so, how many months or years is it?

    - What is the general process you follow for archiving data?

- Data integration

    - Do you have a preference for any particular CRM architectural style?

    - What are the preferred methods for integrating data between systems in the organization?

    - Are integrations typically developed using in-house resources?

    - Does your organization intend to integrate CRM via a services-oriented architecture? If so, is that an initial or long-term goal?

Technology Futures

- Initially, do you intend to use CRM for analytic, operational, or reference data (or some blend)?

- Are there any pertinent strategic shifts in your IT strategy that would affect the overall architecture of a CRM solution? Common examples:

    - The implementation of a new integration pattern (e.g., the purchase of an ESB platform)

    - A move toward cloud computing

    - A move toward virtualization

- Are any of the technologies that would interact with an MDM solution slated for retirement or replacement?

Project Status Guideline

Status Summary

- Is the project on track for delivery as expected?

- What is the final date for delivery?

- What are the final cost estimates?

- Status against any other high-level goals

  - Manufacturing rate

  - Delivery

  - Partners

Progress

- List achievements and progress since the last status update was given.

  - Address schedule implications.

- Highlight those things that made progress possible.

Attention Areas

- List delays and problems since the last status.

  - List corrective actions being taken.

  - Address schedule implications.

- Make sure you understand

  - Issues that are causing delays or impeding progress

  - Why the problem was not anticipated

  - If a customer will want to discuss an issue with upper management

Schedule

- List top high-level dates.

- Keep it simple, so the audience does not get distracted with details.

- Distribute a more detailed schedule if appropriate.

  - Make sure you are familiar with the details of the schedule so you can answer questions.

Deliverables

- List main critical deliverables.

  - Yours to client

  - Client to you

  - Yours to outside services

  - Outside services to you

- Understand the confidence rating of each deliverable.

  - Indicate the confidence level on slides if appropriate.

Costs

- List new projections of costs.

  - Include original estimates.

    - Understand the source of differences in these numbers (anticipate questions).

- If there are cost overruns

  - Summarize why.

  - List corrective or preventative actions you've taken.

  - Set realistic expectations for future expenditures.

Technology

- List technical problems that have been solved.

- List outstanding technical issues that need to be solved.

  - Summarize their impact on the project.

- List any dubious technological dependencies for the project.

  - Indicate the source of doubt.

  - Summarize the action being taken or back up plan.

Resources

- Summarize project resources.

  - Dedicated (full-time) resources.

  - Part-time resources.

  - If the project is constrained by a lack of resources, suggest alternatives.

- Understand that the customer may want to be assured that all possible resources are being used, but in such a way that costs will be managed appropriately.

Upcoming Goals

- Date of the next status update.

- List goals for the following review.

  - Specific items that will be done

  - Issues that will be resolved

- Make sure anyone involved in the project understands the action plan.

Decision-Making Framework

A decision-making framework (DMF) would power you with a well-disciplined plan for your project, approach, and solution you build. I find the market-based management (MBM) principles and philosophy by Charles Koch an excellent source of management philosophy for building a data-driven Front Office platform.

The framework (Figure 8-6) is divided into eight areas. I will outline key considerations and high-level definitions of each of these categories I learned during my time at Koch Industries directly from the leaders in Wichita, Kansas.

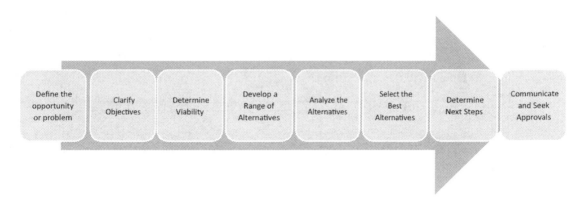

Figure 8-6. *Decision-making framework (DMF) powered by Charles Koch's market-based management (MBM) philosophy*

1. Define the opportunity or problem.

    a. Succinctly identify the opportunity or problem.

    b. Focus on the desired outcome, not possible solutions.

2. Clarify your objectives.

    a. What are you trying to accomplish?

    b. What do you care about the most?

3. Determine viability.

    a. Stop the process if it should not be a priority.

    b. Estimate the value of the opportunity or problem.

    c. Brainstorm the preliminary views on critical issues, including risks and long-term consequences.

    d. Does addressing the opportunity or problem fit our business vision?

    e. Will it build a competitive advantage?

    f. Are we the logical owners? Why us? Why now?

    g. Is future work justified? Who can help you decide?

    h. Identify likely winners and eliminate losers early.

    i. Avoid incremental investment in a "lost cause."

4. Develop a range of alternatives.

   - Be creative; think beyond the obvious!

   - Brainstorm ways the opportunity or problem could be addressed.

   - What is the "optimize base case"?

   Tips:

   - Create alternatives first; evaluate later.

   - Ask "How?" using your objectives.

   - Do your thinking first.

   - Ask others for suggestions.

5. Analyze the alternatives.

   Consider the pros/benefits/positives and the cons/difficulties/obstacles of each reliable alternative.

   - Consider second and third consequences (including intangible).

   - What about creative destruction? How could the pros and cons change the future? Who has expertise? Who can help?

   - Identify key drivers.

   - What will make the venture successful? Unsuccessful? Select the few critical success drivers. What assumptions are we making? Can they be tested?

Manage risk and upside:

- What is the full range of possible outcomes? What do we need to do to capture the potential upside?

- What are the critical areas of risk? What could go wrong? Are there any potentially catastrophic risks?

- Can the risks be mitigated? Should they be mitigated? Can we cap the downside? How will others (customers, competitors, policymakers, etc.) respond?

- How will we adapt if the unexpected occurs? What is our exit strategy?

- Can we embed options? Should we?

Explore capabilities and resources:

- Do we possess the capabilities needed to implement the venture? If not, should we hire, train, or contract the capabilities?

- What capabilities will we acquire or build?

- What is the opportunity cost of the needed resources?

Perform economic analysis:

- What level of analysis (including risk assessment) is needed for this venture? Apply marginal analysis. Avoid false precision.

6. Select the best alternatives.

   a. Focus on your objectives, the value created, and return on resources.

7. Determine next steps.

   a. What is required to advance to the next stage?

   b. Who will own each step?

   c. How will we measure success?

   d. How will we know if we must "course correct"?

8. Communicate and seek approvals.

    a. Communicate early and often; do not wait until the end of the process.

    b. Seek input from others, including those who will need to approve the venture.

    c. Prepare a write-up only if needed to.

    d. Clarify and communicate your thinking.

    e. Facilitate change.

    f. Request authority.

    g. Improve decision-making.

Summary

We discussed the core offering of Marketing Cloud by Salesforce and its use cases in the Front Office environment. In the next chapter, we will begin exploring the concept of Master Data Management, a key offering of Dun & Bradstreet (D&B) Hoovers, and Informatica Cloud Customer 360.

CHAPTER 9

Data Management

In the previous chapter, we reviewed a few concepts and frameworks, including customer segmentation, executive scorecard, and framework for business development owners. We also covered Net Promoter Score (NPS), dashboard design, how to architect top line revenue growth in Salesforce, and in-depth CRM design questionnaires. In this chapter, we will review and study the data aspect of Salesforce that includes data export, mass delete, native integration, duplicate management, and the state and country picklist enablement process. We will briefly discuss D&B Hoovers and Informatica Cloud from a Salesforce perspective.

Data

Once Salesforce is implemented for any organization, managing data becomes one of the higher priorities from an organization perspective. Life happened, people change jobs and relocate, and company shuts down...whatever the reason may be, it has become necessary to update and manage your data. Salesforce provides data management capabilities natively including a desktop tool called data loader which could be downloaded and configured to perform basic level ETL (extract, transform, load) work.

Data Export

Salesforce Data Export lets an administrator prepare a copy of the entire Salesforce database in CSV format and create a zip file to download from the system. From this page (Figure 9-1), you can start the export process immediately or schedule it to run automatically.

© Rashed A. Chowdhury 2021
R. A. Chowdhury, *Building a Salesforce-Powered Front Office*, https://doi.org/10.1007/978-1-4842-6676-2_9

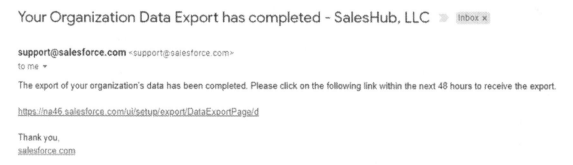

Figure 9-1. *Salesforce Data Export – monthly export service definition*

The export files are also available on this page for 48 hours, after which time they are deleted. When an export is ready for download, you will receive an email (Figure 9-2) containing a link that allows you to download the file(s).

Your Organization Data Export has completed - SalesHub, LLC » Inbox ×

support@salesforce.com <support@salesforce.com>
to me ▾

The export of your organization's data has been completed. Please click on the following link within the next 48 hours to receive the export.

https://na46.salesforce.com/ui/setup/export/DataExportPage/d

Thank you,
salesforce.com

Figure 9-2. *Your Organization Data Export has completed – confirmation email*

I recommend that you schedule a weekly data export routine (Figure 9-3) and download the files somewhere else as your backup mediums. In this process, you will get a zipped folder containing all of the selected objects in CSV (comma-separated values) format. It is important to note here that there is an enterprise-grade database backup solution in Salesforce AppExchange which you could consider implementing. Own Backup is a popular choice in AppExchange. Spanning, Odaseva, CopyStorm, and so on are a few alternatives that you could consider from the Salesforce AppExchange as well.

If you need to integrate SQL Server with Salesforce and perhaps back up Salesforce in SQL Server, I found that the DBAmp solution (`https://forceamp.com`) is strong and affordable.

Figure 9-3. *Salesforce Data Export – schedule data export*

Also, you can download your data classification information into a .csv file. The .csv file includes the object and field names and the field-specific data sensitivity value. Only fields that have an associated data sensitivity value are included in the downloaded file. The .csv file includes the first 2000 records for each data sensitivity value.

Mass Delete

For one reason or another, you will have incomplete, inadequate, bad, or irrelevant data in your system, and it will be necessary to clean up your database by deleting those records. Your user can delete one record at a time in the front-end user interface if they are the record owner, but to be able to quickly delete hundreds of stale contacts or trade show Leads, it will be time-consuming for your administrator to delete records one at a time. Salesforce provided mass delete records (Figure 9-4) capabilities for accounts, Leads, activities, contacts, cases, solutions, products, and reports. The deleting process is very similar for each of these objects.

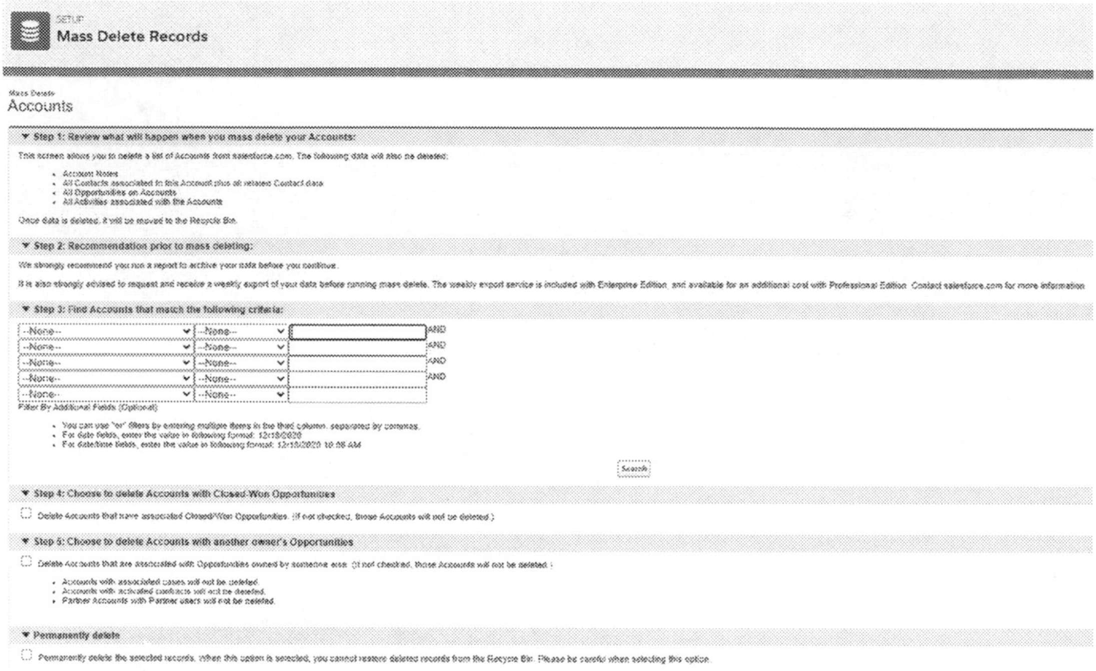

Figure 9-4. *Mass Delete Records – Account*

Once launched, the wizard-driven process will walk you through a few steps to complete the transactions. For example, if you want to perform a mass delete account, you have to complete the following steps:

- You will have to review what will happen when you mass delete your Accounts. The first section of the Mass Delete account (Figure 9-4) wizard allows you to delete a list of Accounts and its associated data as follows:

  - Account Notes

  - All Contacts associated to this Account plus all related Contact data

  - All Opportunities on Accounts

  - All Activities associated with the Accounts

  - Once data is deleted, it will be moved to the Recycle Bin.

- Salesforce recommends that your administrator run a report to archive your data before carrying out this exercise. It is also strongly advised to request and receive a weekly export of your data (we discussed this in the previous section) before running mass delete.

- Find Accounts that match your specific criteria. For example, your administrator can select all accounts that are inactive more than one year or so. Add additional criteria if desired.

- Your administrator may also want to select the delete Accounts with the Closed-Won Opportunities option which will ensure to delete the accounts with a closed won opportunity.

- Finally, since your administrator is mass deleting to clean up your entire organization, they may want to select to delete Accounts with another owner's Opportunities with the following criteria:

    - Accounts with associated cases will not be deleted.

    - Accounts with activated contracts will not be deleted.

    - Partner Accounts with Partner users will not be deleted.

Finally, permanently delete the selected records. When this option is selected, the administrator cannot restore deleted records from the Recycle Bin.

All Data Integration Rules

Data integration keeps your data up to date so that your data remains accurate and relevant and provides value to the enterprise. When activated, these rules check existing Salesforce records with any running data services for updates and append based on the defined business rules.

Basically, in data integration rules (Figure 9-5), you have to identify the source data and destination object, define all the related fields that may need the updates, and finally define the rules on how these updates will be made. You can also invoke Salesforce triggers and advanced workflow rules for the updated record.

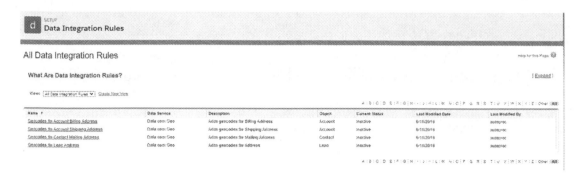

Figure 9-5. *Data integration rules*

Data integration rules can assess your data, enhance, enrich, standardize, and complete for accuracy. You can even run a Salesforce data integration report to understand the value proposition aspect of the updated database record.

For example, let's review the Geocodes for Account Billing Address (Figure 9-6) rule configured here.

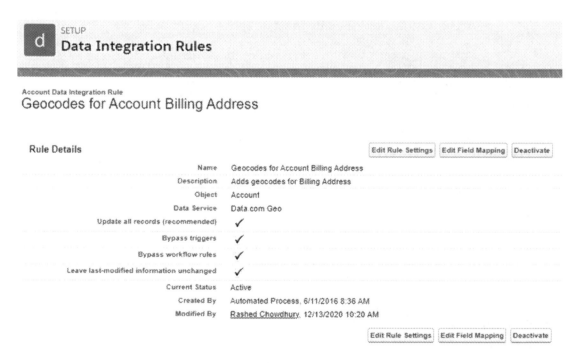

Figure 9-6. *Data integration rules definition*

Giving a logical name and entering a good description is straightforward. Then we have to select all the options. Updating all records is highly recommended. If your administrator deselects this option, this rule doesn't update records when new data is available, and there should be a very good reason for deselecting this option.

Your administrator then has to define the field mapping between the Salesforce object and the data service of your choice in the match tab of the Data Integration Rule Field Mapping (Figure 9-7). There are many data services that are available in the marketplace: Data.com, D&B Hoovers, and so on, to name a few.

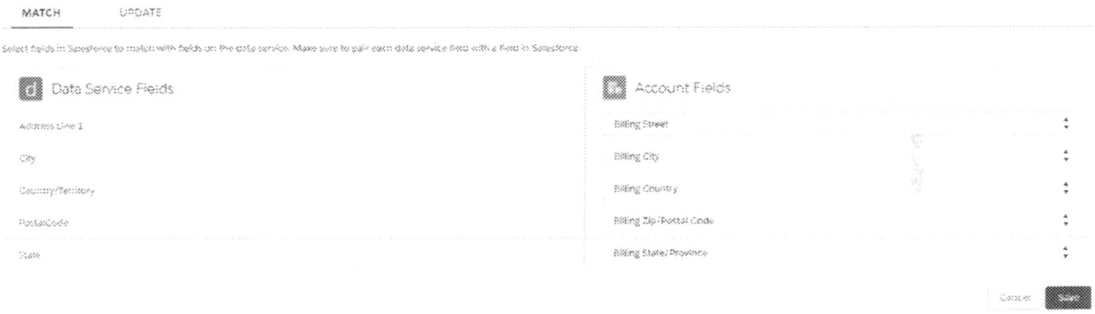

Figure 9-7. *Integration Rule Field Mapping (match)*

In this step, your administrator has to select fields in Salesforce to match with fields on the data service. We used Address line 1, city, state, zip, and country to match with Data.com service fields and Salesforce Account fields. One thing we need to make sure is to pair each data service field with a field in Salesforce.

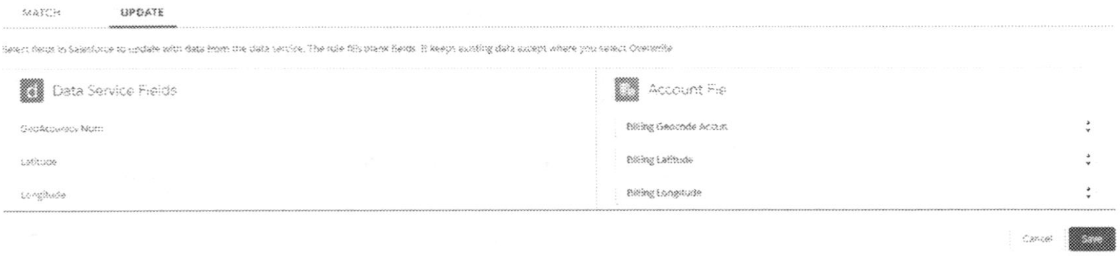

Figure 9-8. *Data Integration Rule Field Mapping (update)*

Finally, we have to identify what fields to update in Salesforce. The administrator has to identify and select fields in Salesforce to update with data from the data service. In this example, we choose GeoAccuracy Num, Latitude, and Longitude (Figure 9-8).

Salesforce Duplicate Management

Salesforce duplicate rules (Figure 9-9) work together with Salesforce matching rules to prevent users from creating duplicate records in the system.

A matching rule decides if the record a user is creating or updating is comparable enough to other records to be considered as a duplicate, though a duplicate rule discloses to Salesforce what move to make when duplicates are identified in the database.

Figure 9-9. *Duplicate Rules*

For instance, a duplicate rule can impede users from saving records that have been recognized as potential duplicates or simply alert users that they may be creating a duplicate but allow them to save the record at any rate.

Other third-party solutions within the Salesforce AppExchange and its ecosystem could be purchased and integrated as part of the org-wide duplicate management effort. For example, Cloudingo, DemandTools, Informatica Cloud, DupeCatcher, and so on, to name a few of the duplicate management tools available in the Salesforce AppExchange.

Contact Duplicate Rule – Standard Rule for Contacts with Duplicate Leads

Specify how your organization's sharing rules determine which records the matching rule compares.

Enforce sharing rules: The matching rule compares only records that the user has access to, and the resulting list of possible duplicates includes only records the user has access to.

Bypass sharing rules: The matching rule compares all records, regardless of user access, but the resulting list of possible duplicates includes only records the user has access to.

Figure 9-10. *Contact Duplicate Rule – Standard Rule for Contacts with Duplicate Leads*

There are three parts to the Duplicate Rule – Standard Rule for Contacts with Duplicate Leads (Figure 9-10) rule:

- Rule Details: In this section, you simply name the rule and enter a good description. One of the main tasks here is to specify how your organization's sharing rules determine which records the matching rule compares. It is recommended to enforce the sharing rules for the record-level security.

- Actions: Your administrator has to specify what happens when a user tries to save a duplicate record. The action on creating and editing should be set to allow. The alert should set to read as to use one of these records. Your administrator needs to tell users why they can't save the record and what you'd like them to do.

- Matching Rules: You have to define how duplicate records are identified. We compared contacts with Lead records and enforced a matching rule for Lead records.

Finally, set the order flag that determines the order in which duplicate rules are processed. A newly created rule is automatically processed last, but you can reorder the rules. Tell users why they can't save the record and what you'd like them to do.

All Matching Rules

A standard matching rule (Figure 9-11) compares field values to assess if a record is similar enough to existing records to be considered a duplicate in Salesforce.

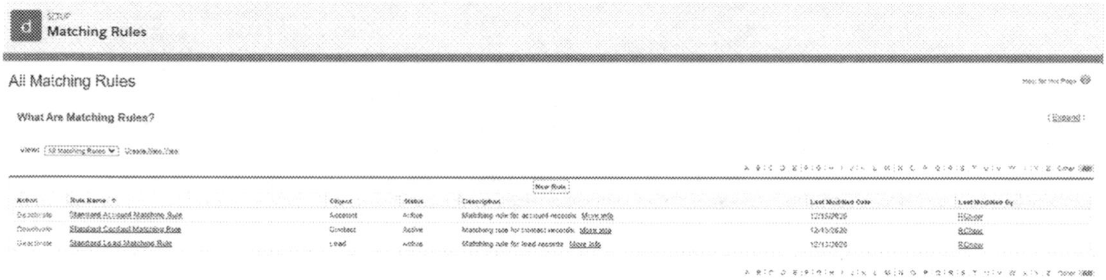

Figure 9-11. *Matching Rules*

For example, a matching rule can specify that if the Email and Phone values of two records match exactly, the records might be duplicates in Salesforce.

Your administrator should use matching rules with duplicate rules to define what happens when duplicates are identified.

Enable State and Country/Territory Picklists

Before switching to state and country/territory picklist (Figure 9-12) fields, your administrator must find and convert existing state and country/territory text data into standard picklist values. Your administrator should also find where state and country/territory data are used in customizations such as reports and list views, because you may need to update them when you enable the picklists.

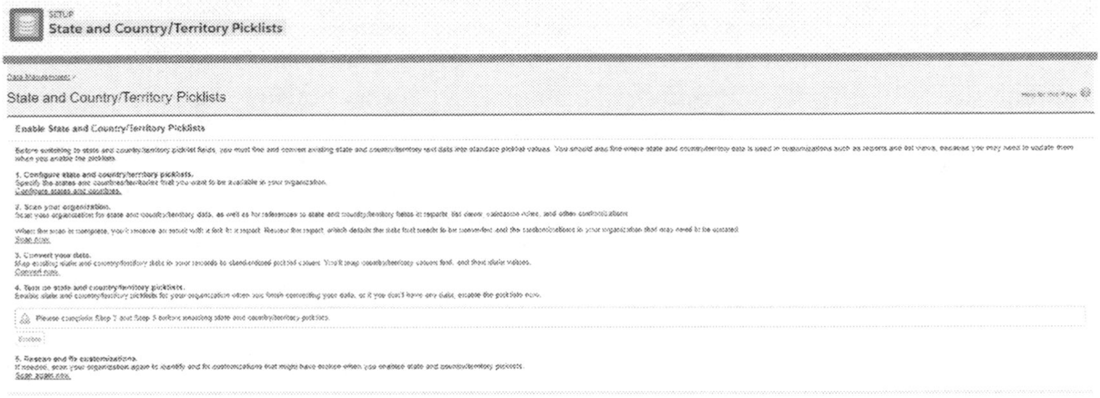

Figure 9-12. *State and Country/Territory Picklists*

Before switching to state and country/territory picklist fields, your administrator must find and convert existing state and country/territory text data into standard picklist values. You should also find where state and country/territory data are used in customizations such as reports and list views, because you may need to update them when you enable the picklists.

1. Configure state and country/territory picklists: Specify the states and countries/territories that you want to be available in your organization.

2. Scan your organization: Scan your organization for state and country/territory data as well as for references to state and country/territory fields in reports, list views, validation rules, and other customizations. When the scan is complete, you'll receive an email with a link to a report. Review the report, which details the data that needs to be converted and the customizations in your organization that may need to be updated.

3. Convert your data: Map existing state and country/territory data in your records to standardize picklist values. You'll map country/territory values first, and then state values.

4. Turn on state and country/territory picklists: Enable state and country/territory picklists for your organization when you finish converting your data, or if you don't have any data, enable the picklists now.

Scan Your Organization

Your administrator needs to identify where state and country/territory text data is used in your organization and find customizations that you may need to update when you switch to picklists.

1. Click Scan. You'll receive two emails when the scan is complete: one regarding affected address data and one regarding affected customizations.

2. Click the links in the emails to see how your data and customizations are affected.

SaaS Databases

There are a variety of tools to manage your data in Salesforce. One such tool is D&B Hoovers. D&B Hoovers is a business intelligence solution created by Dun & Bradstreet to accelerate sales, identify the best prospects, and use data to better engage with customers.

The solution uses sophisticated analytics combined with an extensive commercial database to deliver quality business intelligence. It integrates with Salesforce to help save time and improve records for your company.

Dun & Bradstreet Hoovers

Dun & Bradstreet (D&B) Hoovers has many features to help you analyze data and make decisions. The following features are just a few examples of what this tool can do:

- Business Signals: Monitors the behavior of other businesses and their activities to find opportunities.

- Conceptual Search: This allows you to search for a concept and receive a list of companies related to or involved with that concept. For example, searching blockchain will return all companies who are concerned with that topic. From there, the results can be saved and filtered.

- Ideal Profile Scoring: This allows you to specify specific criteria you want to be targeted when looking for new companies with whom to do business and then scores companies based on these criteria to find the best prospects.

- One-Stop Reports: One-stop reports usually create a consolidated information from a list of other reports. This report is generated in a PDF format.

- Smart Lists: These are dynamically generated and updated lists that contain information about new opportunities. New businesses and contacts relevant to the criteria you set are automatically added to your Smart List.

- Triggers: A trigger is an automated alert that fires when specific terms or events come up in the news. With triggers, the user can watch trends unfold and gain critical insights into the market. These alerts may be customized and emailed to the user.

Informatica Cloud MDM – Customer 360

Cloud MDM – Customer 360 is a Master Data Management (MDM) tool created by Informatica, which integrates with Salesforce. MDM tools are designed to regulate, cleanse, standardize, and manage data. It ensures data is not duplicated, and versions of the data do not drift and end up not matching each other in different areas of the organization.

With Informatica's Cloud MDM – Customer 360, you can keep your data up to date and visible in a single customer view. This means customer data from different systems may be merged and shown in one picture. This ensures users within your business have a single trusted source of information when they need to look up customer information within Salesforce.

Ensuring your data is not fragmented or duplicated within your different data systems is essential and helps you better sell to customers. For example, if a sales representative is preparing a price quote for a customer and there are errors in the system from which they're pulling, those errors will hurt your bottom line. That data needs to be accurate across the whole organization.

The following are a few features that Cloud MDM – Customer 360 provides:

- Data cleansing: Cleans data immediately whenever accounts, Leads, and contacts are created or updated based on corporate standards for customer data, such as country names, ISO codes, street suffixes, and legal forms.

- Deduplication: Automatically dedupes duplicate accounts, Leads, or contacts in SFDC and other data sources using its configurable, fuzzy Duplicate Detection process. Cloud MDM also prevents users from creating duplicate records.

- Consolidation: Enables you to consolidate and enrich customer data across other corporate databases, external databases, or other sources. Also builds hierarchy.

- Role-based dashboards: Provides configurable dashboards tailored to different roles within your organization. This allows your customer view to be differentiated and provides the best customer engagement.

- Identify relationships: Visualizes customer connections and relationships. Aggregates data from prospects, customers, transactions, products, and more.

Summary

In this chapter, we reviewed Salesforce data management offering, a key offering of Dun & Bradstreet (D&B) Hoovers, and Informatica Cloud Customer 360 and Salesforce data management.

In the next chapter, we will introduce you to proposal development and building sales pipeline by leveraging technology.

CHAPTER 10

Proposal Development and Sales Pipelines

In the previous chapter, we reviewed and studied the data aspect of Salesforce that includes data export, mass delete, native integration, duplicate management, and state and country picklist enablement process. We briefly discussed D&B Hoovers and Informatica Cloud from a Salesforce perspective. What does the sales pipeline look like today? How should you structure your proposals? How can you manage your pipeline and proposals? We will investigate these questions in this chapter. The last question can be answered right now: With Salesforce and other applications, you can create proposal templates and utilize proposal automation. You can track and generate reports on your sales pipeline. The following topics will be covered in this chapter:

- Proposal automation

- Sales playbook

- Sales pipeline challenges and trends

- Market noise

- Buying power spread out

- Involved buying process

Proposal Automation

Drafting up a proposal to send to a Lead can be time-consuming. The last thing you want to do is start from scratch every single time you need to send a proposal. This will severely slow down the sales process. The solution to this problem is to create a sales proposal template.

© Rashed A. Chowdhury 2021
R. A. Chowdhury, *Building a Salesforce-Powered Front Office*, https://doi.org/10.1007/978-1-4842-6676-2_10

A template is a predesigned document that has your company's branding on it. Fields are set to be populated using data from the prospect's Opportunity record. Several tools integrate with Salesforce that can create these proposal templates. Since the template is a predesigned document, you will ensure your company upholds a consistent image with every proposal sent out. Fields automatically filled out using Salesforce data saves your sales team time. Of course, they can always manually edit fields where they are missing data or it does not quite fit the proposal.

With proposal tools, you can also create and send proposals in just a few clicks, taking out much of the manual effort which might usually go into the proposal-sending process. Plus, not only does having automatically filled-out fields save time, but it also can lead to better accuracy, as there is no human error from manual editing.

Sales Playbook

You have several members of your sales team. How do you keep them all focused on selling when they are busy creating content, such as developing messaging or resources? The answer is by creating a sales playbook.

A sales playbook is a standardized document which details your sales process. It is meant to be used as a reference for your sales team. It can have examples of emails, questions to ask Leads, and guidelines for creating a proposal. Having a sales playbook allows your sales team to be more cohesive and better represent the company. They save time by not having to create content that is already in the sales playbook and can instead focus on selling.

When creating your sales playbook, you need to remember the use case. It is supposed to be a reference for your sales team. Keep the book concise and clearly labeled for the best readability. Make it easily accessible to your sales team. What use is having the book at all if there are several hoops a salesperson must jump through before they can use it? At that point, they are just wasting time. Consider hosting it in the cloud, so it is always available to everyone.

The content of your sales playbook is not set in stone. Treat your sales playbook as a living document. As your business develops new products, strategies, target customers, and compensation plans, you should update your sales playbook to reflect that information.

If your document is hosted on the cloud and is easily editable in real time, it is that much easier to update your playbook and get the changes out to your whole team. Just make sure when you make significant changes or add large sections to the document, you notify the team so they are aware.

Sales Pipeline Challenges and Trends

Knowing possible challenges to your sales pipeline is key to combating them and coming out on top. You want to stay on top of current trends and leverage technology as best you can.

Market Noise

Today, the market is boisterous. Every day, consumers are continually being inundated with ads, messages, and images. People spend a lot of time looking at their phones, watching Netflix or cable television, browsing the Internet and social media, looking at the news, and checking emails. It can be hard to find a way to break through the noise and reach your customers.

You can stick out on social media by merely creating quality and unique content. If all your competitors are sharing the same things, you will stand out by having your content. Consider making your content more visual, too, as that more easily gets people's attention. When not sharing your content, try to share news and other items which are different than your competitors. Try not to make any content you create or share too long (or at least the meta description of it). Keep the word count low on a visual, for example. People may only pay attention to your post for a few seconds, and it's essential they get the gist of it quickly.

Lastly, provide value to the consumer. If they are seeing as much content as they are per day, they do not want to feel like your offering is useless to them; or even worse, it comes at a cost to them. Please provide them with valuable content to reward them for taking the time to see what you are offering.

Buying Power Spread Out

There is rarely a single decision-maker at a company making a purchasing choice anymore. Instead, companies will have buying committees requiring several signatures before a purchase may be signed off. According to CEB research, in 2017, a business had an average of 6.8 people involved with a single purchasing decision.

This means you cannot just focus your efforts on selling to a single member of an organization. You must build your relationship with several figures at once. When you create your proposal, it is not going to be sent to and looked at by just one person.

B2B purchasing decisions are also all being heavily considered before businesses ever contact a sales representative as well. The Internet makes it easy to do independent research, and purchasers generally will not rely on getting information from a sales rep anymore. By trying to reach and build relationships with more people, the businesses who are fond of you can instead be the source of useful information for other purchasers.

Involved Buying Process

As you can see, the buying process for a business is complicated. Having several people involved with a purchasing decision is just one small part of the process. Figuring out how to work around this process is critical.

If a business is looking to make a purchase, it is because they have a problem for which they want to find a solution. To best sell your product, it is essential to know what issue it is solving. Show everyone you are marketing to the problem they have, even if they did not realize they had it. Then show them that the best way to solve their problem is to use your product or service. As this is the first part of the buying process, it is essential to get the prospect's attention here and have them become interested in you.

Following discovering they have a problem to solve, they will next research solutions. As businesses and consumers alike do more and more independent research online before making purchases, you must make yourself visible at this stage. If your marketing had already shown the purchasers the problem in the first place, then you are a step ahead. If this has not happened, then try to let your content help you establish yourself as an industry expert.

Keep in mind there is not just one person to whom you are marketing while a business is evaluating all its options. There are usually several people within the buying committee who have different needs and will be impressed differently.

It is also essential to make the actual purchase easy. Picture this: You have been looking for a product online. You do some research and finally narrow it down to two different brands. After careful consideration, you decide on Product A rather than Product B. It was close, and the product's price and quality seem similar, but A won you over in the end. You go to their website to make your purchase, and you cannot figure out how.

Eventually, you find where to add the product to your cart, buried under seemingly unrelated pages. You proceed to try and check out, but the website is unresponsive. After several minutes, you have not made any progress. You decide to try buying Product B instead and find no issues. Even though you had initially chosen Product A, the actual act of purchasing it was so tricky you eventually decided something else.

When selling your products or services, keep the process clear, fast, and straightforward. Make sure your website is quick and that it is easy to navigate. Ensure your website is usable and still sprints on a mobile device. You do not want to lose what was almost a sale because of a frustrating purchase experience.

Finally, you want your customer to evaluate their purchase positively. If they are not satisfied with their purchase, you may have lost their loyalty (or have not been able to build it in the first place). Send thank you emails to the customer and surveys to gather information on how they feel about their purchases.

Challenges and Trends

Having too much information and white noise makes it difficult to determine what's essential to the market. In today's market, it is more difficult to convince a buying committee and not just a buyer. Companies don't have a single decision-maker any longer, and the buying committee replaces them. The buying process is much more involved in the current business climate.

The selling team should consider asking questions like what is involved in the process and what problem are we solving. Someone from the selling team has to be that knowledgeable guide who will convince the buying team to come into the curiosity focus area, and that's where today's sales development kicks in.

Everybody has to start somewhere. Marc Benioff started his career at Oracle as the youngest corporate executive, and then later in his life, he began Salesforce from his apartment with a single 1-800 number. The conversation is rapidly changing and has evolved so much. Companies these days are asking way more from the sales development team than ever before.

Solution Approach

It is imperative to think about the buyer journey in today's sales process. Instead of how you want to deliver your products or services, you should ask your buyer how they want the product or service to be delivered. What would help move the mind of the buyer and where you waste their time. It should be all about the buyer in your solution approach.

Also, you need to focus on the individual customer and personalize their experience – the better the customer experience you can deliver, the better the chance to win the deal.

The professional maturity of the Sales Development Representative (SDR) is essential. The core values of a strong brand are imperative to leverage for the brand as we are witnessing a new type of sales user is engaging.

Leverage Technology to Sell More

As part of the corporate marketing and communication strategy, companies often use the email campaign to promote its products and services to the prospects. Most of the mass email communications follow corporate marketing guidance and use tools like Salesforce Pardot or Marketing Cloud. Oftentimes, the nature of those communications are more generic and address the broader communication demands. Salesforce provides an array of technology stacks in Salesforce Sales Cloud for business development and sales team to take advantage of those solutions to resolve relevant sales challenges as follows:

- To build up the pipeline, the sales team will need to send their own personalized email communication to their contact as sales ultimately own the relationship and should remain in contact with buyers. Salesforce Engage (mini Pardot) that comes with Salesforce Sales Cloud (when you sign up with Pardot) uses marketing-approved content in the hands of the sales development rep. This is a win-win setup; marketing-curated content makes marketing compliant and sales get the freedom to customize the copies of the email following corporate branding guideline. As a sales manager, you should know which email templates are working and which aren't from Salesforce Engage.

- For the high velocity sales development rep (SDR) team, you may want to consider introducing the sales console, a high productivity sales development tool with multiscreen capability. The sales console is a tool that has multiple screens with a customer list. Sales rep can quickly highlight each customer record which is then used to populate all the screens in the console while recording conversation from the phone. By reducing the number of clicks and navigation, the sales console enables the high speed of sales rep and improves the overall sales process. This is designed to expedite the SDR working with the prospects and customers.

- It is essential for the sales development team to get on a call with prospects and customers. If you are not talking, then you are not moving the customer through the pipeline. Using the Salesforce Lightning Voice, your administrator can configure a lightning voice for the rep to automatically log a call or email using Inbox.

- Today's rep needs intelligent tools to sell smarter. Agents need to sell the channel they are comfortable selling and serving the customer. You can have your Salesforce developers build custom experiences for different teams with improved overall user experience. New Salesforce Lightning components have a lot of inside sales capabilities built within the platform. The new and improved Salesforce Lightning Experience helps the sales development team in a great deal using out-of-the-box functionalities, and the sales team should leverage this technology to sell more.

Summary

In this chapter, we reviewed the sales proposal automation and basics of sales playbook. We also reviewed current market challenges, trends, and solution approach and leveraged technology to improve sales. We also covered the core buying power and buying process concepts. In the next chapter, we will introduce you to governance, customization trends, system, setup, and configuration best practices.

CHAPTER 11

Configuration Best Practices, Customization, and DevOps

In the previous chapter, we reviewed with Salesforce you can create proposal templates and utilize proposal automation. We also covered sales playbook, sales pipeline challenges and trends, buying power, and buying process. In this chapter, we will be discussing more on key configuration, setup home, customization consideration, DevOps, and governance framework to support the enterprise Salesforce practice.

Key Configuration and Setup

Authentication and authorization are two very critical concepts you should have a good idea of, not just from the Salesforce perspective, but IT in general. We will be discussing authentication settings and password policies.

Login and Authentication Settings

Securing the application is one of the critical capabilities software company has to think through very carefully. In the login and authentication settings (See Table 11-1) of the Salesforce organization, Salesforce provides the ability to restrict how, when, and from where the users are accessing the application. Access control from an IP address, time of the day, and single sign-on perspective are few necessary settings to note here.

© Rashed A. Chowdhury 2021
R. A. Chowdhury, *Building a Salesforce-Powered Front Office*, https://doi.org/10.1007/978-1-4842-6676-2_11

Table 11-1. *Login and authentication settings*

Settings Name	Description	Recommended
IP address restrictions	Salesforce administrator can restrict the user access to a range of IP addresses including any specific IP address.	For multiregional global implementation, consider IP restriction
Time of day restrictions	Salesforce administrator can restrict user access to specified time of the day or night.	For multiregional global implementation, consider time of the day restriction
Single sign-on options	Salesforce administrator can enable delegated authentication via SAML*.	Complex network environment, implement enterprise grade single sign-on (SSO) capabilities

*SAML:

- SAML is the standard for federated single sign-on.

- OASIS standard: Commercial and open source support.

- An authentication interface is hosted by a customer.

SAML workflow: A user requests a secure resource. Salesforce redirect to customer IDP. The customer authenticates the user. The user returns to Salesforce with SAML and is granted a session.

Password Policies

There are controls available for enabling password restrictions and account lockout settings. All of these settings are available for administrators under Setup ➤ Security Controls ➤ Password Policies (See Table 11-2).

Table 11-2. *Password policies*

Settings Name	Description	Recommended
User password expires in	Frequency to automatically expire passwords	90 days
Enforce password history	How many previous passwords to save to prevent password reuse	Five passwords remembered
Minimum password length	Minimum length of a password	Eight characters
Password complexity requirements	Should a password contain a mix of letters and numbers	Mix alphanumeric
Password question requirements	Require the user's password hint not to contain the password	Cannot contain the password
Maximum invalid login attempts	How many invalid logins are allowed before locking out the account	5
Lockout effective period	How long should an account remain locked out	30 minutes

Session Settings

There are controls available for enforcing session handling and session timeout (See Table 11-3). All of these settings are available for administrators under Setup ➤ Security ➤ Session Settings.

Table 11-3. *Session settings*

Settings Name	Recommended
Timeout value	2 hours
Disable session timeout warning pop-up	Yes
Force logout on session timeout	Yes
Lock sessions to the IP address from which they originated	Yes
Lock sessions to the domain in which they were first used	Yes

(*continued*)

Table 11-3. *(continued)*

Settings Name	Recommended
Require secure connections (HTTPS)	Yes
Require secure connections (HTTPS) for all third-party domains	Yes
Force relogin after Login-As-User	Yes
Require HttpOnly attribute	Yes
Enforce login IP ranges on every request*	Yes
Enable caching and autocomplete on login page	Yes
Enable secure and persistent browser caching to improve performance	Yes
Enable user switching	Yes
Require identity verification during multi-factor authentication (MFA) registration	Yes
Require identity verification for email address changes	Yes
Allow Lightning Login	Yes
Enable clickjack protection	Yes
Enable Stricter Content Security Policy	Yes
Enable XSS protection	Yes
Enable Content Sniffing protection	yes
Hide this site's URL from other websites (including Visualforce pages)	Yes

Enforce IP addresses in Login IP Ranges for all Salesforce access requests. If you don't select this option, Login IP Ranges are enforced only when users log in.

Setup Home (for Salesforce Administrator)

Setup Home (Figure 11-1) is a starting point for getting your Salesforce administrator navigate the advanced configuration and system administration aspect of the Salesforce platform. Salesforce has done a great job with the Setup Home for the administrator or advanced user.

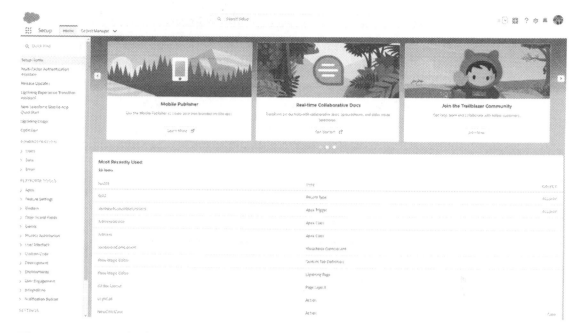

Figure 11-1. *Salesforce Setup Home*

There is no reason to memorize click paths to access different configurations and features within Salesforce. The left pane of the Setup Home consists of the following three main menus primarily:

- Administrator (User, Data, and Email)

- Platform Tools (Apps, Feature Settings, Einstein, Objects and Fields, Events, Process Automation, User Interface, Custom Code, Development, Environments, User Engagement, Integrations, and Notification Builder)

- Settings (Company Settings, Data Classification, Identity, and Security)

On the left pane, up in the top left-hand corner, you will find the *Quick Find* where an admin user can type any feature, and if it is available in your Salesforce organization, it will show up along with the click path.

Top menu areas, you will find *Object Manager, Search Setup,* and *Quick Create* menus. *Object Manager* is available next to Setup Home where an admin user has full access to customize standard objects and add custom objects. Right above the *Object Manager, Search Setup* is located.

Middle of the Setup Home, the carousel menu (*Mobile Publisher, Real-Time Collaborative Docs, Trailblazer Community, Go Mobile, App Exchange, Customize*) is available.

At the bottom of the Setup Home menu, the *Most Recently Used* feature is listed. I will explain most of these common features here.

Quick Find

The easiest way to find a setup page is in *Quick Find* where the administrator user can simply type the desired page; you don't have to memorize the click path of the page.

Figure 11-2. *Salesforce Quick Find under Setup*

As the admin user begins to type, the list of menu options (page link) that matches your search term will appear as shown in Figure 11-2. Simply click the page link, and the page link will take you to the desired setup page.

Object Manager

The Object Manager will provide you the access needed to all the standard and custom objects within your Salesforce organization (Figure 11-3). The Salesforce platform is highly customizable and lets administrators modify the data model with features like custom fields, page layouts, record types, and triggers.

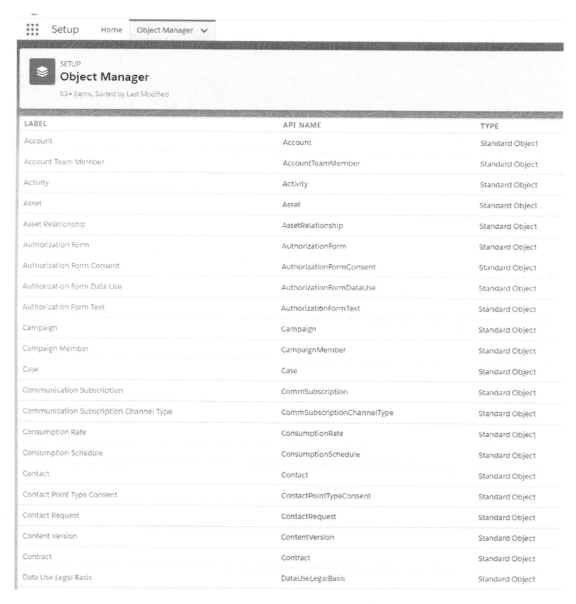

Figure 11-3. *Object Manager in Salesforce Setup Home*

To access Object Settings of a given object (e.g., Account) like fields and relationships, page layouts, lightning record pages, triggers, record types, buttons, links, and actions are available once you click the object link itself (as shown in Figure 11-4).

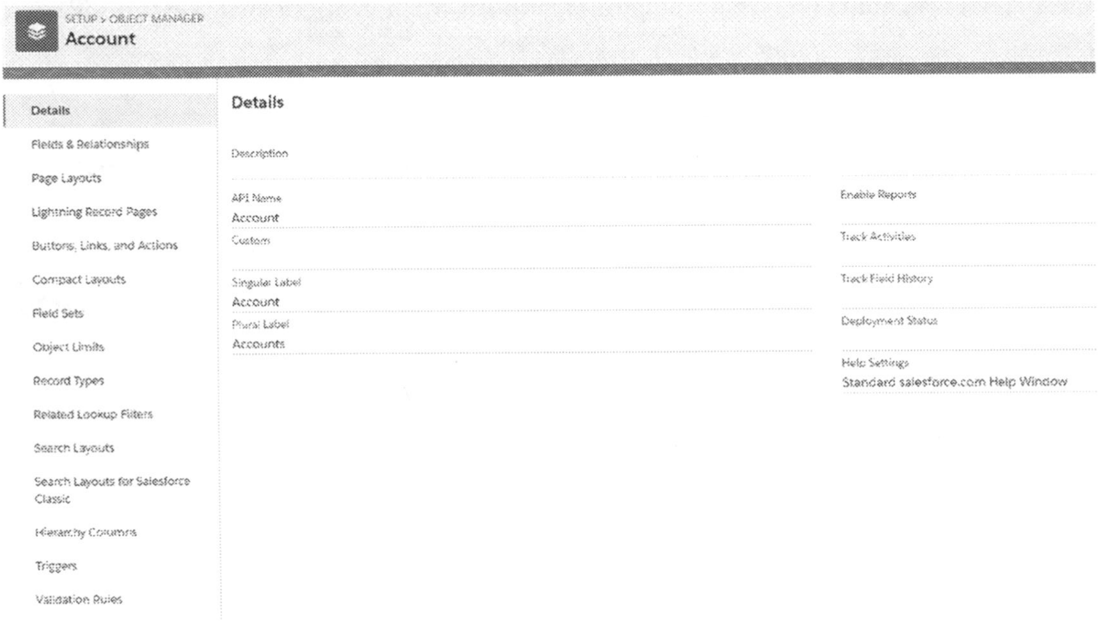

Figure 11-4. *Object Manager – Account object*

Global Search

Whether a custom account record type or custom tab definition all the way to page layout or custom case action setup, a global search (Figure 11-5) for Setup could provide the unparalleled search capability within the scope of Setup.

Figure 11-5. *Global search*

With global search, the administrator can search record across many objects within Salesforce. The administrator can also search records only available and limited to Setup. The search algorithm for Quick Find however focuses on the setup page (Web to Lead, Lead Settings, Roles, etc.) only, whereas Global Search looks for database records across Salesforce objects and setup.

It is important to call out here that not all Setup components and settings are searchable. The administrators can only match the results against the name of the record.

Create Shortcut

There are about six common tasks that a Salesforce administrator carries out in a daily basis, and Setup Home has these tasks listed under the Create drop-down as follows:

- User

- Multiple User

- Custom Object

- Custom Tab

- Email Template

- Workflow Processes

Carousel

The carousel of quick access tiles is way more than the latest and greatest feature offering from Salesforce (Figure 11-6).

Figure 11-6. *Setup Home – carousel*

With the tiles, you get an easy way to

- Mobile Publisher: Salesforce has its own mobile app which could be downloaded from both Google Play and Apple App Store. Companies can use the Mobile Publisher to create branded mobile apps and customize the look and feel.

- Real-time Collaborative Docs: Salesforce provides real-time collaboration opportunity that improves productivity significantly with collaborative documents all within Salesforce.

- Join the Trailblazer Community: The Trailblazer Community is a vibrant online community which consists of customers, suppliers, vendors, Salesforce employees, and partners across the globe. You should consider joining the Trailblazer Community to connect, give back, have fun, collaborate, and learn together with fellow trailblazers. You can also join your local Trailblazer Community Groups to learn Salesforce with peers, build your network, and find mentors.

- Go Mobile: This quick access link would take you to the preparation plan and implementation approach of the new Salesforce Mobile App. Your users can have a seamless digital experience with the new mobile app which enables your users to have a truly seamless experience across any devices. The new and improved mobile app will have built-in Lightning experience and smart navigation.

- Visit AppExchange: You can navigate directly to Salesforce AppExchange, an online portal of Salesforce-based solutions. Once you sign up with AppExchange, you will get personalized recommendations and tailored news, tips, and the latest solutions that match your profile.

- Click to Customize: This link will essentially take you to the Object Manager setup where you can modify standard objects to suit your processes and add custom objects, custom fields, a clean page layout, and a dedicated record type for each business process as part of your unique solution for your organization.

- Download SalesforceA: This mobile app is for the Salesforce administrator where the admin user can perform key admin activities (reset passwords, lock an account, freeze users, create new users, run a report, etc.) and monitor the organization remotely.

- View Release Notes: This link will take you to the current Salesforce release with the Release Notes where you can learn new functionalities that deliver innovations across the Salesforce platform to help connect you to your customers.

- See System Status: You can get real-time information on Salesforce performance, compliance, and security any time of the day by going into the Salesforce trust site (`https://trust.salesforce.com/en`) as shown in Figure 11-7. The status sites also provide transparency around service availability and performance for Salesforce products like Tableau, Pardot, MuleSoft, Heroku, and Data.com.

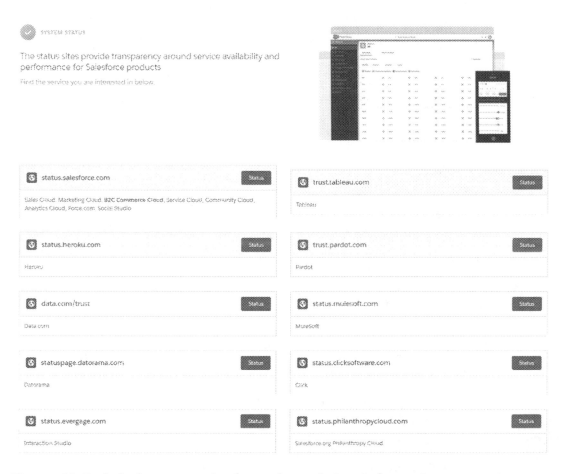

Figure 11-7. *Salesforce trust site, home for real-time information on system performance and security*

Setup is more than just your home base. It's also a portal to all the sites you commonly used as a Salesforce administrator.

Most Recently Used

The Most Recently Used list at the bottom of the page shows some of the Setup records that you recently viewed, edited, or created (Figure 11-8).

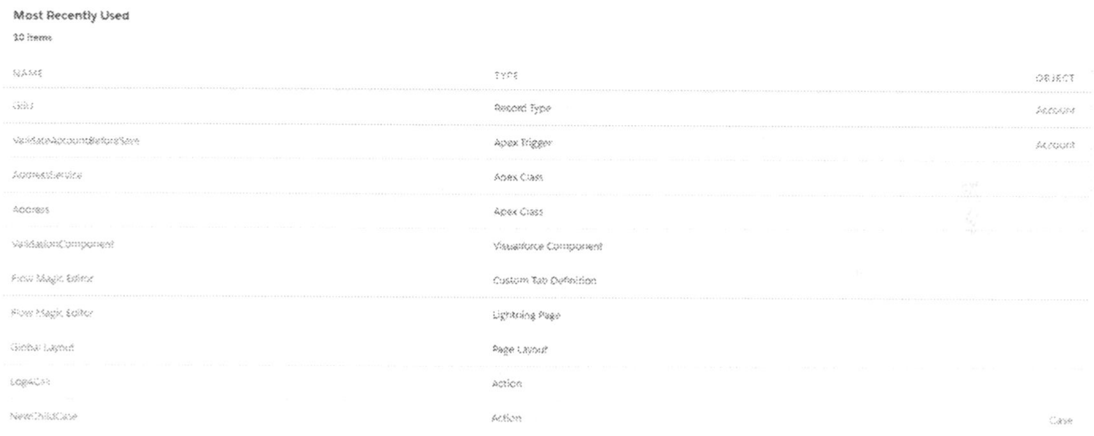

Figure 11-8. *Setup Home – Most Recently Used items*

You can use it to quickly jump back to what you were working on with a single click. You can also understand the type of items and objects you were working. Oftentimes, I find this feature very helpful especially if you have to manage multiple orgs.

Salesforce Enhancements and Customization – Consideration

Due to the nature of an initial business use case, Salesforce used to be implemented to solve CRM-related challenges. Over time this initiative has become beyond a CRM solution and turned into a full-blown platform service. It is necessary for big and complex implementation to launch CRM development and maintenance work to improve overall competitive effectiveness. Here are a few areas an organization can consider exploring to launch Salesforce-related projects.

Data Quality

- Prepare dashboard to monitor and measure key data quality metrics.

- Merge duplicate accounts, contacts, and Leads.

- Ensure complete data on account and contact pages, including contacts on all clients and prospects.

- Confirm account teams on all client accounts.

- Flag inactive (out of business) accounts.

- Reduce the number of expired opportunities.

Simplification

- Simplify account and opportunity pages to eliminate unnecessary fields and mandate essential data.

- Reduce actions required to provide complete data.

Standard Process and Protocols

- Document and communicate "Rules of the Road" for creating and maintaining an account, contact, and opportunity information.

- Document and communicate the marketing operation team's standard operating procedure, especially how to manage campaigns and Leads in Salesforce.

- Customize the Lead conversion process for your organization.

- Customize the sales opportunity management and opportunity close (won or lost) process.

Account Ownership

- Identify one account owner for paying clients and identify the account team.

- Introduce the account organization process whether to turn a trusted data source like D&B Hoovers or Data.com as a system of record for new prospects and existing clients.

Training and Support

- Revise training format to include live and virtual sessions, videos, quick reference cards, and so on.

- Reinvigorate the global Salesforce administrator network (confirm roles and responsibilities, ensure adequate training, and reestablish monthly network calls) to provide on-the-ground support for field staff and leadership.

Sales Enablement

- Create a "Colleague Current Year Initiatives" dashboard to improve the ability of sales and relationship management colleagues to track account activity and opportunities.

- Leverage sales library functionality to house sales and marketing materials, including collaterals, presentations, sales toolkits, and so on that can be accessed via laptop or mobile devices.

At-Risk Management

- Improve the ability to identify and manage vulnerable and at-risk accounts.

- Create the ability to track and report on at-risk and lost business reasons, revenue, competitors, and so on.

Competitor Management

- Create a competitor management process which will enable you to keep a close watch on market intelligence by maintaining competitive pricing, tracking which account is selling which competitor products and comparing them with your products and services. You can capture pricing of competitive products, associate competitive products to accounts, and maintain strategic information like competitor product positioning and whether the competitor product is gaining or losing and maintaining its market share.

DevOps

DevOps combines organizational practices, development methodologies, and tools that efficiently improve application delivery efficiency. The core objective of the DevOps process is to manage the software development, maintain the infrastructure operation, and use the tool that supports the interface to implement newly created deliverables effortlessly.

Unlike traditional IT systems, DevOps for Salesforce is a bit different from other platforms. DevOps for Salesforce empowers admins, developers, and architects with a common platform to plan, build, test, deploy, and monitor changes across the entire enterprise.

In traditional IT application development platform (See Figure 11-10), there are several on-premises database environments involved:

- Production database: End-users in business and tech use the live environment to carry out transactions are typically supported by a production-grade database.

- Development database: This is necessary for the development teams to build new application features.

- Test and QA database: An environment where end users test to verify the new capabilities against original requirements.

Similar to these traditional IT practices, Salesforce introduces its own terminologies and principles with a little twist. Let's review a few core items that will assist you in understanding Salesforce terminologies and its DevOps practices:

- Org: An "org" means a specific hosted environment of the Salesforce organization in the cloud for your company which could be used as production, development, or test. In traditional IT terms, an org means a specific business application supported by a database instance or schema.

- Sandbox: Salesforce-specific development environment that used to develop and test new and existing capabilities.

- Change set: Administrators and developers make changes to a Salesforce org that include configuration, setup, security settings, Apex code, visual force pages, page layout, record type, custom profiles, custom objects and fields, and so on to achieve a specific customization objective. Collecting the definitions of all these changes (oftentimes referred to as metadata) and combining them in a package to ship from one Salesforce environment to another is called change set.

- Declarative: A method (user interface–based elements) to develop a new process or further tailor to an existing capability to meet your own requirements without code development or using programming within a Salesforce environment.

Developers and administrators create and work on their own sandbox environment and move the deliverables in the QA environment (as shown in Figure 11-9) to make sure their individual code or changes work with the rest of the team members in the higher environment.

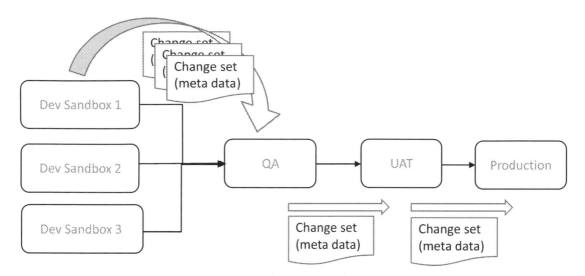

Figure 11-9. *Salesforce DevOps processes*

Once the overall testing effort is completed and the QA sandbox receives all clear signal from the change management (the team that controls and approves changes among systems), a new change set gets created. The DevOps team takes the changesets and deploys them in a higher environment like UAT (User Acceptance Test). End-users come together and test the changes in the application from both functional and technical test perspectives. Once end users accept the functional changes, the DevOps team then works with the development team, release manager, and end users and communicates a production deployment schedule. In a set schedule and controlled environment, the DevOps team then carries out the deployment procedures and implements brand-new changes in the production environment and communicates to the entire organization.

Typical activities for the development teams are plan, build, code, and test where teams follow a preset development schedule in an agile development environment. Two weeks of sprint developing the deliverables and then performing a show and tell demo is common in Salesforce agile practice.

Common activities for the operation team are release, deploy, operate, and monitor the application whether manually or using a system like Copado, Prodly, AutoRabit, Flosum, Odaseva, and so on, to name a few. Most of these applications are available to download from AppExchange and can integrate with your Salesforce org. Common features you will get from these solutions are version control, data loader, sandbox management, test automation, deployment automation, backup, and recovery.

Development Environment

It all starts with Salesforce's multitenant cloud infrastructure – which lets you focus on your business while Salesforce manages the infrastructure required to run apps and a billion transactions a day. All of Salesforce's customers share the same infrastructure and core codebase, which makes the platform massively scalable and secure. A lot of companies rely on Salesforce's service every day and have made sure it meets all of their strict requirements.

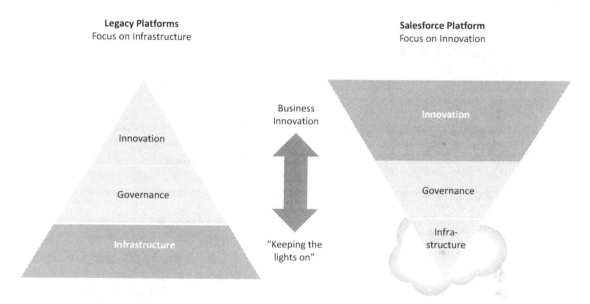

Figure 11-10. *Traditional IT platform vs. Salesforce platform dilemma*

Then you get a Cloud database architecture that's metadata driven – so you can add all the data and customizations you want without anything ever breaking.

Salesforce upgrades their service; you upgrade an app or back office system – no problem. Everything just works because of the flexible design. You can use the platform to connect to any external social network through any device and give users control, simplicity, and peace of mind with Salesforce cutting-edge identity technology.

You can also connect with any back-end system, partner app, or AppExchange you want through Salesforce's REST APIs.

Then you have Force.com and Heroku – which provide the architecture (See Figure 11-11) and the tools to help you build apps. Force.com is decisive for both developers and business analysts who can use point-and-click tools, while Heroku lets developers build in whichever language they prefer and prototype apps incredibly fast.

And for any app you build on the Salesforce platform, Chatter's enterprise social collaboration comes standard. You can even extend it out to public or private communities outside your company to connect and collaborate with customers or partners.

Finally, every app is easy to make a mobile. With Salesforce mobile SDK and back-end services, it's easy to build scalable and secure mobile apps that tie into your customer data and leverage all the latest authentication, mobile app policy management, geolocation, and offline capabilities.

Sandbox Use Case

As the name suggests, a sandbox is a copy of your Salesforce organization in a separate test environment where you can use for any number of purposes and use cases. Each sandbox comes with standard Salesforce functionalities to mirror your production org in a separate environment, and you can perform any type of test and development activities which do not affect your production Salesforce org.

There are four different types of sandboxes (Table 11-4) offered by Salesforce.

Table 11-4. *Sandbox types*

Sandbox Type	Refresh Interval	Storage Limit	What's Copied
Developer sandbox	1 day	200 MB	Metadata
Developer Pro sandbox	1 day	1 GB	Metadata
Partial Copy sandbox	5 days	5 GB	Metadata and sample data
Full sandbox	29 days	Same as production	Metadata and all data

Note   When storage limits are reached to the maximum, Salesforce sandboxes don't send email notifications typically. So, if you have reached the maximum storage limit, you can't save new data in your sandbox any longer. You should consider looking up Storage Usage from the Setup menu.

A sandbox is a copy of your organization in a separate environment that you can use for a variety of purposes, such as testing and training (Table 11-5).

- A developer sandbox is good for build and some individual QA work. Any of the other sandboxes can also be used for these use cases.

- You would need a Partial Copy sandbox for integration test, batch test, training, or UAT (User Acceptance Test) at minimum due to its sample data and storage capability.

Table 11-5. *Sandbox use case*

Use Case	Developer	Developer Pro	Partial Data	Full Copy
Build	✓	✓	✓	✓
QA	✓	✓	✓	✓
Integration test	✗	✗	✓	✓
Batch data test	✗	✗	✓	✓
Training	✗	✗	✓	✓
UAT	✗	✗	✓	✓
Performance/load test	✗	✗	✗	✓
Staging	✗	✗	✗	✓

- For the performance/load test or staging use case, you must have a Full sandbox because you need metadata and a copy of all the production data.

Sandboxes are completely isolated from your Salesforce production organization, and as such, the operations you perform in your sandboxes do not affect your Salesforce production organization. You can create different sandbox environments for your org, depending on your business needs.

What to Consider for Setting Up a Sandbox Environment?

There are tons of things to think through when setting up your company's sandbox development environment, especially if you have a large and complex enterprise-grade Salesforce implementation. Also, you have to consider the types of the sandbox and its usage, Salesforce's release preview schedule, user's community communication, organization identification, integration with internal applications like a data warehouse, product catalog, and whether to turn on single sign-on (SSO) not. I have seen companies that are committed to operational excellence and serious about their IT investment have a dedicated release manager who sits on the DevOps team and coordinates the entire code deployment and data movement aspects of Salesforce org enterprise wide.

Types of Sandbox

You have to identify and match up the use cases against the sandbox depending on your business and org demand. I will outline a typical setup, and you can then get an idea from here to design your own. A lot of time for test and training, you have to load sandboxes with data. Careful coordination and communication are necessary with other application owners to make sure you have a fully integrated test environment with data so that users can validate the new functionalities.

Depending on your organization, complexity of data, and business requirement, you may have to refresh or update your sandbox with production data. There are tools like data loader, demand tool, Informatica Cloud, Jitterbit, Dataloader.io, and so on available in Salesforce AppExchange which could be subscribed and downloaded to automate your testing environment. Some of these tools also provide test automation capabilities.

Sandbox Planning and Options

Salesforce typically provides three different application releases in a given year to improve application performance, new capabilities, and reported bug fixes. In order to have a robust DevOps environment, you may want to consider enabling the release preview with your sandbox environment. This would help your operation and solution to stay aligned with Salesforce's release schedule and overall solution to be future proof. If you have other managed packages installed in your environment, you have to consider the release preview for those managed packages as well.

Also, for a sandbox to refresh, it may take anytime from 1 day all the way to 29 days. For performance test and staging use cases, your sandbox (Full copy) prep time should be at least 29 days plus any other organizational procedural time. For testing, training, and UAT use cases, your sandbox (Partial copy) preparation time should be at least 5 days plus any other organizational procedural time. A dedicated DevOps team is the key to have a smooth operation with much needed communication channels in place to prevent any unwanted glitches (wipe out changes accidentally, etc.).

Sandbox Communication Plan

It is imperative to have your communication out to all the relevant parties to make sure all teams that support or use the sandbox are aware of the planned refresh, especially if you require something from them as part of your deployment process. Also, understand how they were using it. This will provide you with great deal of clarity when designing the sandbox refresh and related operational activities. It is also important to know which users don't exist in production. Consider reviewing and documenting all sandbox users' additional access and permissions required for a working sandbox environment. Finally, notify your users when the sandbox environment is refreshed and ready with data for use.

Sandbox Org ID

Did you know that Salesforce Org ID is different than the production org and changes each time the sandbox is refreshed? Also, object IDs are copied from production when the sandbox is created and refreshed only. However, record IDs will be the same in a full sandbox at the point when the sandbox is created. If your org has any hard-coded URL, you must update the org IDs in the sandbox, so they do not point to production.

Sandbox Users, Contacts, and Access

In Salesforce, it is a standard process that the sandbox name (e.g., dev) is appended to the end of the username (rashed.chowdhury@salesforce.com.dev). If the username is still not unique, then characters and digits are prepended to the username.

As a precaution, Salesforce adds "invalid" at the end of the user email addresses so that accidental email doesn't reach to a user's email address from the sandbox environment. However, other email address fields across other objects in the org are not invalidated. So, you may want to double check your workflow or any other automated process not to accidentally send any email.

A quick and easy way to access your sandbox is by typing `https://test.salesforce.com` directly to your browser as a URL. If you have my domain enabled in your org, you have to enter mydomain.sandboxname.my.salesforce.com where mydomain is the name of your domain and sandboxname is the name of your sandbox.

Case Study: Healthcare Payers' Digital Transformation

Let's take healthcare payers as an example. How can we provide a digitally transformed, superior customer experience to this community? To provide personalized, real-time care for members in your community, here are a few solutions you could develop using Salesforce:

- Enrollment app: We could improve the enrollment process of any given community member experience by digitally inputting necessary member information on the fly and connecting them with the nearby service provider.

- Telehealth app: Let's examine the way telemedicine and telehealth are evolving. It is now possible to expand care through Salesforce health cloud features like enhanced care coordination, nurse chat, check-ins with patient's diagnosis, and treatment plan.

- Member portal: Combined with the community and Marketing Cloud, it is now possible to extend all your care services to the patient network via interactive, on-demand journeys for healthcare offerings like fertility tracking, weight loss program, and so on.

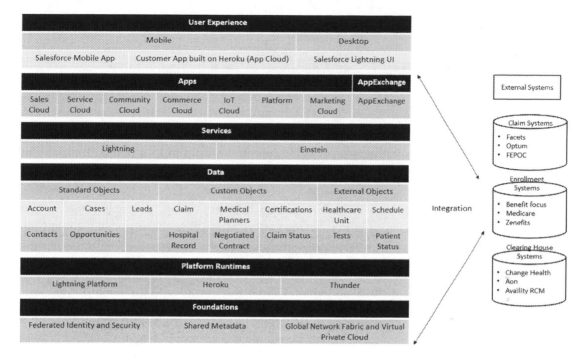

Figure 11-11. *Architecture diagram*

How to streamline and improve IT processes to free up IT employees for other value-added initiatives:

- Service desk: It is now possible to provide a centralized service desk solution by offering self-service case logging capability across any device.

- Concierge: New and improved intranet replacement solutions can enable employees to find and access all your internal company information in one place. The self-service artificial intelligence (AI)–powered concierge service can be configured to improve its knowledge base by enabling the machine learning (ML) feature. Users can search and find their answers by capitalizing on the self-service knowledge base features.

- Software development: It is now possible to automate the DevOps process by taking every user story in place, from creating a product backlog to developing sprint, outlining all the requirements in epic, feature, and user story format using the Salesforce platform and its ecosystem. IT leaders now can spend more time on strategy and value-added service offerings and less time in operation by reducing DevOps time and improving the overall efficiency of the software development lifecycle (SDLC).

The Salesforce platform allows you to develop your custom solutions based on your company's needs. There is also a plethora of existing apps, bolt solutions, lightning data, flow solutions, and components available on Salesforce AppExchange, which could be downloaded to your Salesforce ORG and customized to fit your requirements. Here are a few popular solutions in the healthcare payer's area:

- SpringCM Contract Management

- TalkDesk for Contact Center Management

- Sage People for Global HR and People System

The possibilities of building on the Salesforce platform are limitless. The platform empowers developing desktop to mobile apps for any industry – with click-not code and using underlying Customer Relationship Management (CRM) technology that powers the core application your user already knows.

Case Study: IT Challenges Related to Salesforce Desktop Add-On

To apply the Salesforce updates (Add-On, Salesforce Chatter, etc.), Enterprise IT Desktop Support needed to assign temporary admin access to a list of Salesforce users and, upon completion of the software updates, turn the access off. It was realized that this manual process is labor intensive and not the most optimal way to accomplish the task, especially in a corporate enterprise environment.

Use the System Center Configuration Manager (SCCM) tool to administer Salesforce packages or push any applicable updates to the user community, much like what an IT department uses today to manage other software updates. This centralized package management method has several benefits that include (a) empowering user productivity, (b) unifying management and security infrastructure, and (c) simplifying IT administration.

Deploying Salesforce updates via SCCM to the user community is the most effective and profitable option. IT managed a new deployment package for Salesforce that may cost somewhere between $200 and $400. New Salesforce updates to the existing SCCM package may cost somewhere between $100 and $200. Periodic Salesforce updates may occur five to six times a year.

Summary

In this chapter, we reviewed key configuration, setup home, customization consideration, and DevOps to support the enterprise Salesforce practice. We also studied real-world digital transformation using the Salesforce platform and IT challenges related to Salesforce desktop add-ons. These concepts and setup best practices will help you build a highly efficient Salesforce organization. In the next chapter, we will introduce you to the Salesforce platform, security, email, Salesforce mobile app, and a few resources that are available to us.

CHAPTER 12

Salesforce Platform

In the previous chapter, we reviewed key configuration, setup home, customization consideration, and DevOps and studied the real-world digital transformation case study to support the enterprise Salesforce practice. We also learned more on the key configuration and setup and recommended approach. In this chapter, we will cover Salesforce Experience Cloud (community cloud), security, email, Lightning Usage, and key Salesforce resources.

Salesforce Experience Cloud

Creating a community with Salesforce is a great way to improve your brand and customer service. Salesforce Experience Cloud combines websites, portals, and social media. A self-service community is even better, as enabling your customers to fix problems on their own (or with each other's help) saves your company time and money. By using Flow, Lightning Bolt, and custom actions, you can build a process-driven self-service community. We will cover the following topics in this chapter:

- Lightning Bolt
- Process Builder
- Flow
- Putting it all together

Lightning Bolt

Lightning Bolt is a feature within Experience Cloud that acts as a community template. Previously, templates for your community were only provided by Salesforce. With the introduction of Lightning Bolt, partners may also create templates for you to use, increasing the number of options available to you by quite a lot. Use Bolts to easily preassemble and preconfigure your new communities.

229

© Rashed A. Chowdhury 2021
R. A. Chowdhury, *Building a Salesforce-Powered Front Office*, https://doi.org/10.1007/978-1-4842-6676-2_12

A Lightning Bolt includes a theme, layout, pages, and components. A piece is a way the community site looks and has CSS. Pages hold components, and components are the building blocks of the page. Several elements may be combined on pages to get the output you want.

An easy way to build your Bolt is to start with another Bolt as a base. Remove pages you do not need for your specific use cases and add on new pages where necessary. Change existing pages if they are close to what you need. Add, remove, and modify components on each page to further customize and tailor the Bolt to your needs. After you have made all your changes, you now have a Bolt of your own, which you can export as your package.

Process Builder

Process Builder is a simple point-and-click development tool provided by Salesforce to drive business process automation. It is differentiated from Flow by being more straightforward as well as quicker to use. However, it is not as powerful.

Processes are made up of a trigger, a criteria node, and at least one action. Triggers identify when a process should be run. As an example, a trigger can be set to run a function when a record is updated or created. Criteria set the rules for whether the process should be run after a trigger is hit. These can be data validation rules, for example. Finally, Actions are what the function does after the criteria have been met. Actions may be scheduled or taken immediately and can do things such as create records, send emails, or post messages to a Chatter feed.

Consider using the Process Builder for your community to update child cases as parent cases are changed. It can also be used to create new cases and automate the process. Finally, use it to update your solutions and add comments to your cases.

Flow

Flow is the most powerful business process automation tool used in Salesforce. It is more potent than Process Builder and more complicated to use due to that. Use Flow (Figure 12-1) when you need more complex automation than what you can achieve with Process Builder.

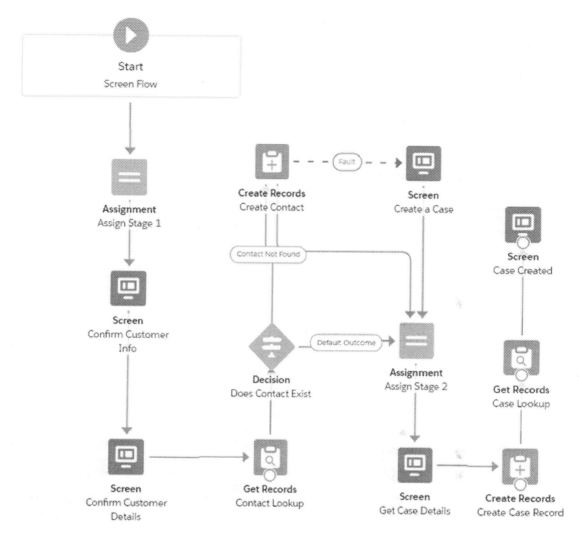

Figure 12-1. *Flow design in Salesforce*

To give an example, Flow includes screen interactions, while Process Builder cannot. Screen interactions (Figure 12-2) are the screens the user can see. Information is displayed, which the user can then click and interact with items on the page. User interface screen elements collect information from the user and pass it to other components in your Flow to be processed.

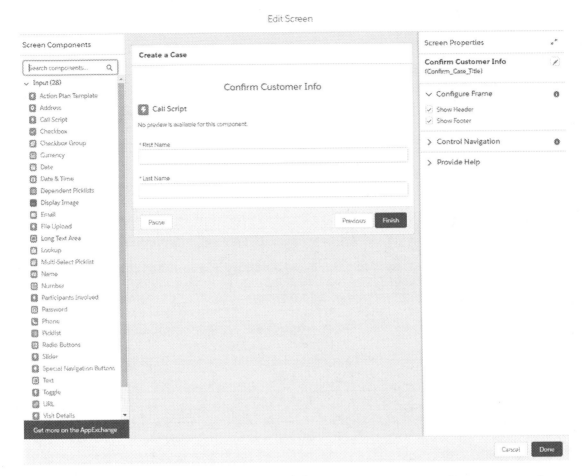

Figure 12-2. *Flow Builder User Interface (screen components, edit screen, and screen properties)*

A Flow is comprised of elements that represent actions, connectors to show the path of the Flow, and finally resources, which are values the Flow references throughout its courses. All of these come together to manipulate data in Salesforce in an intelligent, controlled manner.

As Flow goes through its paths, it uses logic elements to help make decisions and changes. The decision element is self-explanatory. It is used to make the Flow determine the direction in which it will continue. The assignment element (Figure 12-3) is used to change the value of variables. The loop element goes through the importance of a variable that holds a collection. Finally, the waiting factor will cause the flow to wait for an event to occur. All of these help the Flow progress using logic.

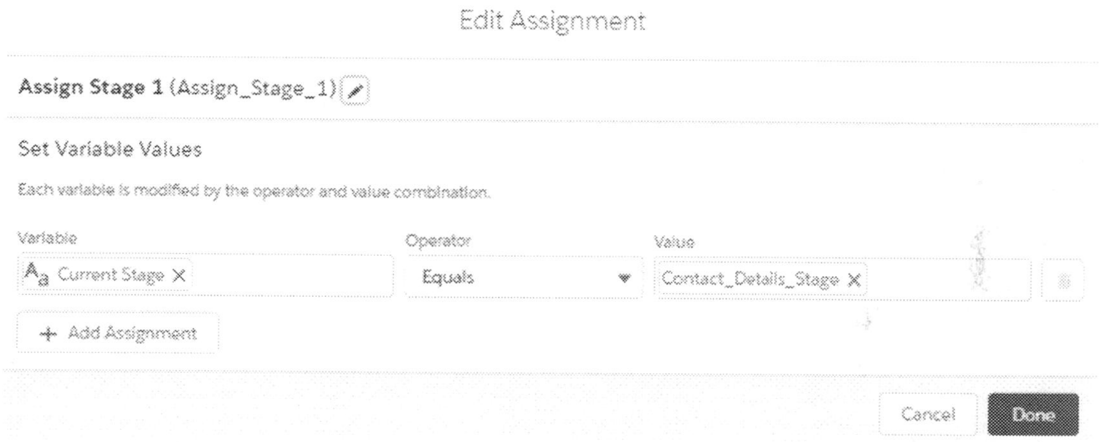

Figure 12-3. *Assign Stage – Flow Builder designer*

Your Flow can also utilize data manipulations. These include standard manipulations, such as record (Figure 12-4) update, delete, and create. Email alerts are available as well and are like Process Builder.

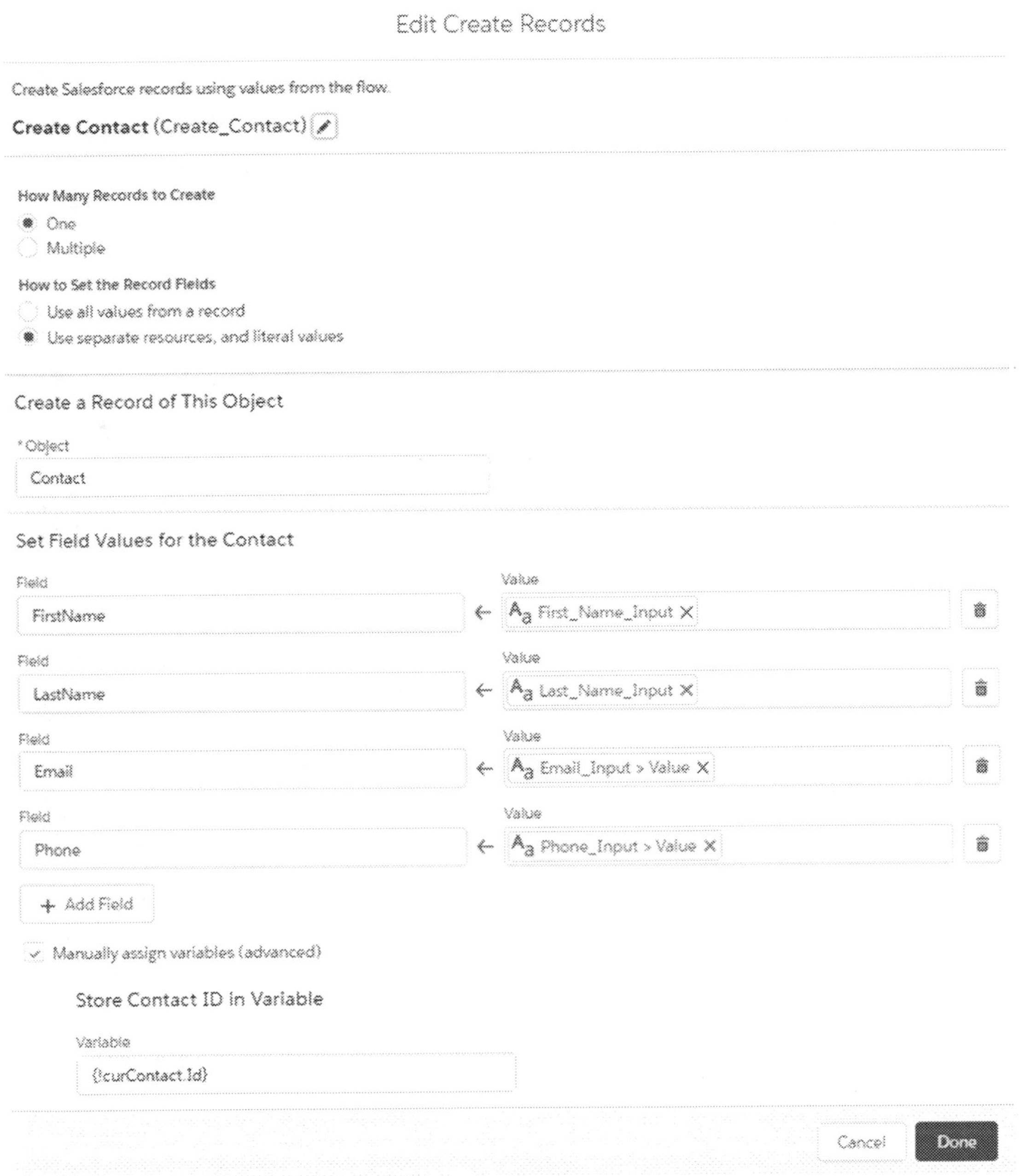

Edit Create Records

Create Salesforce records using values from the flow.

Create Contact (Create_Contact) 🖊

How Many Records to Create
◉ One
◯ Multiple

How to Set the Record Fields
◯ Use all values from a record
◉ Use separate resources, and literal values

Create a Record of This Object

* Object

| Contact |

Set Field Values for the Contact

Field	Value	
FirstName	← Aₐ First_Name_Input ×	🗑
LastName	← Aₐ Last_Name_Input ×	🗑
Email	← Aₐ Email_Input > Value ×	🗑
Phone	← Aₐ Phone_Input > Value ×	🗑

+ Add Field

☑ Manually assign variables (advanced)

Store Contact ID in Variable

Variable

| {!curContact.Id} |

Cancel   **Done**

Figure 12-4. *Flow Builder create records*

Any quick actions you have created within your organization are also available to use in your Flows.

The last main element of a Flow is, again, Resources. These are the objects which hold the data which gets passed around and altered. One widely used Resource is the variable. It contains values that get passed throughout the Flow. These values can also change both due to the Flow and through external input. Collection variables are similar, but instead are a series of variables with the same data type.

A subject variable is like a regular variable, but it holds a record of a specific object type. This means that while a variable has one value, a subject may have several values, and you can access all the record's fields. There are also subject collections of which you can probably guess the purpose – they hold multiple records of the same type.

There are many more Resource types, but here are just a few more. A Constant is a value, similar to a variable, except it never changes throughout the Flow. A Formula uses Resources in the Flow as input to generate an output value. Lastly, there is the Choice. This is simply an individual choice to be made in the Flow.

Putting It All Together

Now that we have gone over the different components which can go into creating your Salesforce Community, it is time to put it all together. Hopefully, you have a pretty good understanding of the different parts which go together to make your Bolt page. For more in-depth explanations, you can always find online help from Salesforce and Trailhead.

To start, find a preexisting Bolt that is close to what your business needs. Make changes to it, such as adding, removing, or changing pages and components. Once you have the Bolt in a state which works best for you, create Processes using the Process Builder that it will need to run. Implement those, and then use Flow to create more powerful Processes.

Once your Processes have been integrated, it is time to finalize the creation of your Bolt. Export the Bolt and then build a package. Finally, install that package. Once that has been done, your Bolt is finished and ready to use. Your business has its very own self-service community, prepared to go.

Security – Health Check

How well does your org meet Salesforce security standards? This is an important topic of interest for many IT organizations, especially for the IT executives. What and how many security risks does your org have and how to mitigate them. Before you solve the problem, you have to identify the problem. The Salesforce Health Check page has the answer which you will find under security settings. Here is the click path: Settings ➤ Security ➤ Health Check. Let's reduce your security risk and limit data loss by optimizing the following areas.

When I ran the Salesforce baseline standard, the system generated a health check report (Figure 12-5) and scored my org 59% – poor.

The entire assessment was divided into four major categories: (1) high-risk security settings (15 items), (2) medium-risk security settings (11 items), (3) low-risk security settings (8 items), and (4) information security settings (3 items). The report listed the following fields of each setting and provided a status of compliant (green) or critical (red):

- Status

- Settings

- Group

- Your value

- Standard value

- Action

Figure 12-5. Health check

For any critical (red) settings, you will also notice that your value is not matching with the standard value (the recommended value). You can go to each setting one at a time, or you can press the Fix Risk button which will automatically set all your values for all the critical settings to match with standard values and thus fix the problem (See Figure 12-6).

How well does your org meet Salesforce security standards? Reduce your security risk and limit data loss by optimizing the areas below

Salesforce Baseline Standard ▼   ⚙ ⌄

100% Excellent

of the standard met
How did we calculate this score?

Figure 12-6. *Health check status*

I recommend after reviewing all the critical settings (red), press the Fix Risk button which will fix the security setting issues and will provide a new and improved health score.

Login Access Policies

Sometimes, it is necessary for users to reach out to support organizations, and support personnel may have to remotely access the end user's desktop to carry out troubleshooting activities. Your administrator can control which support organizations your users can grant login access by setting up the login access policies (Figure 12-7).

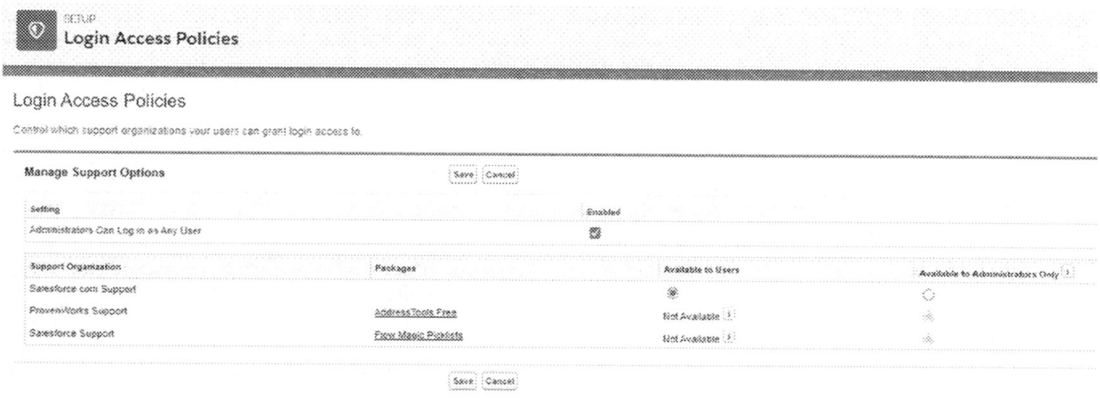

Figure 12-7. *Login access policies*

Administrators Can Log in as Any User should be selected. I also recommend Salesforce support to be available to users, and this option should be checked. This way, your users can open up a support case with Salesforce directly to resolve issues without involving your Salesforce administrator.

Lightning Usage

The new and improved Salesforce provides a built-in Lightning Usage App that tracks the adoption and usage of Lightning Experience, so you can monitor the progress of your transition and understand your users' needs. The Lightning Usage page can be accessed from the Setup Home.

To learn more tips and tricks, check out the Lightning Experience Rollout Specialist on Trailhead or run the Salesforce Optimizer to receive a personalized report highlighting exactly how you can improve your org.

The key metrics this app tracks are monthly active users and daily active users as shown in Figure 12-8. In this specific instance, this is my development organization and showing only one active user (me).

Figure 12-8. *Lightning Usage key metrics*

In the org Lightning Usage page, you can view the browser usage by month for the past 3 months and browser usage for the past 7 days (Figure 12-9).

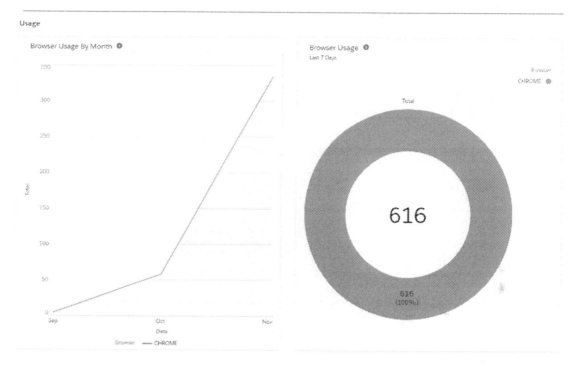

Figure 12-9. *Lightning Usage by month and last seven days*

You may also want to check out the Lightning Experience Rollout Specialist on Trailhead or run the Salesforce Optimizer to receive a personalized report highlighting exactly how you can improve your org today!

Salesforce Optimizer

You can have your administrator analyze your implementation to find ways to simplify customizations and drive feature adoption. Consider running Salesforce Optimizer as part of your monthly maintenance, before installing a new app, before each Salesforce release, or at least once a quarter. I highly recommend this practice.

The Salesforce Optimizer app covers features analyzed in the existing PDF report in a more interactive and actionable format.

- Allow access to enable the Salesforce Optimizer app. This step is required to use the app.

- Decide if the app should automatically run and update.

- Run monthly.

Pro tip   You can always open Salesforce Optimizer from the App Launcher.

Salesforce Optimizer PDF

Salesforce generates a PDF report (Figure 12-10) with recommendations to improve your implementation and then saves the report to Salesforce Files.

Figure 12-10. *Salesforce Optimizer*

When you work through each of the feature items listed in the report, you will be presented with status and result.

For example, an optimizer with an immediate action and recommendation (Figure 12-11) is telling me the results (immediate action required) and the recommendations with approximate time to carry out these recommendations to resolve the issue.

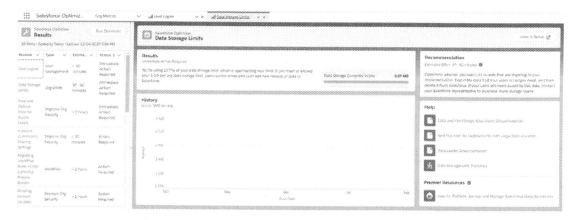

Figure 12-11. *Salesforce Optimizer with immediate action and recommendation*

It would be best if you considered having your administrator run the optimizer at least once a month and identify immediate action and action-required items at a minimum. Review required and not currently enabled should be next in line once the first two sets of critical item sets are resolved.

Email

Email plays a huge role at Salesforce, and it is an important platform offering as part of Salesforce's core capabilities. There are a few things to consider when setting up email in Salesforce that include a letterhead for classic email, org-wide email footer, enhanced email, outlook configuration, and more.

Classic Letterheads

Letterheads (Figure 12-12) are applicable only for classic email templates. Your administrator can set up your Letterhead to standardize the look and feel of HTML email templates.

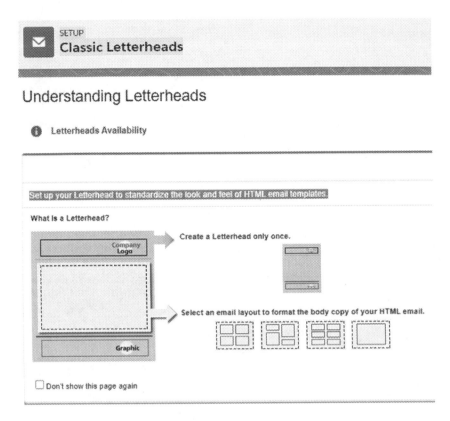

Figure 12-12. *Classic email letterheads*

You have to create a letterhead only once. There are three main parts to a letterhead – header, body, and footer. Your administrator can customize the look and feel of your letterhead.

Unfiled Public Classic Email Templates

There are a number of email templates (Figure 12-13) that come with Salesforce out of the box. The classic email templates you create here can be used with the following features, in both Salesforce Classic and Lightning Experience. The Salesforce Lightning Desktop offers a new email experience where administrators and end users can write email and create templates directly from records in Salesforce:

- Approvals

- Big Deal Alert

- Cases

- Case Assignment Rules

- Case Escalation Rules

- Communities

- Email to Case

- Lead Assignment Rules

- Process Builder

- Web to Lead

- Workflow

- Lightning Email Action (in Lightning Experience only)

- Lightning List Email Action (in Lightning Experience only)

- Salesforce Classic Email Author (in Salesforce Classic only)

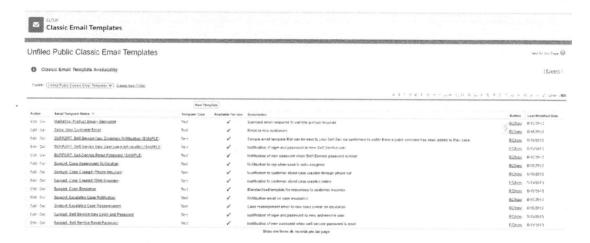

Figure 12-13. *Unfiled public classic email templates*

Marketing: Product Inquiry Response

You can have your administrator use merge fields to personalize your email (Figure 12-14) content. Your administrator can add substitute text to any merge field. Substitute text displays only if the merge record does not contain data for that field. Have your administrator enter substitute text after a comma in the merge field, for example,

{!Contact.FirstName,Sir or Madam}. When you save the template, the merge field will appear in the email body of the template with the following syntax: {!NullValue(Contact.FirstName,"Sir or Madam")}. Click the following link to see a sample email template.

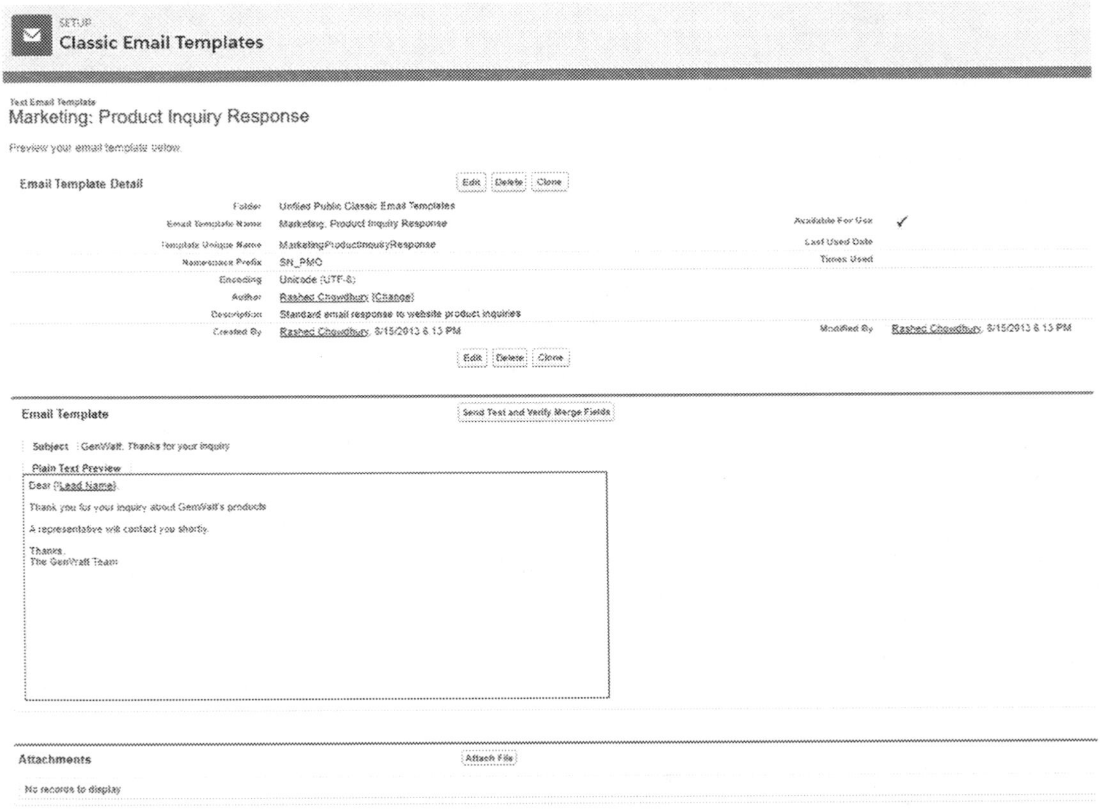

Figure 12-14.   Classic email templates definition

Note that the description field is for internal use only. It will be listed as the title of any email activities you log when sending mass email.

The following is an example template:

```
{!Today}

Dear {!Contact.FirstName,Sir or Madam},

Thank you for your interest in {!Organization.Name}. We look forward to
working with {!Account.Name, your company}. You will be receiving an
information packet in the mail shortly. In the meantime, please review the
attached company overview.
```

244

Sincerely,

{!User.FullName}
{!Organization.Name}
{!User.Email}

This yields the email shown in Figure 12-15.

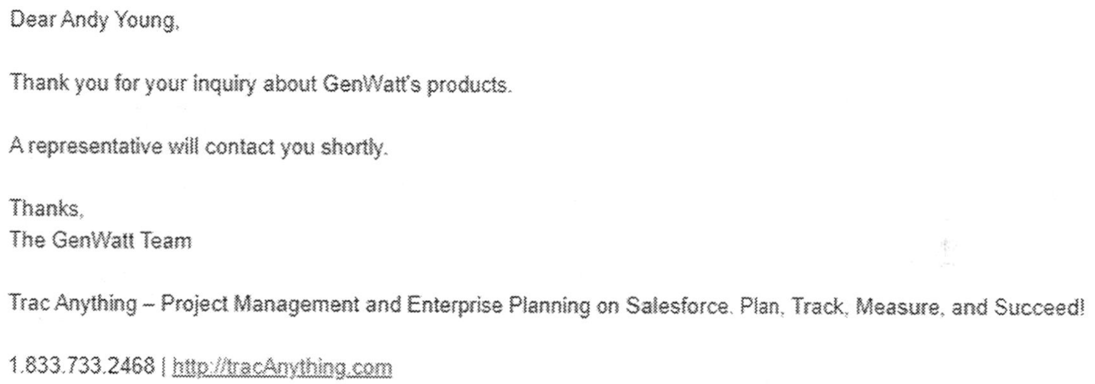

Dear Andy Young,

Thank you for your inquiry about GenWatt's products.

A representative will contact you shortly.

Thanks,
The GenWatt Team

Trac Anything – Project Management and Enterprise Planning on Salesforce. Plan, Track, Measure, and Succeed!

1.833.733.2468 | http://tracAnything.com

Figure 12-15. *Sample template*

Email to Salesforce

Email to Salesforce allows you to automatically log emails you send from third-party email accounts as activities on Lead and contact records in Salesforce.

After Email to Salesforce is activated, users can access the My Email to Salesforce page to view their unique Email to Salesforce address and customize their settings. You should send the notification email (Figure 12-16) to the users to notify them that Email to Salesforce has been activated.

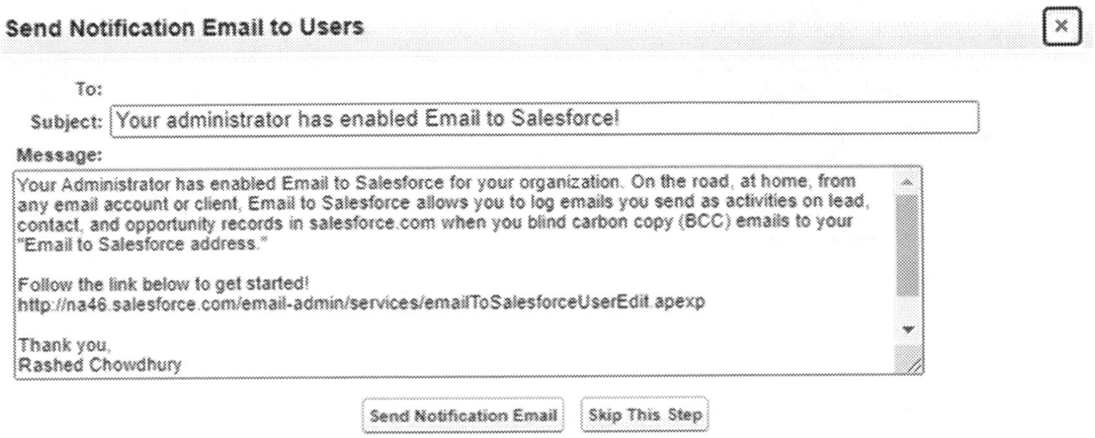

Send Notification Email to Users   [×]

To:

Subject: Your administrator has enabled Email to Salesforce!

Message:

Your Administrator has enabled Email to Salesforce for your organization. On the road, at home, from any email account or client, Email to Salesforce allows you to log emails you send as activities on lead, contact, and opportunity records in salesforce.com when you blind carbon copy (BCC) emails to your "Email to Salesforce address."

Follow the link below to get started!
http://na46.salesforce.com/email-admin/services/emailToSalesforceUserEdit.apexp

Thank you,
Rashed Chowdhury

[Send Notification Email]   [Skip This Step]

Figure 12-16. *Email notification to users within Salesforce*

Organization-Wide Email Footers

Your administrator can add footers to emails sent from Salesforce. The administrator can create default footers (Figure 12-17) – one for single emails and one for mass emails – or create one for each character encoding (General US and Western Europe, Korean, etc.).

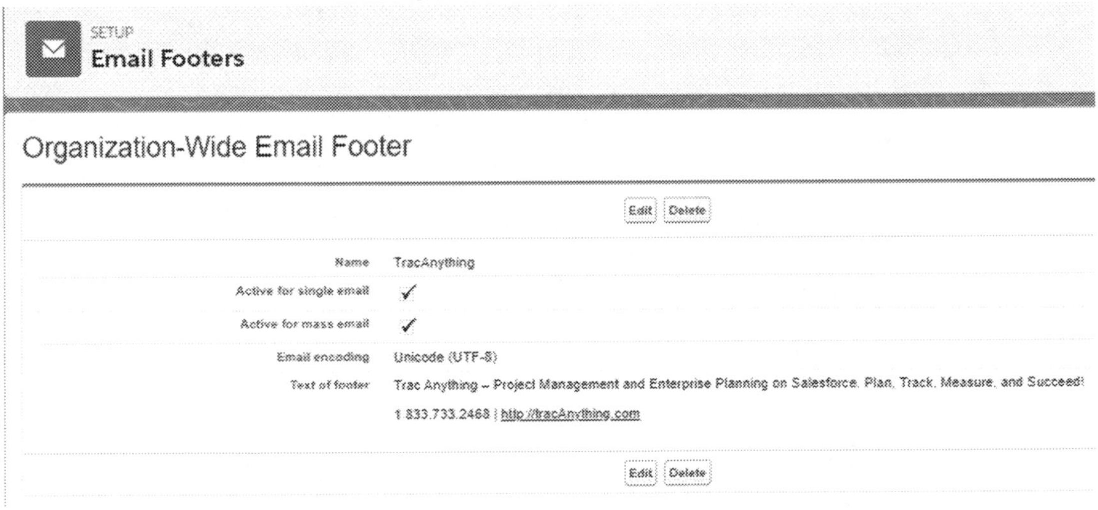

SETUP
Email Footers

Organization-Wide Email Footer

[Edit] [Delete]

Name	TracAnything
Active for single email	✓
Active for mass email	✓
Email encoding	Unicode (UTF-8)
Text of footer	Trac Anything – Project Management and Enterprise Planning on Salesforce. Plan, Track, Measure, and Succeed! 1 833.733.2468	http://tracAnything.com

[Edit] [Delete]

Figure 12-17. *Organization-wide email footer*

Default footers are used if no footers match the outgoing email's character encoding.

Enhanced Email

Your administrator can enhance email or elevate email to a standard Salesforce object, with customization options and an API. Emails are no longer stored as tasks, but as full-featured records, complete with details, related lists, and collaboration tools. On email records, users can view their messages exactly as their customers do, complete with formatting.

Organization-Wide Email Addresses

An organization-wide email address (Figure 12-18) associates a single email address to a user profile. Each user in the profile can send email using this address. Users will share the same display name and email address.

Figure 12-18. *Organization-wide email address*

You will have to verify the email link which will be sent from Salesforce.

Outlook Configurations

Microsoft Outlook integration improves the productivity and synchronization of the team. Salesforce contacts and Leads can be easily added to email recipients. New outbound emails can be added as tasks in Salesforce, ensuring effective monitoring and execution of important action items. Similarly, sent or received emails can also be added as tasks or cases. Furthermore, Outlook items like contacts, events (Figure 12-19), and tasks (See Figure 12-20) can be easily associated with Salesforce records, ensuring end-to-end management of activities, events, and tasks.

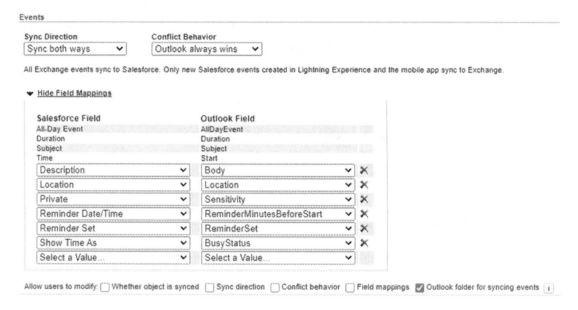

Figure 12-19. *Microsoft Outlook synchronization – Events*

Outlook configurations define the settings that are applied to Salesforce for Outlook for specific groups of users. Setting up an outlooking configuration in Salesforce is straightforward. You have to define the options like Side Panel, Add Email, Create Case, or Default Sync rules in the email settings to control the services' behavior. You also have to consider defining the rules under Sync Settings to control the behavior of Contacts, Events, and Tasks objects. Let's talk Sync direction for a moment. In this setting, your Salesforce administrator has to define which direction record will sync: Salesforce to Outlook, Outlook to Salesforce, or Sync both ways. Another important setting is conflict behavior. Who wins when there is sync conflict. You could set Outlook always wins, or Salesforce always wins depending on the business strategy and system you trust as the authoritative system of record.

Create Case is an essential setting for the customer service team. If you want customer and service agents to create cases, it may require turning on Email-to-Case, which is currently disabled for your organization. To use this feature, you must enable Email to Case.

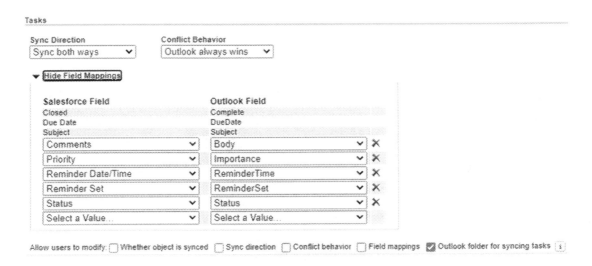

Figure 12-20. *Microsoft Outlook synchronization – Tasks*

There are few options under Email Settings in Outlook Configuration we have to walk through. For example. Set default sync setting to Sync All Outlook Items. It takes effect the next time users update their Salesforce for Outlook configuration and settings (See Figure 12-21) from the Windows system tray, even with the option "Overwrite configuration changes made by users" selected. Another option under Email Settings doesn't let users change their sync setting; this setting, if selected, prevents users from changing between Sync All Outlook Items and Sync Only the Outlook Items I Select. It takes effect the next time users update their Salesforce for Outlook settings from the Windows system tray.

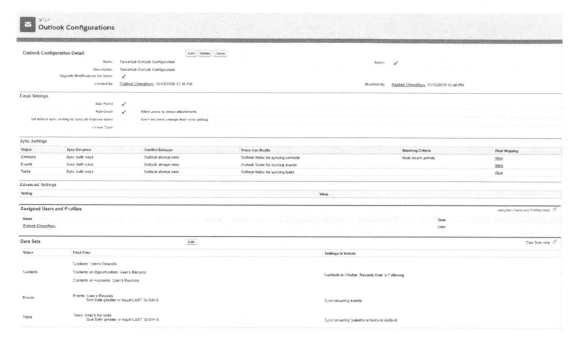

Figure 12-21. *Microsoft Outlook configuration*

Salesforce Mobile App

With the new Salesforce mobile app (Figure 12-22), your users can have a truly seamless experience across desktop and mobile devices. Users will have access to their favorite Lightning apps, improved navigation, and deeper functionality on every page.

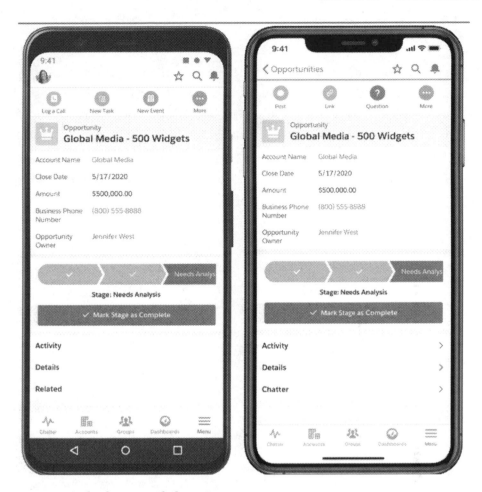

Figure 12-22. *Salesforce mobile app*

With the new Salesforce mobile app, you can

- Build fast: Build Lightning apps, pages, and components once, then make them available on a desktop, mobile, or both!

- Build custom: Use Lightning tools to tailor experiences for your mobile users, whether you create a mobile-only experience or simply hide components that don't make sense for mobile.

- Empower users: Put users in control of their workflows with desktop navigation personalizations that sync with mobile.

Schema Builder

Schema (See Figure 12-23) means a representation of a plan or theory in the form of a model. In the world of database, the database architect constructs the tables to hold business data and defines the relationship of the table with other tables and business objects within the database. Often, IT engineers refer to the database table and object as entities, and these entities may have one-to-one, one-to-many, or many-to-many relationships. The visual representation of the relationship of these entities often is referred to as the entity relationship diagram.

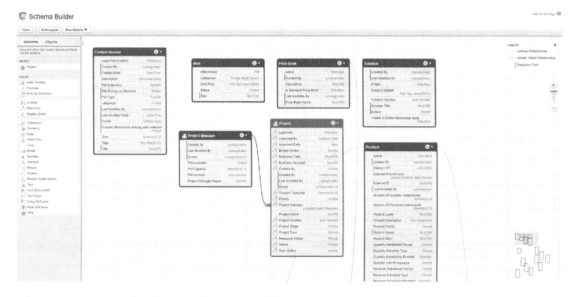

Figure 12-23. *Salesforce Schema Builder*

In Salesforce, Schema Builder provides an interactive environment to be able to view and edit all the existing objects and relationships of a given Salesforce organization (database instance).

There is a lot of work that goes behind the scene to design and implement a solid data model to support the business application. Schema Builder provides an easier and simpler way to manage the entire data model including building it from scratch.

You can drag and drop new custom objects (Figure 12-24) and fields into the schema. This is another way of creating or modifying custom objects in Salesforce. A few key activities you can carry out using Schema Builder to your database schema:

- Creating custom objects

- Defining relationships (Lookup relationships, Master-detail relationships)

- Creating all custom fields (checkbox, currency, date, email, number, percent, phone, picklist, multiselect, text, rich text area, URL, etc., except geolocation). See Figure 12-25 for reference.

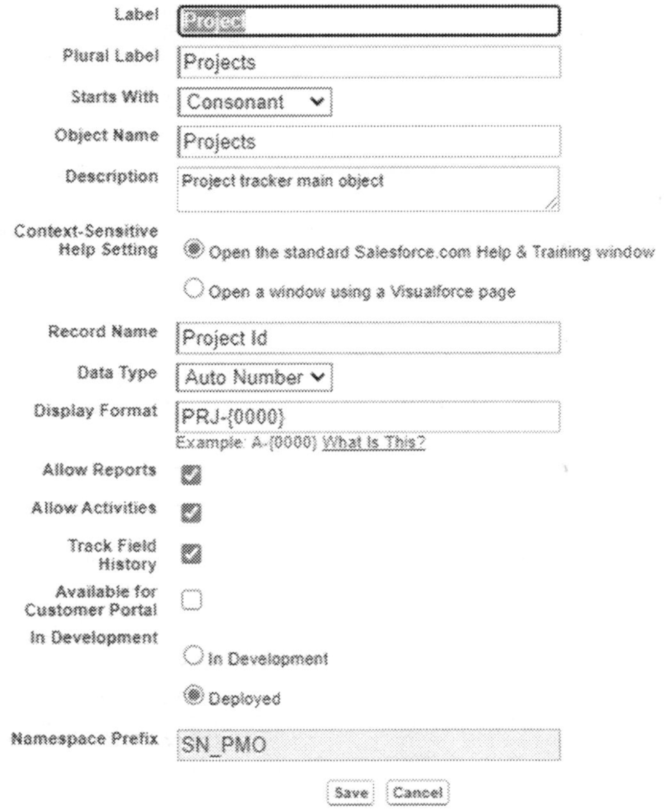

Label	Project
Plural Label	Projects
Starts With	Consonant ∨
Object Name	Projects
Description	Project tracker main object
Context-Sensitive Help Setting	⦿ Open the standard Salesforce.com Help & Training window
	◯ Open a window using a Visualforce page
Record Name	Project Id
Data Type	Auto Number ∨
Display Format	PRJ-{0000}
	Example: A-{0000} What Is This?
Allow Reports	☑
Allow Activities	☑
Track Field History	☑
Available for Customer Portal	☐
In Development	
	◯ In Development
	⦿ Deployed
Namespace Prefix	SN_PMO

Save   Cancel

Figure 12-24. *Create new object using Schema Builder*

When creating a new object, using some type of primary key (unique number) other than the Salesforce system–generated unique record ID is something I found to be very helpful.

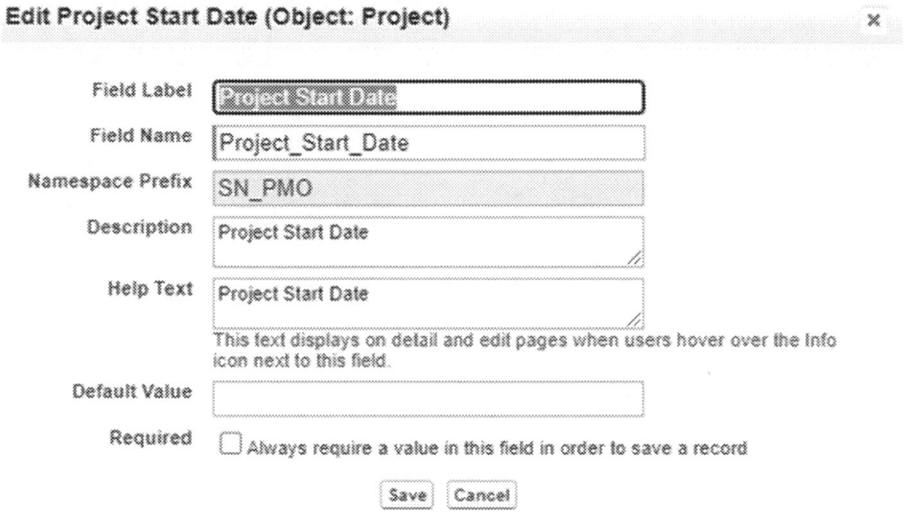

Edit Project Start Date (Object: Project)   ✕

Field Label	Project Start Date
Field Name	Project_Start_Date
Namespace Prefix	SN_PMO
Description	Project Start Date
Help Text	Project Start Date

This text displays on detail and edit pages when users hover over the Info icon next to this field.

Default Value	
Required	☐ Always require a value in this field in order to save a record

Save   Cancel

Figure 12-25. *Create new custom field using Schema Builder*

Also, if you set the first Record Name to be a number field, consider using a display format. For example, in this case, I used PRJ- {0000}, so that all of the database record for this field will follow a standard format (PRJ-0001, PRJ-0002, etc.) which in turn will be easy to recognize. The Allow Reports option will ensure you can report on this field in the future. Allow Activities will ensure setting up a task or creating a calendar event in the custom object is available.

Developing an App

To get your very own Developer Edition, a full-featured copy of Lightning Platform, for free, go to https://developer.salesforce.com and sign up. The tutorials and resources in Salesforce show you how to create an application (See Table 12-1) from start to finish with less code. You can follow these free tutorials and use the Salesforce platform to build any cloud-based application. The fundamental idea remains the same, develop an application with less code, and most apps share the familiar architecture:

- Database: The database is the host of the data model of the application.

- Logic: Business logic and automation (workflow, advanced configuration, etc.) to execute specific business scenarios in given conditions.

- User interface: To surface and present data to the app user so that the user can work with the data using prebuilt functionalities.

- Website: Expose your data-driven app on the Web to show external-facing capabilities and interact with the exterior world.

Table 12-1. *High-level app development activities*

Create the App	Create a Project Management Application
Data model	Develop custom objects
	Develop custom fields
	Define data model and add relationship
	Create tabs
	Create users and permissions and establish security
Add logic	Add formulas and validation rules
	Add workflow and approval process
	Develop email template
	Add business rules and advanced logic using Apex code
	Add tests
	Develop tests
	Evaluate code coverage
	Iterate and improve
Develop user interface	Develop a custom page layout
	Develop roles and profiles
	Create user assignments
	Develop custom user interface using a visual force page (VFP)
	Add Lightning web components (LWC)
Integration	Integrate with core CRM functionalities

(*continued*)

Table 12-1. (*continued*)

Create the App	Create a Project Management Application
	Define relationship with Account, Contact, and other standard CRM objects
	Customization to connect with ERP system
Website	Enable Salesforce mobile app
	Create a public website using Sites

Salesforce Service Cloud – Core Offering

Salesforce service cloud accepts support inquiries from most of the channels where your customers are active, including your website, email, phone, chat, and relevant online communities. Any organization can support these channels by using the automation features to create and assign support cases.

Salesforce service cloud manages your support processes by establishing support statuses for your support processes and automatically escalating cases based on the criteria you define. Also, you can set up entitlements to enforce your support processes. You can monitor your overall support activities through reports and dashboards.

You can boost engagement and productivity by promoting case deflection through community engagement. Salesforce service cloud can deliver a 360-degree view of your customer using the service console. You can do more from within the console, including making and receiving phone calls and accepting knowledge articles.

Key Salesforce Resources

Trailhead: Trailhead is a fun way of learning Salesforce. `https://trailhead.salesforce.com/en/home`

- Trailblazer Community: `https://trailblazers.salesforce.com/`

- AppExchange: `https://appexchange.salesforce.com/`

- IdeaExchange: `https://trailblazer.salesforce.com/ideaSearch`

- Events: `www.salesforce.com/events/`

- Help Portal: Documentation, Trailhead, Trailblazer Community, track progress. `https://help.salesforce.com/home`

- Developer Portal: Development with Salesforce is free and easy. Anyone can sign up with a Salesforce development environment with an email address. `https://developer.salesforce.com`

Summary

In this chapter, we covered Salesforce Experience Cloud (community cloud), security, email, Lightning Usage, and key Salesforce resources. In the next chapter, you will learn how companies can partner with Salesforce and become an independent software vendor (ISV). We will discuss partner designations, partner onboarding, channel management, channel sales, and AppExchange app development processes.

CHAPTER 13

Helping Companies Grow as a Salesforce Partner

In the previous chapter, we reviewed Salesforce Experience Cloud (community cloud), security, email, Lightning Usage, and essential Salesforce resources. Companies can partner with Salesforce and become an independent software vendor (ISV). The Salesforce Partner programs offer a set of resources, training materials, and tools to ISVs for them to be profitable and best serve their customers. As an ISV, you will build enterprise apps for Salesforce, using their technology and marketing resources to find success. The following topics will be covered in this chapter:

- Partner designations
- Your digital experience
- Partner onboarding
- Channel management
- Channel sales and marketing
- AppExchange app development

Partner Designations

For the Salesforce Partner Program year 2020, there are two different partner designations: AppExchange Partner and AppExchange Premier Partner. By default, a partner is considered an AppExchange Partner. A partner can become a Premier Partner if they receive an invite from Salesforce and accept the terms and conditions that come along with it.

© Rashed A. Chowdhury 2021
R. A. Chowdhury, *Building a Salesforce-Powered Front Office*, https://doi.org/10.1007/978-1-4842-6676-2_13

Being a Premier Partner comes with several benefits. To start with, you get a 30% discount on Salesforce Certification Vouchers as opposed to the 15% discount regular partners receive. Also, as a Premier Partner, you will receive priority when it comes to Salesforce working with you to comarket your apps. You will also get access to a Partner Enablement Manager. Their sales expertise will help you sell more and scale your partnership. Lastly, you will receive ten technical support case packs as opposed to the five regular partners receive, allowing you to get more support from Salesforce when you need it.

Your Digital Experience

With your role as an independent software vendor (ISV), you can help other companies grow their business and scale revenue. Ensuring that you have an excellent digital experience (Figure 13-1) is key to gaining new partners yourself. Your business should make it easy for your customers to onboard. Other companies grow and scale because of your apps, but you benefit as well, gaining new Leads through the AppExchange (`https://appexchange.salesforce.com`).

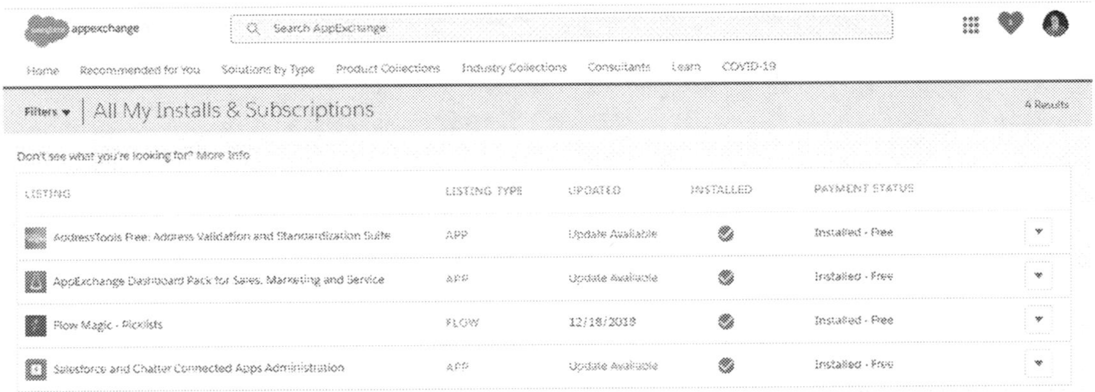

Figure 13-1. *All my installs and subscriptions in Salesforce AppExchange*

Having a well-branded experience online is key to attracting companies to use your products and work with you. You could create a Lightning community and customize it for your business. Consider using existing content from your content management system (CMS) to further personalize your community. You should look to optimize your site with search engine optimization (SEE) and useful URLs.

Partner Onboarding

Salesforce Partner Relationship Management (PRM) is a great tool to help onboard your partners as well as to recruit them in the first place. Branded recruitment sites help capture prospective partners, and automated approvals streamline the whole process. It can create role-specific tasks and timelines for your partner program. Different levels of onboarding may have various assignments. The progress is tracked for all of it using Lightning Components.

Partner portal (`https://partners.salesforce.com`) is an excellent resource for Salesforce partners (ISV AppExchange, consulting partners, and resellers) where partners can carry out critical business activities that include collaboration, managing users, publishing apps in Salesforce AppExchange, and keeping track of the latest conversations.

Salesforce PRM lets you set up partner certification, as well, to ensure your partners are properly onboarded. Within PRM is a learning management system you can use to create learning activities for your partners to complete. These keep your users current and knowledgeable about your products through training.

Channel Management

Keep your channel well managed with Salesforce PRM. It provides you with plenty of insights into your channel with a 360-degree view so that you can make the most informed decisions. The picture provided stats such as Lead flow, conversion rates, channel ROI, and more in real time to analyze partner performance.

You may also integrate with Google Analytics to have even more information at your disposal. Track how your partners are using your channel by seeing their page views, what they are searching for, and whether they are a new or returning visitor.

Support your partners using your channel with tools given directly by PRM. Answer your partners' questions with FAQs, Q&A forums, articles, and answers on demand. Allow an individual partner to gather wisdom from all your partners to help answer their questions. Also, partners can create cases. Assign priority to these cases, either automatically or manually. If a partner needs more immediate help, they can utilize a live chat, which can be initiated by the system based on their activity on your channel.

Channel Sales and Marketing

Keep your partners engaged with better marketing and sales. Throughout your partner lifecycle, use automated triggered events to perform actions when the user logs in or reaches various milestones within the training. This helps to create a personalized experience for your partners.

Use PRM to help your partners create marketing journeys of their own without needing to be marketing experts. Partners can personalize emails and track their results. They can also get new marketing collateral quickly. They just must upload their logo, and PRM will automatically convert it into a material such as product brochures or banners.

Distributing Leads when working with multiple partners is made a lot easier with PRM. Automate which Sales Qualified Leads to get sent to which partners based on set workflows. You may also mark Leads as exclusive to different partners using Deal Registration.

PRM also streamlines the quoting process. Your partners can be connected to your own quoting processes and resources, such as price books, and help them create their quotes. PRM offers discount approvals as well as contract management and sales recommendations, making it a significant improvement to partner sales processes.

In this section, I will discuss and demonstrate how to build and list an app in Salesforce AppExchange in a high level. The first step is to secure a Developer Edition Salesforce organization. As part of the partner agreement with Salesforce, you will get a Partner Business Organization (PBO). Salesforce partner can run their business from this organization which comes with a few special applications with it. Environment Hub is one of those special apps where you can create and manage development, test/demo, and trial org.

Besides the Environment Hub app, there are a few other special apps that I think are important to discuss here. One is the License Management App (LMA) which tracks the installs of your package and allows you to manage the license for them. The other one is the Checkout Management App (CMA) which enables customers and end users to complete the download of your app from Salesforce AppExchange and payment processing according to a licensing agreement. I will discuss this topic later in this chapter after we build our app and create the package.

Design and Build

In your development organization, based on your data model and design blueprint, you build custom objects, custom fields, page layouts, record types, validation rules, and the relationship among your custom objects. Once you have your basic data model, you probably want to build out the page layout (user interface).

I am going to explain how we build Trac Anything (Figure 13-2), a Project Management and Enterprise Tracking Solution for the Front Office natively built in Salesforce. A modern project management platform to manage the iterative development sets the value-based prioritization, improves collaboration, and brings traditional waterfall principles to effectively manage the overall project in a hybrid environment.

Figure 13-2. *Trac Anything, custom Salesforce app. Exhibiting custom visual force page*

The main object for the Trac Anything app is the project object, and to display the list of projects in different stages, we choose to use the Kanban view (Figure 13-3) that summarizes the project costs by stages. The Kanban board view will show project records in a graphical way that helps you monitor your project and keep the project moving forward.

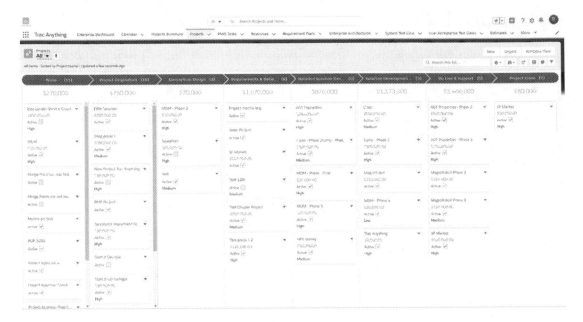

Figure 13-3. *Trac Anything, custom Salesforce app. Exhibiting project by stage with summarized dollar values in Kanban view*

We created relevant data fields following Project Management Institute (PMI) best practices and organized them in functional sections (objective, team, financials, business case, approval, etc.) to build the Project detail screen (Figure 13-4). Custom related lists have also been created to complement the project object.

We added an approval process using Salesforce's declarative approval automation tool and built email templates to communicate project update to stakeholders. Custom functionalities such as one-click status update in PDF have been incorporated. We used the Apex and Visualforce page to build these functionalities.

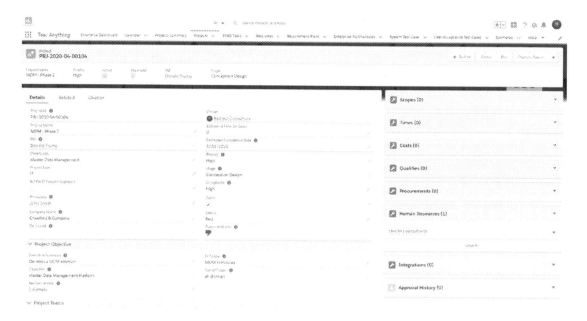

Figure 13-4. *Trac Anything, custom Salesforce app. Exhibiting main project object with custom related list and custom formula fields*

The custom formula field has been incorporated to display a visual status indicator and to calculate financials as part of the business case automation effort.

Communication is the key in any business, and that's especially true for a project management and enterprise planning solution. We used a custom email header and pulled project-related data fields from Salesforce to incorporate them in the email body when generating the project update as part of the official Project Management Office (PMO) communication. We used the custom Salesforce email template feature to develop the Email Alert: PMO task due date is closing in 7 days (Figure 13-5).

Alert :PMO task due date is closing in 7 days

?   noreply@salesforce.com on behalf of PMO Admin   ↩ Reply   ↩ Reply All   → Forward   ···
To

Mon 10/26/2020 2:30 AM

ⓘ If there are problems with how this message is displayed, click here to view it in a web browser.
We could not verify the identity of the sender. Click here to learn more.
The actual sender of this message is different than the normal sender. Click here to learn more.

PMO Communication
Project Management Office

Dear Automated Process,

This is to inform you that, the following PMO task's due date is on 10/26/2020.

Here is the Project Summary:

Project Number:	PRJ-2020-09-00162
Project Name:	Trac Anything
Project Manager:	Rashed Chowdhury
Project Type:	Capital Investment
Project Status:	Red
Created By:	Rashed Chowdhury
Project Owner:	Rashed Chowdhury
Estimated Time:	15
Estimated Completion Date:	10/7/2020
Priority:	High
Project Stage:	Solution Development & Testing
Project Complexity:	Medium
Last Modified:	Rashed Chowdhury
Approved:	1
Approved By:	
Active:	1
Record Id:	a006g00000Ct62c

Please click on this link to Update the PMO Task in salesforce: Click here!

Figure 13-5. *Trac Anything, custom Salesforce app. Exhibiting Project Management Office (PMO) communication generated from Salesforce using custom email template*

We also added the Salesforce record link in the email, so that when the user receives the email, the link will bring the user to the exact same record in Salesforce.

Finally, once all the functionalities, business rules, and automation were built, we then used the Salesforce package manager to build the package (Figure 13-6) for our app.

Figure 13-6. *Trac Anything, custom Salesforce app. Exhibiting Project Management Office (PMO) app package using Salesforce Package Manager*

Here are our current developer settings listed as follows for the Trac Anything app. These settings determine the types of packages you can create and upload.

- Package Types Allowed – Managed and Unmanaged: Your organization is configured to contain one managed package and an unlimited number of unmanaged packages. Only managed packages can be upgraded.

- Managed Package – ETS: You have selected the following as the only managed package for this Salesforce.com organization: ETS.

- Namespace Prefix – SalesHub: Salesforce.com prepends this prefix (along with two underscores, "__") to components that need to be unique such as custom objects and fields.

According to Salesforce, a package contains components such as apps, objects, reports, or email templates. This is the package we uploaded on AppExchange to share with potential customers. Once the package is created and ready to upload, this concludes the initial development activities.

Key Activities – Listing

Now that the development of the app and package is completed, we have to list the app in Salesforce AppExchange. In order to accomplish that, there are a few activities we have to complete as follows:

- Create your listing.

- Connect your package.

- Pricing your app.

- Set up Stripe.

- Establish your pricing.

- Confirm your status as a checkout partner.

- Submit for security review.

Create your listing. Articulate and explain what business problem you are solving and list key features of your solution. It is a good idea to have a website for your product where you can publish all the product-related information which will serve as a reference for your customers as well.

Salesforce partner agreement, legal review, and partner branding agreement: These documents are very legal centric and easy to understand. Someone with legal knowledge should review for you if possible. Once all of these are completed, your business plan (Figure 13-7) is done.

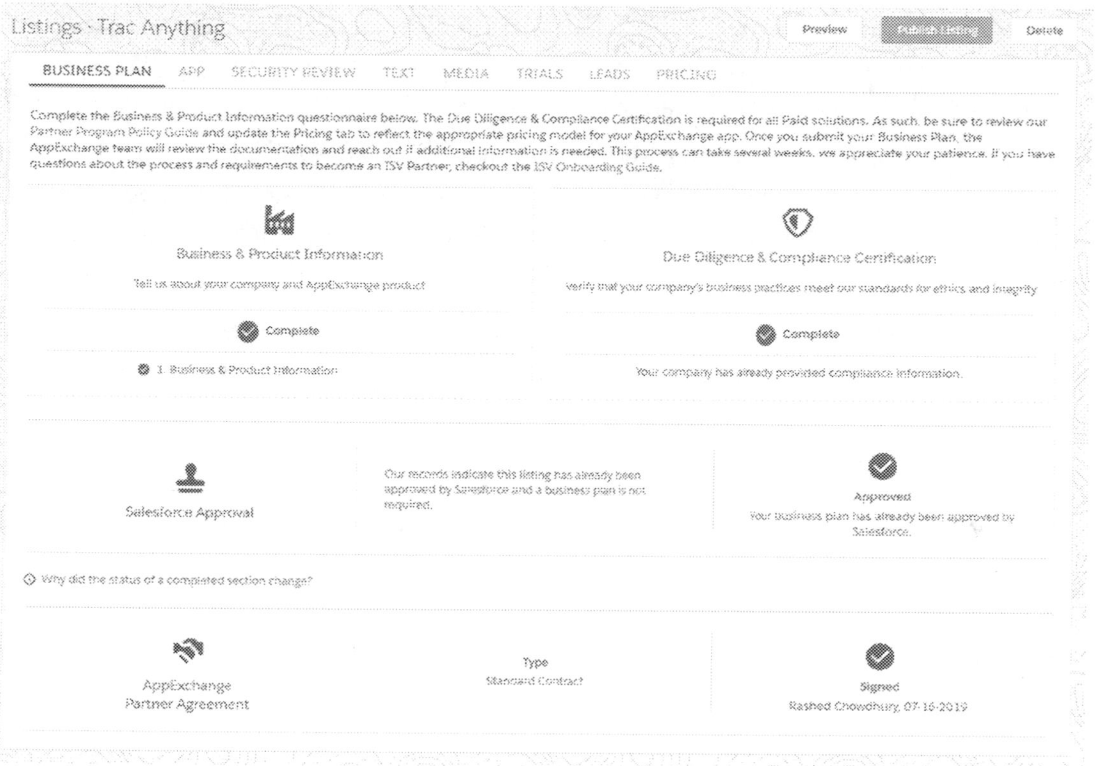

Figure 13-7. *Trac Anything listing in Salesforce Partner portal under publishing tab - Business Plan details of the listing.*

You will have to work your way to the next tab in the listings; in this case, App (Figure 13-8) is the next tab. You have to choose a package for your listing (Trac Anything in this case as an example).

Information about the package, such as version number and contents, appears on the Details tab of the listing. If the package is installed directly from the AppExchange, customers will receive the version that you select.

How should customer install your app? Directly from the AppExchange is recommended because that's the easiest and fastest way to list your app. I would also recommend to select the first option: by default, install this app only for the system administrator in the customer org.

Make sure to select supported editions of Salesforce and language. Don't forget to select Lightning Experience as your supported feature under the specification of the app section.

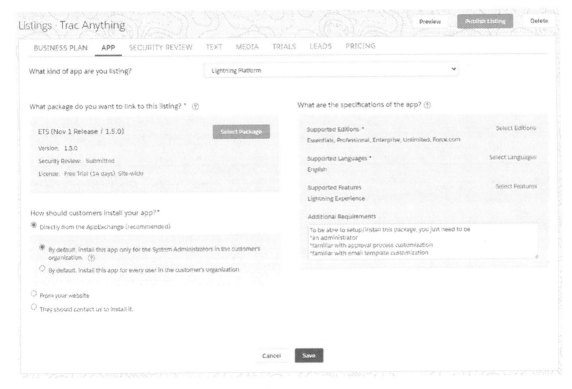

Figure 13-8. *Trac Anything listing in Salesforce Partner portal under publishing tab - App details of the listing*

If you don't see the package you're looking for, go to the organizations tab to connect the organization that contains the package. Be sure to upload the package to Partner Portal from your Salesforce development org.

Security Review: To promote trust in the AppExchange ecosystem, all publicly listed solutions must pass Salesforce's comprehensive security review (Figure 13-9). You have to provide your contact info, security compliance, questions, documents, test environment (login information), and summary and make a payment.

You can expect to pay a one-time, upfront total of $2700 to initiate the security review process with Salesforce. The total payment includes a $2500 security review fee and $150 first year listing fee in Salesforce AppExchange. You can expect to pay a $150 listing fee annually after the first year.

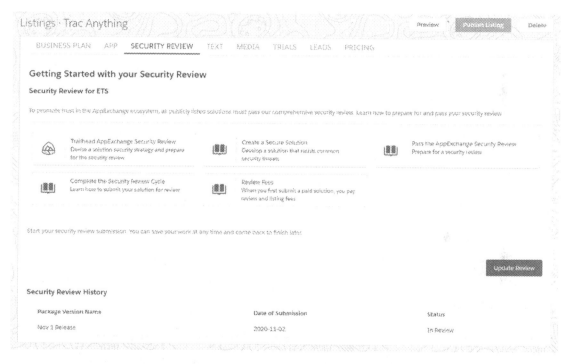

Figure 13-9. *Trac Anything listing in Salesforce Partner portal under publishing tab - Security Review details and history*

Listing title, a catchy tagline, and a crisp description are next under the Text (Figure 13-10) tab. Essentially, the use cases, product benefits, and any content marketing assets should be listed here. Also, list your support and service model so that the customer knows how to reach out to you in the event the customer may need any services.

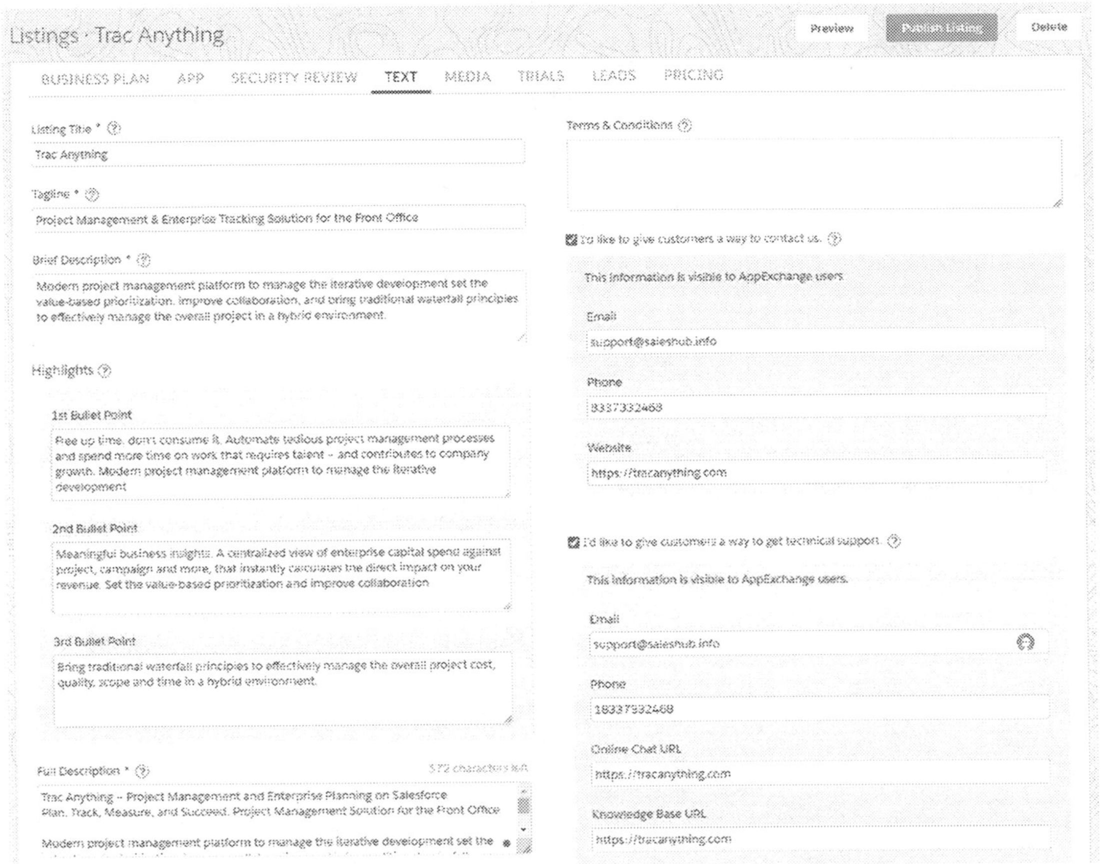

Figure 13-10. *Trac Anything listing in Salesforce Partner portal under publishing tab - Details listing information*

I personally like the media tab (Figure 13-11), because you get to show off your creativity, branding style, screenshots of your app, and product video. Here are the marketing assets Partner Portal is going to need to help with completing the listing:

- Logo (60X60 pixels) in PNG format

- Tag image 224X164 (pixels) in PNG format

- 15 screenshots 700X467 pixels in PNG format

- One video

- One demo – link to YouTube

- Data sheet

- Customization guide

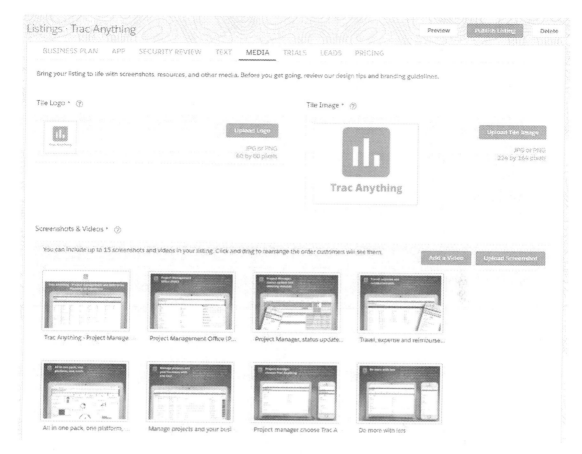

Figure 13-11. *Trac Anything listing in Salesforce Partner portal under publishing tab - Details media and marketing assets for the app*

Finally, set the pricing (Figure 13-12) in the pricing tab. You have to let customers buy the product with a credit card or bank transfer on AppExchange; choose Paid, using Checkout in the pricing tab under the publishing menu. Next, select to collect payment details before installation. If you select this option, you must use Stripe to manage trial periods.

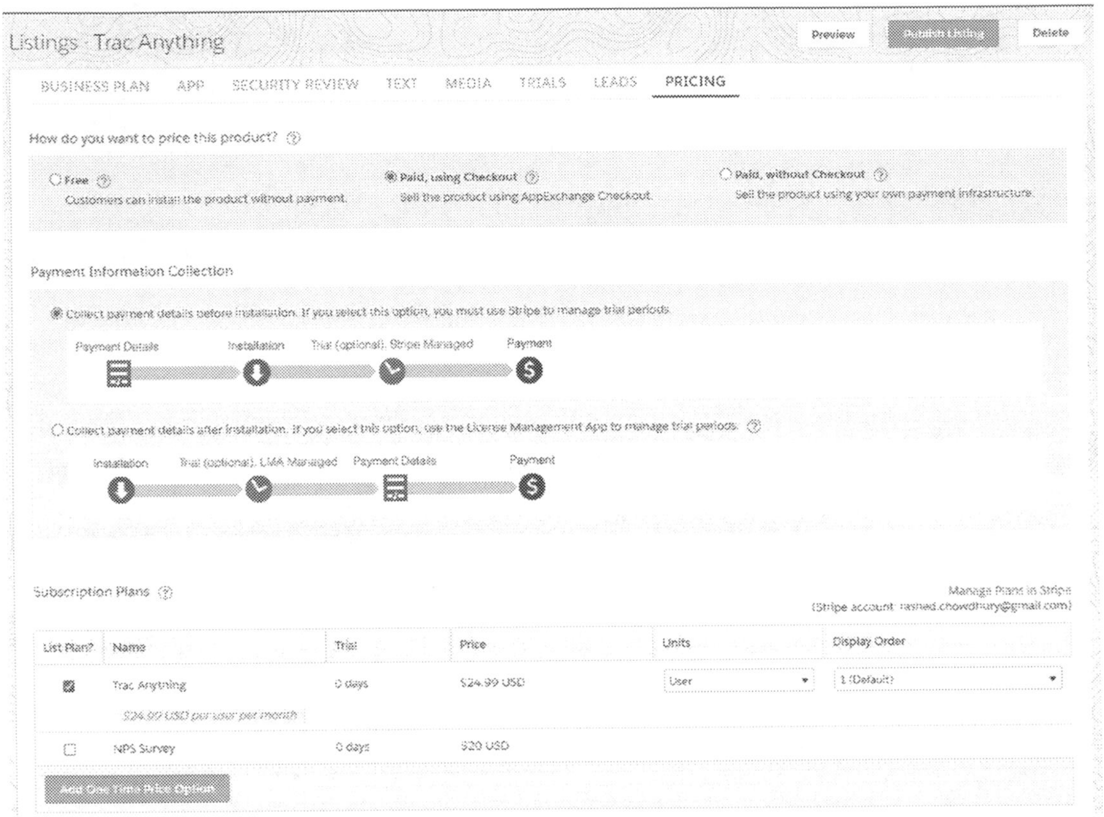

Figure 13-12. *Trac Anything listing in Salesforce Partner portal under publishing tab - Pricing Plan details of the listing*

If you charge customers a recurring fee to use your product, create a subscription plan. Identify and list your list price plan ($?/month).

Finally, a good published listing should look like Figure 13-13 which has all the necessary components of a listing, price/user/month, description of the solution, watch demo, screenshot and solution video, solution highlights, and description.

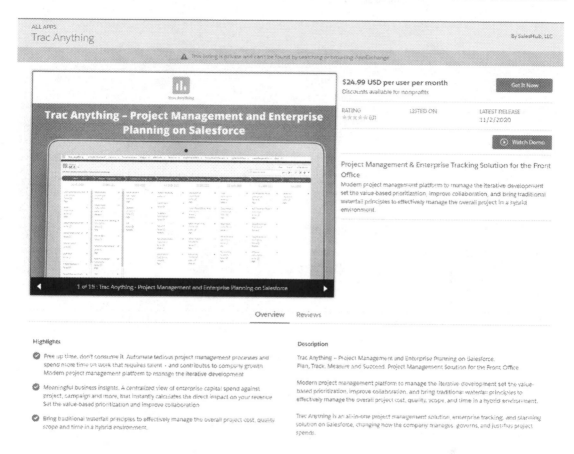

Figure 13-13. *Trac Anything listing in Salesforce Partner portal under publishing tab - Overview details of the listing*

Checkout Management App

Checkout (Figure 13-14) is Salesforce's fastest path for partners to get their application listed on the Salesforce AppExchange. Checkout is for AppExchange Partners that are selling their applications to existing Salesforce customers (ISVForce Partners). Checkout Partners list their solution on the Salesforce AppExchange and enter into a 15% revenue share with Salesforce to access programmatic benefits.

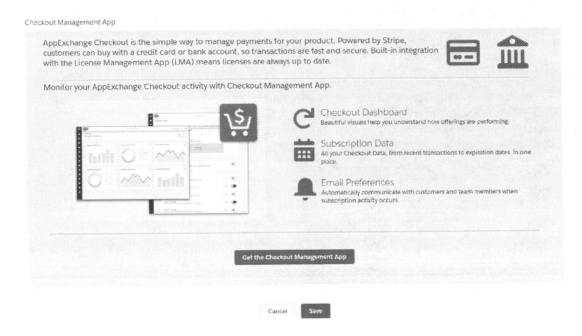

Figure 13-14. *Checkout Management App*

For Checkout Partners, the only distribution channel for your application is to be downloaded directly from the Salesforce AppExchange. To use Checkout, you must distribute your app as a Salesforce managed package.

Checkout Enabling

Checkout Partners transact with their customers through the Stripe payment platform. Stripe Checkout supports six pricing models:

- Per user per month

- Per company per month

- Per user per year

- Per company per year

- Per user one time

- Per company one time

Signing up for Checkout is straightforward – no merchant bank accounts or payment gateways are required.

- Start on the Publishing Console.

- Select "Paid, using Checkout" in the Pricing tab.

- After you agree to the terms and conditions, you can create your Stripe account.

- Connect your checking account, authorize the AppExchange to use your new Stripe account, and you're ready to use Checkout!

To activate Checkout for your app, first create your subscription plans in Stripe, then go back to your publisher home screen to edit your listing and choose which plans to offer on the Pricing tab. After you select your plans and associate them with your listing, your app is ready for Checkout. Customers who buy your app on the AppExchange will be asked to provide their credit card information. If they install your app, they'll be charged according to the payment details you specified.

What Are the Steps for the Security Review Submission Process?

Confirm these action steps before you click submit for Security Review:

- Are you attaching clean Checkmarx results for apps with Native Force.com components? If Checkmarx returns anything besides "code quality" issues, you must either resolve or provide a document detailing false positives.

- Are you attaching clean Web App Scanner results for apps with Composite components? If the Web App Scanner returns anything besides "information" issues, you will need to resolve or explain in a false positive document as well.

Note   The scans will not catch everything. Too much reliance on tools and not enough on secure design, secure development, and manual testing will likely result in a fail.

- Are you providing working credentials to an end-to-end test environment with only the package submitted for review installed? (Exception: If the package depends on other packages to function.) It is strongly recommended that partners create a new test org from the Environment Hub for this purpose. Note: Sandboxes, active production orgs, or packaging DE orgs where the app was developed cannot be accepted.

- Are you providing working credentials to all Composite components of your offering, such as web services?

Note   If you are not sure if something is in scope, include it anyway. If the Security Review team determines something is missing, there will be delays.

If you are confident that you've met these requirements, then proceed to submit your app for Security Review. You will receive an email within 48 business hours to confirm that your app is submitted into the security team's queue. Please retain this email as evidence of your submission with the time/date stamp.

Key Resources

The following are resources for further reading:

- Checkout Homepage: `https://partners.salesforce.com/s/education/appinnovators/Checkout`

- Security Review Homepage: `https://partners.salesforce.com/s/education/appinnovators/Security_Review`

- Security Review Trailhead: `https://trailhead.salesforce.com/modules/isv_security_review`

- Security Review Collaboration Group: `https://partners.salesforce.com/_ui/core/chatter/groups/GroupProfilePage?g=0F9300000001s8Y`

- Security Review Office Hours: `https://partners.salesforce.com/s/education/general/Partner_Office_Hours`

- Create Your Listing: `https://partners.salesforce.com/s/education/general/AppExchange_Listing`

- Tip Sheet (has all of the links): `www.slideshare.net/partnerforce/partner-community-tip-sheet`

- Submit a Case: `https://partners.salesforce.com/partnerSupport`

Summary

We reviewed Salesforce Partner designation and some of the benefits that come with it. We also discussed partner onboarding activities, channel management, and channel sales core concepts. We walked through the practical exhibit and demonstration of an app, its design concepts, build process, and finally created a managed package using the Package Manager.

We then reviewed and discussed listing the app in Salesforce AppExchange, the key activities necessary to be able to successfully upload the app package to Salesforce Partner Portal, marketing materials for the app, and the checkout process from AppExchange and finally covered the security review details.

We also listed some of the key resources to become a successful Salesforce AppExchange partner.

Index

© Rashed A. Chowdhury 2021
R. A. Chowdhury, *Building a Salesforce-Powered Front Office*, https://doi.org/10.1007/978-1-4842-6676-2

When coral dies, reefs change.
Other animals lose it as a
home and as food.

It's sad, but coral reefs are at risk.
Global warming is a threat to them.
It makes sea temps rise. Coral
can't survive in hot seas.

global warming: GLOH-buhl WORM-ing

These reefs can get quite
biodiverse. Many kinds of plants
and animals make it their home.

Coral reefs get built in
warm, tropical seas.

This algae is quite small. You can't see
it with just your eyes. It spreads. It
grows in coral. It makes it bright colors.

Look! These plants
seem nice!

Those are not plants!
These things get built by tiny
animals—coral! This whole
ecosystem is known as
a coral reef.

OUR CHANGING WORLD

Earth's climate can change. It has in the past. When dinosaurs lived, most of Earth was warm. Its poles were warm, too!

But 11,500 years ago, Earth's climate got cold. Big sheets of ice covered huge swaths of land.

fossil fuels: FAH-suhl FYOOLZ

Change should take a long time. Right now, it is changing too fast. Since the mid-1800s, humans made big changes. They cut trees. They burnt **fossil fuels**.

Carbon dioxide is set free when coal and oil burn. It mixes with other **greenhouse gasses**, such as methane. This gas is made by livestock farming.

ATMOSPHERE

HEAT FROM THE SUN

These gases trap heat. They trap it close to land. This then makes temps rise. It makes Earth hot, like in a greenhouse.

Earth would not be the same. We must all work to slow global warming and keep the future of this planet safe.

drought: DROWT

High temps and drought kill grasslands.

If we can't fix this, and people keep burning fossil fuels, temps will keep rising. They will rise 2.0–11.5°F (1.1–6.4°C) by 2100.

Ice at the poles is melting.

This might not seem bad, but it is. It makes biomes change. They change too fast. Living things can't adapt that fast. They die.

The whole of Earth's surface temp rose 2°F (1°C) since the mid-1800s.

WORDS TO KNOW

adapted able to live well in an environment because of changes that have happened to it over time.

aquatic growing or living in water.

biodiverse having many different types of animals or plants.

bog an area with soft, wet ground.

deforestation cutting down a forest or a large area of trees.

desertification when land changes into a desert.

drought a long period with little or no rain.

ecosystem all of the living things in an area and the way they affect each other.

elevation how high a place is above sea level.

equator an imaginary line around the center of Earth.

erosion the process by which Earth's materials are worn away by wind, water, gravity, or ice.

fossil fuels fuels such as coal, natural gas, and oil that are formed from the remains of ancient plants and animals.

global warming the increase in temperature on Earth.

greenhouse gas a gas, such as carbon dioxide, that traps heat in Earth's atmosphere and contributes to global warming.

hemisphere one of the two halves of Earth.

latitude the position north or south of the equator.

lichen a plant-like organism.

nocturnal active during the night.

oasis a place in the desert where there is water.

permafrost land that is permanently frozen beneath the surface.

plain a large area of flat land.

predator a hunting animal.

temperate not too hot or too cold.

topography the arrangement of physical features in an area.

tropical the region of Earth just north and south of the equator. Tropical climates are usually hot and humid.

wetland an area of land that is particularly wet.

ANTONIO VIVALDI

Par che tardo oltre il costume
CANTATA
PER SOPRANO E BASSO CONTINUO
RV 662

EDIZIONE CRITICA
A CURA DI
FRANCESCO DEGRADA

RICORDI

Prefazione generale

I criteri che guidano la nuova edizione critica delle opere di Antonio Vivaldi sono analiticamente esposti nelle Norme editoriali, *redatte a cura del Comitato Editoriale dell'Istituto Italiano Antonio Vivaldi. Se ne offre qui un estratto che descrive, nei termini indispensabili alla comprensione della partitura, la tecnica editoriale adottata.*

L'edizione si propone di presentare un testo il più possibile fedele alle intenzioni del compositore, così come sono ricostruibili sulla base delle fonti, alla luce della prassi di notazione contemporanea e delle coeve convenzioni esecutive.

La tecnica di edizione adottata per opere singole o gruppi di opere è illustrata nelle Note critiche. *Esse contengono di norma:*

1. *Una trattazione dell'origine e delle caratteristiche generali della composizione (o delle composizioni).*
2. *Un elenco delle fonti (comprese le fonti letterarie quando rivestano particolare importanza).*
3. *Una descrizione di tutte le fonti che il curatore ha collazionato o consultato, comprese le più importanti edizioni moderne.*
4. *Una relazione e una spiegazione relative alle scelte testuali derivanti dallo stato delle fonti e dalle loro reciproche relazioni e alle soluzioni adottate per composizioni particolarmente problematiche, non previste nella* Prefazione generale. *In particolare viene specificato quale fonte è usata come* fonte principale *dell'edizione, quale (o quali) sono state* collazionate, *consultate o* semplicemente *elencate.*
5. *Una discussione sulla prassi esecutiva relativa alla composizione o alle composizioni edite.*
6. *Un apparato critico dedicato alla lezione originale e alla sua interpretazione, contenente la registrazione di tutte le varianti rispetto alla fonte principale e alle fonti collazionate.*

Ogni intervento del curatore sul testo che vada al di là della pura traslitterazione della notazione antica o che non corrisponda a un preciso sistema di conversione grafica qui segnalato, viene menzionato nelle Note critiche *o evidenziato attraverso specifici segni:*

1. *Parentesi rotonde (per indicazioni espressive o esecutive mancanti nelle fonti e aggiunte per assimilazione orizzontale o verticale; per correzioni e aggiunte del curatore laddove nessuna delle fonti fornisce, a suo giudizio, un testo corretto).*
2. *Corpo tipografico minore (per l'integrazione del testo letterario incompleto o carente sotto la linea o le linee del canto; per le indicazioni «solo» e «tutti» aggiunte dal curatore; per la realizzazione del basso continuo per strumento a tastiera).*
3. *Linee tratteggiate* ‑ ‑ ‑ ‑ ‑ *per legature di articolazione o di valore aggiunte dal curatore.*
4. *Semiparentesi quadre* ⌐   ⌐ *per il testo musicale o letterario di un rigo derivato in modo esplicito (mediante abbreviazione) o implicito da un altro rigo.*

Non vengono di norma segnalati nell'edizione gli interventi del curatore nei casi seguenti:

I) *Quando viene aggiunta una legatura tra l'appoggiatura e la nota principale. Questa regola vale anche nel caso di gruppi di note con funzione di appoggiatura.*

II) *Quando segni di articolazione (per esempio punti di staccato) sono aggiunti a una serie di segni simili per assimilazione, sulla base di inequivocabili indicazioni della fonte.*

III) *Quando la punteggiatura viene corretta, normalizzata o modernizzata; lo stesso vale per l'ortografia e l'uso delle maiuscole.*

IV) *Quando abbreviazioni comunemente usate vengono sciolte.*

V) *Quando pause di un'intera battuta mancanti nella fonte vengono aggiunte, e non c'è alcun dubbio che una parte del testo musicale sia stata inavvertitamente omessa.*

VI) *Quando vengono introdotti dal curatore segni ritmici indicanti modalità di esecuzione.*

L'ordine delle parti strumentali nella partitura segue la prassi editoriale moderna.

La notazione trasposta dell'originale (per il violone, il flautino, il corno) viene mantenuta nell'edizione; nelle Note critiche *viene specificato l'intervallo di trasposizione dei singoli strumenti (con l'eccezione del violone). Parti in notazione di «bassetto» (violini, viole, clarinetti, chalumeaux, ecc.) sono trascritte nelle chiavi di violino e di contralto e nell'ottava appropriata.*

Nelle Note critiche *l'altezza dei suoni viene così citata:*

do¹ —— si¹   do² —— si²   do³ —— si³   do⁴ —— si⁴   do⁵

Le armature di chiave sono modernizzate per intere composizioni o per singoli movimenti, e l'armatura di chiave originale è indicata nelle Note critiche. *L'edizione usa le seguenti chiavi: per le parti strumentali, le chiavi di violino, di contralto, di tenore e di basso secondo l'uso moderno; per le parti vocali, la chiave di violino, la chiave di violino tenorizzata e la chiave di basso. Le chiavi originali o i cambiamenti di chiave sono registrati nelle* Note critiche.

Per quanto concerne il trattamento delle alterazioni, le fonti settecentesche della musica di Vivaldi seguono l'antica convenzione secondo la quale le inflessioni cromatiche mantengono la loro validità solamente per il tempo in cui la nota alla quale è premessa l'alterazione è ripetuta senza essere interrotta da altri valori melodici, indipendentemente dalla stanghetta di battuta. Pertanto la traslitterazione nella notazione moderna comporta l'automatica aggiunta di certe alterazioni e la soppressione di altre. Inflessioni cromatiche non esplicite nella notazione della fonte originale, ma aggiunte dal curatore, sono segnalate, quando è possibile, nella partitura, mettendo tra parentesi l'alterazione o le alterazioni introdotte. Se la stessa alterazione è presente nell'armatura di chiave, ovvero appare precedentemente nella stessa battuta, mantenendo dunque, secondo le convenzioni moderne, la propria validità, l'intervento del curatore viene segnalato nelle Note critiche, *dove viene offerta la lezione originale.*

Il basso continuo per strumento a tastiera è notato su due righi. Il rigo superiore contiene la realizzazione del curatore stampata in corpo minore. Essa non è da intendersi tout-court come una parte per la mano destra, dato che alcune note potranno legittimamente essere intese per la mano sinistra dell'esecutore. Il rigo inferiore che, in quanto parte di basso si riferisce spesso non solo agli strumenti del continuo, ma a tutti gli strumenti gravi dell'orchestra, è fornito di tutte le numeriche del basso esistenti nell'originale, stampate sotto di esso. Queste numeriche possono essere, se necessario, corrette dal curatore, che tuttavia non ne aggiungerà di nuove. Le alterazioni sono apposte davanti alle numeriche cui si riferiscono e i tratti trasversali indicanti l'alterazione cromatica di una nota (δ) sono sostituiti dal diesis o dal bequadro corrispondenti. L'abbassamento di un semitono di una cifra del basso precedentemente diesizzata, è sempre indicata col segno di bequadro, anche se le fonti, talvolta, usano per lo stesso scopo il segno di bemolle. Le indicazioni « solo » e « tutti » nel basso, sempre in carattere minore se aggiunte dal curatore, si riferiscono a cambiamenti nella strumentazione della linea del basso, descritti più analiticamente nelle Note critiche. *Particolari figurazioni ritmiche nella linea del basso non devono necessariamente essere eseguite da tutti gli strumenti del continuo: così, veloci disegni in scala possono essere affidati ai soli strumenti ad arco; a sua volta il clavicembalo può suddividere in valori più brevi lunghe note tenute dal basso, dove questo si addica alla generale struttura ritmica del brano.*

Quando la ripetizione del « Da Capo » non è scritta per esteso (come avviene per lo più nelle composizioni vocali), la prima sezione deve essere ripetuta dall'inizio o dal segno ✕ , sino alla cadenza della tonalità fondamentale, contrassegnata generalmente da una corona, o sino al segno ✕ . Nelle arie e in composizioni vocali simili, il « Da Capo » deve essere eseguito dal solista (o dai solisti) con nuovi abbellimenti, in armonia con il carattere ritmico e melodico del brano.

Nei recitativi, le appoggiature per la parte di canto non vengono indicate una per una nel testo dell'edizione; pertanto il cantante deve compiere sempre una scelta giudiziosa del luogo ove introdurle. Di norma sono richieste in tutte le formule cadenzali nelle quali c'è un intervallo discendente prima dell'ultima sillaba accentata di una frase; se l'intervallo è una seconda o una terza maggiore o minore, la sillaba accentata è cantata un tono o un semitono sopra (secondo l'accordo sottostante) rispetto alla nota successiva; se l'intervallo è più ampio di una terza, la silla-

ba accentata è intonata alla stessa altezza della nota precedente. Questo vale sia che il basso abbia o non abbia una cadenza, sia che la nota dell'appoggiatura sia consonante o meno col basso. Talvolta si possono introdurre appoggiature anche all'interno di una frase, per dare importanza a certe parole, anche quando l'ultima sillaba accentata è raggiunta partendo da una nota inferiore. Ma anche in questo caso, la nota dell'appoggiatura deve essere più alta rispetto alla nota successiva; appoggiature ascendenti possono essere consigliabili in frasi che terminano con un punto di domanda o che richiedano una particolare espressività. Nei recitativi, quando non altrimenti indicato, tutte le note del basso e gli accordi corrispondenti del rigo superiore devono essere eseguiti come « attacchi » di breve durata; questo, in particolare, nella musica vocale profana. Devono essere tenuti solo gli accordi alla fine di un recitativo, segnalata da una corona. Il trattamento ritmico degli accordi delle cadenze nell'accompagnamento dei recitativi è generalmente suggerito, nell'edizione, dalla realizzazione del basso continuo; ritardare troppo gli accordi sulle cadenze non è consigliabile nei recitativi di composizioni profane. Le « cadenze posposte », nelle quali la nota del basso entra dopo che la voce ha smesso di cantare, sono suggerite nell'edizione solo per conclusioni cadenzali particolarmente importanti, mediante l'inserzione di una virgola tra parentesi sopra il rigo superiore e inferiore. Dopo una cadenza, nel corso di un recitativo, è da evitare un ritardo nell'attacco della frase successiva, a meno che una virgola tra parentesi non lo richieda espressamente.

Gli abbellimenti vocali e strumentali diversi da quelli da impiegarsi nel « Da Capo » e nei recitativi, sono aggiunti dal curatore (tra parentesi) se assenti nella fonte, nei punti in cui sono di norma richiesti dalle convenzioni esecutive dell'epoca di Vivaldi. Se la fonte indica o sottintende una cadenza, questo verrà specificato nelle Note critiche, *ma di norma non ne verrà offerta una realizzazione. Nelle arie con « Da Capo » è richiesta di solito una cadenza almeno alla fine dell'ultima sezione, e spesso anche alla fine della seconda (quella centrale); ciò non verrà specificato caso per caso nelle* Note critiche, *salvo laddove occorra chiarire l'esatta posizione della cadenza stessa.*

General Preface

The guiding principles behind the new, critical edition of the works of Antonio Vivaldi are set out in detail in the *Editorial Norms* agreed by the Editorial Committee of the Istituto Italiano Antonio Vivaldi. We give below a summary which describes, in terms essential to the understanding of the score, the editorial principles adopted. The editon aims at maximum fidelity to the composer's intentions as ascertained from the sources in the light of the contemporary notational and performance practice.

The editorial method employed for single works or groups of works is described in the *Critical Notes*, which normally contain:

1. A statement of the origin and general characteristics of the compositions.
2. A list of sources, including literary sources when relevant.
3. A description of all the sources collated or consulted by the editor, including the most important modern editions.
4. An account and explanation of decisions about the text arising from the state of the sources and their interrelationship, and of solutions adopted for compositions presenting special problems, unless these are already covered in the *General Preface*. In particular, it will be made clear which source has been used as the *main source* of the edition, and which others have been *collated, consulted* or merely *listed*.
5. A discussion of performance practice in regard to the composition(s) published.
6. A critical commentary concerned with original readings and their interpretation, which lists all variations existing between the main source and the collated sources.

All instances of editorial intervention which go beyond simple transliteration of the old notation or which do not conform to a precise system of graphical conversion described below will be mentioned in the *Critical Notes* or shown by special signs:

1. Round brackets (for marks of expression or directions to the performer absent in the sources and added through horizontal or vertical assimilation; for editorial emendations where none of the sources, in the editor's judgement, provides a correct text).
2. Small print (to complete an underlaid text when some or all words are missing; for the editorial indications "solo" and "tutti"; for the realization for keyboard of the continuo).
3. Broken lines ⌒ for slurs and ties added editorially.
4. Square half-brackets ⌐ ¬ for musical or literary text derived explicitly (by means of a cue) or implicitly from that on (or under) another staff.

Normally, the editor will intervene tacitly in the following cases:

I) When a slur linking an appoggiatura to the main note is added. This applies also to groups of notes functioning as appoggiaturas.
II) When marks of articulation (e.g. staccato dots) are added to a series of similar marks by assimilation and the source leaves no doubt that this is intended.
III) When punctuation is corrected, normalized or modernized; the same applies to spelling and capitalization.
IV) When commonly-used abbreviations are resolved.
V) When whole-bar rests absent in the source are added, there being no reason to think that a portion of musical text has inadvertently been omitted.
VI) When editorial rhythmic signs indicating a manner of performance are added.

The order of the instrumental parts in the score follows modern publishing practice.

Transposing notation in the original (for *violone, flautino*, horn) is retained in the edition; in the *Critical Notes* the interval of transposition of individual instruments (*violone* excepted) will be specified. Parts in "bassetto" notation (violins, violas, clarinets, chalumeaux, etc.) are written out in the appropriate octave using treble or alto clefs.

In the *Critical Notes*, the pitches are cited according to the following system:

The key signatures of whole compositions or individual movements are modernized where appropriate and the original key signature given in the *Critical Notes*. The edition employs the following clefs: for instrumental parts, treble, alto, tenor and bass clefs following modern usage; for vocal parts, treble, "tenor G" and bass clefs. Original clefs or clef changes are recorded in the *Critical Notes*.

In regard to the treatment of accidentals, the 18th-century sources of Vivaldi's music adhere to the old convention whereby chromatic inflections retain their validity for only so long as the note to which an accidental has been prefixed is repeated without interruption, irrespective of barlines. Conversion to modern notation thus entails the tacit addition of some accidentals and the suppression of others. Chromatic inflections not made explicit in the notation of the original source but supplied editorially are shown where possible in the score, the one or more accidentals entailed being enclosed in parentheses. If the same accidental is present in the key signature or appears earlier in the same bar, therefore remaining valid under the modern convention, the editorial intervention is recorded in the *Critical Notes*, where the original reading is given.

The *basso continuo* for keyboard is notated on two staves. The upper staff contains the editorial realization. This should not be understood *tout court* as a part for the right hand, since certain notes may be intended for the performer's left hand. The lower staff, which as a bass part often has to be played not merely by continuo instruments but also by all the "low" instruments of the orchestra, includes all the bass figures present in the original, which are printed below it. Where necessary, these figures may be corrected by the editor, who will not add any new figures, however. Accidentals precede the figures to which they refer, and cross-strokes indicating the chromatic inflection of a note (♭) are replaced by the appropriate accidental. The lowering by a semitone of a previously sharpened bass figure is always indicated by the natural sign, although the sources sometimes use the flat sign synonymously. The indications "solo" and "tutti" in the bass, always in small print if editorial, call for changes in the instrumentation of the bass line, which are described more specifically in the *Critical Notes*. Rhythmic figurations in the bass line are not necessarily meant to be performed on all participating instruments; thus, rapid scales may be left to the stringed bass instruments, while the harpsichord may split sustained bass notes into shorter values, where this conforms to the general rhythm of the piece.

Where the "Da Capo" repeat is not written out (mostly in vocal pieces), the first section has to be repeated, from the beginning or from the sign ⋈ until the tonic cadence at the end of this section, which is usually marked by a fermata, or until the sign ⋈ . In arias and similar vocal pieces the "Da Capo" repeat should be performed by the soloist(s) with new embellishments in accordance with the rhythmic and melodic character of the piece.

In recitatives the appoggiaturas for the singer are not indicated individually in the main text of the edition, as the singer has always to make a judicious selection of the places where to sing them. They are normally expected in all cadential formulas where there is a falling interval before the last accented syllable of a phrase; if the interval is a minor or major second or third, the accented syllable is sung a tone or semitone higher (according to the harmony) than the following note; if the interval is larger than a third, the accented syllable is sung at the same pitch as the preceding note. This is valid whether or not the bass actually cadences at that point, and whether or not the appoggiatura is consonant or dissonant with the bass. Occasionally, appoggiaturas can also be sung within a phrase, to lend emphasis to certain words — even when the last accented syllable is approached from below. Here, too, the appoggiatura should lie above the note following it, but rising appoggiaturas may be appropriate in phrases ending

VIII

with a question mark or where special expressiveness is required. All bass notes of the recitatives, including the corresponding chords in the upper staff, should be performed as short "attacks", at least in secular music, where not otherwise indicated. Sustained chords are limited to those at the end of a recitative, marked by a fermata.

The rhythmic treatment of cadential chords in the accompaniment of recitative is usually suggested in the edition by the continuo realization; longer delays of the cadential chords are not appropriate in secular recitative. "Postponed cadences", where the bass note enters after the voice has finished, are suggested in the edition only at major stopping points, by the insertion of a bracketed comma in the upper and lower staff at this juncture. After a cadence within the course of a recitative there should be no delay in the attack of the next phrase, unless a bracketed comma specifically calls for it.

Other vocal and instrumental embellishments than those in "Da Capo" repeats and in recitatives are supplied editorially (in brackets) if absent from the source, where they are normally required by the performing conventions of Vivaldi's age. If the source indicates of implies a cadenza, this will be pointed out in the *Critical Notes*, but normally no specimen of one will be supplied. In "Da Capo" arias cadenzas are usually expected at least at the end of the last section, and often also at the end of the second (middle) section; this will not be specifically pointed out in the *Critical Notes* except in cases where the exact position of the cadenza needs clarification.

Par che tardo oltre il costume
Cantata per soprano e basso continuo RV 662

Larghetto

Par che

2

tar - do ol - tre il co - stu - me Og - - gi____

scen - da al mar d'A - tlan - te Il__ bel____

dio__ che_____ col su - o lu - me E__ la

ter - ra e il ciel_____

P.R.1314

ri - schia - ra.

Par che

tar - do   ol - tre il co - stu - me   Og - gi

4

scen - da al mar d'A - tlan - te Il bel

dio che_____ col su - o lu - me E la ter -

- ra e il ciel ri - schia - - - -

- - - - -

il ciel ri - schia - - - -

40

- - - ra, il ciel_____

ri-schia - ra.

Ed in -

-tan - to il co - re a-man - te, il co - re a - man - te　Cui l'oc-ca - so ap-pre-sta un

be - ne　Tro-va il duol nel - la sua spe - ne　E a sof-frir go - den-do im-

-pa - - - - - -

-ra, go - den - do im-pa - ra,　Tro-va il duol nel - la sua

8

spe - ne E a sof-frir go-den-do im-pa - - - - - - ra, go-den-do im-pa - ra.

Da Capo

(Recitativo)

Quan-do tu d'An-fi-tri-te In grem-bo gi-a-ce-rai, ce-le-ste au-

-ri-ga, Io del-la bel-la Clo-ri In grem-bo go-de-

10

Al - lor che in cie - lo Not -

P.R.1314

te il suo ve - lo Di - sten - de - rà,

In brac - cio a Clo - ri De' miei do - lo - ri, de' miei do -

- lo - ri Ri - sto - ro a - vrò,

ri - sto - ro a -

vrò.

Al - lor_____ ch'in cie - lo Not -

- - - te il suo ve - lo Di - sten - de -

- rà, In brac - cio a Clo - ri De' miei do -

14

-rà,＿＿＿＿＿ De' miei do - lo - ri, ⌐De' miei do -

- lo - ri⌐ In brac - cio a Clo — ri Ri - sto - ro a -

- vrò,＿＿＿＿＿＿＿＿＿＿＿ Ri - sto — — —

- — — — —

16

De' scor-si af - fan - ni

A - mor i dan - ni Com - pen - se - rà,

100

E la mia fe - de, Dol - ce mer - ce - de,

Dol - ce mer - ce - - - - -

17

Da Capo

P.R.1314

Note critiche

La cantata *Par che tardo oltre il costume*, RV 662, per soprano e basso continuo, è pervenuta attraverso due fonti entrambe autografe di Vivaldi, conservate rispettivamente presso la Biblioteca Nazionale di Torino (Foà 27, cc. 2-5) e presso la Sächsische Landesbibliothek di Dresda (Mus. 1-J-7, 8, pp. 96-101).[1] La prima fonte è costituita da un quaderno composto di due doppie carte di formato oblungo, inserite l'una nell'altra, che misurano cm. 23 per 31 circa, cui corrispondono otto pagine di notazione musicale; della c. 5v sono stati utilizzati solo i primi quattro righi. Nella parte superiore della c. 2r appare, al centro, l'intestazione «Can:ᵗᵃ Del Viualdi». Anche se a c. 5v manca l'indicazione «Finis» (che figura peraltro nell'altra fonte), il fatto che la cantata presenti nel suo insieme, sia dal punto di vista musicale, sia da quello testuale, una struttura coerente, dà la certezza che l'opera sia giunta nella sua integrità.

Ogni pagina comprende dieci pentagrammi e la musica è notata su cinque sistemi di due pentagrammi ciascuno; quello superiore è in chiave di soprano, quello inferiore in chiave di basso, senza indicazioni relative alla voce o agli strumenti di accompagnamento. Si tratta tuttavia chiaramente di una composizione per voce di soprano e basso continuo.

Secondo le ricerche di Paul Everett, questo autografo di RV 662 presenta la stessa qualità di carta di RV 657 e RV 683 (per quest'ultima solo relativamente alla parte per contralto e basso continuo, pervenuta in Foà 27, cc. 258-261) e sembrerebbe attribuibile, a giudicare dalle caratteristiche della grafia musicale, a un periodo compreso tra gli ultimi anni del decennio 1720-30 e i primi anni del decennio successivo.

La seconda fonte, conservata a Dresda, è anch'essa – come si è detto – un autografo di Vivaldi. Si tratta di un manoscritto formato da tre carte, che misurano cm. 23,5 per 32 circa, corrispondenti a sei pagine di notazione musicale; ogni pagina comprende dieci righi, utilizzati come nell'autografo originale. Nella parte superiore centrale della p. 96 appare l'iscrizione «Cantata», e poco più a destra l'attribuzione della paternità del lavoro: «Del Viualdi». Nella parte superiore destra della stessa pagina appare l'annotazione (probabilmente non autografa) «Nᵒ 5ⁿᵗᵒ·», che si riferisce alla posizione della cantata all'interno del manoscritto. Con ogni probabilità Vivaldi realizzò questo manoscritto dopo aver completato la versione consegnata al manoscritto di Torino al solo scopo di limitare l'estensione vocale della cantata al *si⁴ bemolle* (la versione originale giunge al *do⁵*) e di semplificarne alcune figure ritmiche. Il manoscritto di Dresda non offre pertanto una nuova versione della cantata, quanto una versione semplificata ad uso di interpreti non dotati dei mezzi vocali senza dubbio eccezionali della cantante (o dell'evirato) per i quali la cantata fu composta. È molto interessante notare che in questo lavoro di revisione Vivaldi limitò la lunghezza delle due arie della cantata; esse comprendono infatti rispettivamente 53 e 101 battute, contro le 57 e le 120 della redazione di Torino. Tutte le varianti tra le due versioni sono registrate nell'Apparato critico. La nostra edizione segue sempre la prima versione. Se gli interpreti volessero optare per la seconda – desumendola dalle informazioni inserite nell'Apparato critico – sarà preferibile adottare in maniera sistematica le sue varianti piuttosto che utilizzarle in modo parziale, onde evitare un insoddisfacente *mélange* privo della coerenza dell'una e dell'altra versione.

La cantata, basata su un testo di autore ignoto e di modestissimo valore poetico, presenta la struttura Aria-Recitativo-Aria.

La prima aria è costituita da due quartine di ottonari; la seconda da due sestine di quinari (il terzo e il sesto dei quali tronchi). Entrambe prevedono il consueto *da capo*; ciò significa che la prima parte di ogni aria (prima aria, bb. 1-45, terzo tempo; seconda aria, bb. 1-93, primo tempo) deve essere intonata due volte. Poiché non abbiamo modificato in nulla il testo di Vivaldi, pare opportuno avvertire che la corona posta sul terzo tempo della b. 45 nella prima aria e sul primo tempo della b. 93 nella seconda, deve essere considerata, nella prima intonazione, come inesistente. Similmente, la corona posta alla fine della seconda parte di ciascuna aria (rispettivamente alle bb. 57 e 120) ha un valore relativo e non assoluto; spetta all'interprete determinare giudiziosamente la durata dell'ultima nota precedente il *da capo*, tenendo anche conto del carattere tetico o anacrusico dell'inizio dell'aria.

Per quanto riguarda l'interpretazione, occorrerà appena ricordare la necessità di una ripresa variata dei *da capo* (il che non esclude la moderata introduzione di abbellimenti e fioriture anche nelle

20

altre parti dell'aria). Punti opportuni per l'introduzione di eventuali cadenze paiono il secondo tempo della b. 42 e il secondo tempo della b. 57 nella prima aria, e il secondo tempo della b. 119 nella seconda aria. Il recitativo andrà interpretato con molta scioltezza e libertà ritmica. Si raccomanda di iniziare i trilli con una chiara appoggiatura superiore.

Per quanto concerne gli strumenti del basso continuo, dovrebbero comprendere un violoncello e un clavicembalo (un'esecuzione con il solo clavicembalo è da escludere, tenendo conto della scrittura virtuosistica e idiomatica del violoncello in questa cantata). La realizzazione che qui si offre (pensata per il clavicembalo) è ovviamente una delle molte possibili, ed è da intendersi come proposta non vincolante, che l'interprete potrà elaborare o modificare a piacere. Mentre nelle arie l'elaborazione del basso continuo ha una relativa completezza, nel recitativo si propone esclusivamente di suggerire all'interprete lo schema armonico del basso (il tipo di accordo, non la modalità della sua esecuzione, che dovrà conformarsi alle fantasiose convenzioni della prassi esecutiva del primo Settecento).[2]

Altre avvertenze concernenti la prassi esecutiva sono contenute nella Prefazione generale.

Trascriviamo il testo della cantata.[3]

I   *Aria*:   Par che tardo oltre il costume
                   oggi scenda al mar d'Atlante
                   il bel dio che col suo lume
                   e la terra e il ciel rischiara.

                   Ed intanto il core amante
                   cui l'occaso appresta un bene
                   trova il duol nella sua spene
                   e a soffrir godendo impara.

II   *Recitativo*: Quando tu d'Anfitrite
                   in grembo giacerai, celeste auriga,
                   io della bella Clori
                   in grembo goderò felice amante.
                   Di tante pene e tante,
                   per lei sofferte, avrò dolce ristoro
                   de' miei sospir, del duol, del lungo pianto.
                   Deh, a dar pace al mio core
                   affretta, o sol, affretta il corso alquanto.

III *Aria*:   Allor che in cielo[a]
                   notte il suo velo
                   distenderà,
                   in braccio a Clori
                   de' miei dolori
                   ristoro[b] avrò.

                   De' scorsi affanni
                   Amor i danni
                   compenserà,
                   e la mia fede,
                   dolce mercede,
                   ritroverò.

[a] Dresda: II volta: «Allor ch'il cielo».
[b] Dresda: sempre «riposo».

Apparato critico

Indichiamo con T la fonte di Torino, con D quella di Dresda.

movimento, battuta	fonte	strumento, voce	
I	D	Soprano, Basso	Indicazione di tempo: «And:ᵉ».
I, 7	T, D	Basso	Nota 16 senza bequadro.
I, 8-9	D	Soprano	Dalla nota 4 di b. 8 alla nota 2 inclusa di b. 9: all'ottava sotto.
I, 9	D	Basso	Pausa di sedicesimo al posto della nota 8.
I, 10	D	Basso	Pausa di sedicesimo al posto della nota 1.
I, 13	T, D	Basso	Nota 7 senza bequadro.
I, 13-19	D	Soprano, Basso	La fonte di Dresda presenta la seguente versione:

ter - ra e il ciel___ ri - schia - ra.

I, 18	T	Basso	Nota 14 senza bequadro.
I, 20	T, D	Basso	Nota 15 senza bequadro.
I, 21	T, D	Basso	Nota 15 senza diesis.
I, 23	T	Basso	Nota 15 senza bequadro.
I, 26	T	Basso	Nota 14 senza bequadro.
I, 26	D	Soprano	Il trillo sull'ultima nota solo in D.
I, 27-31	D	Soprano, Basso	Queste 3 bb. della fonte D (bb. 26-28) sostituiscono le bb. 27-31 di T:

- ra e il ciel ri - schia - ra. Par che

I, 34-35	D	Soprano	La fonte di Dresda presenta la seguente versione:

22

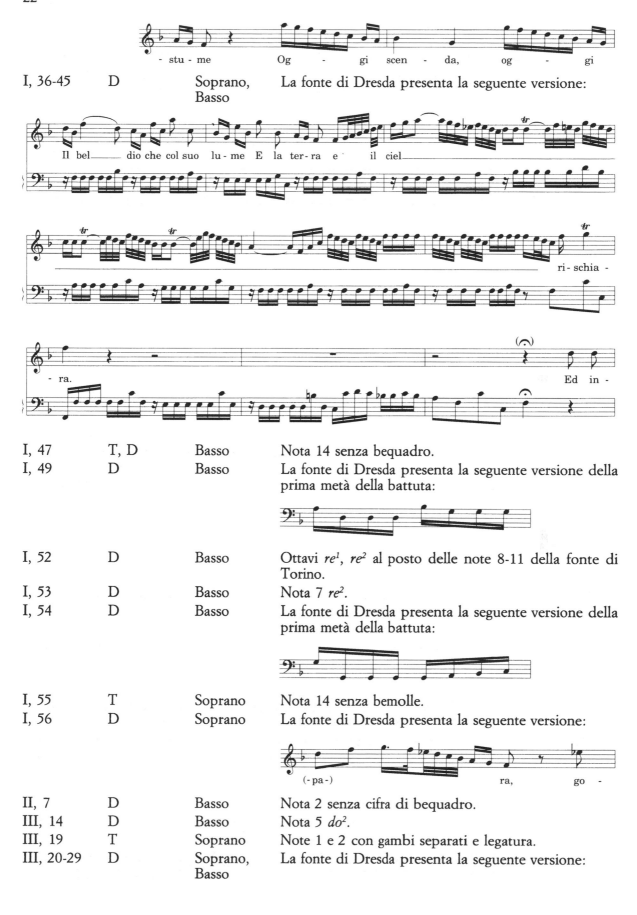

I, 47   T, D   Basso   Nota 14 senza bequadro.

I, 49   D   Basso   La fonte di Dresda presenta la seguente versione della prima metà della battuta:

I, 52   D   Basso   Ottavi *re¹*, *re²* al posto delle note 8-11 della fonte di Torino.

I, 53   D   Basso   Nota 7 *re²*.

I, 54   D   Basso   La fonte di Dresda presenta la seguente versione della prima metà della battuta:

I, 55   T   Soprano   Nota 14 senza bemolle.

I, 56   D   Soprano   La fonte di Dresda presenta la seguente versione:

II, 7   D   Basso   Nota 2 senza cifra di bequadro.

III, 14   D   Basso   Nota 5 *do²*.

III, 19   T   Soprano   Note 1 e 2 con gambi separati e legatura.

III, 20-29   D   Soprano, Basso   La fonte di Dresda presenta la seguente versione:

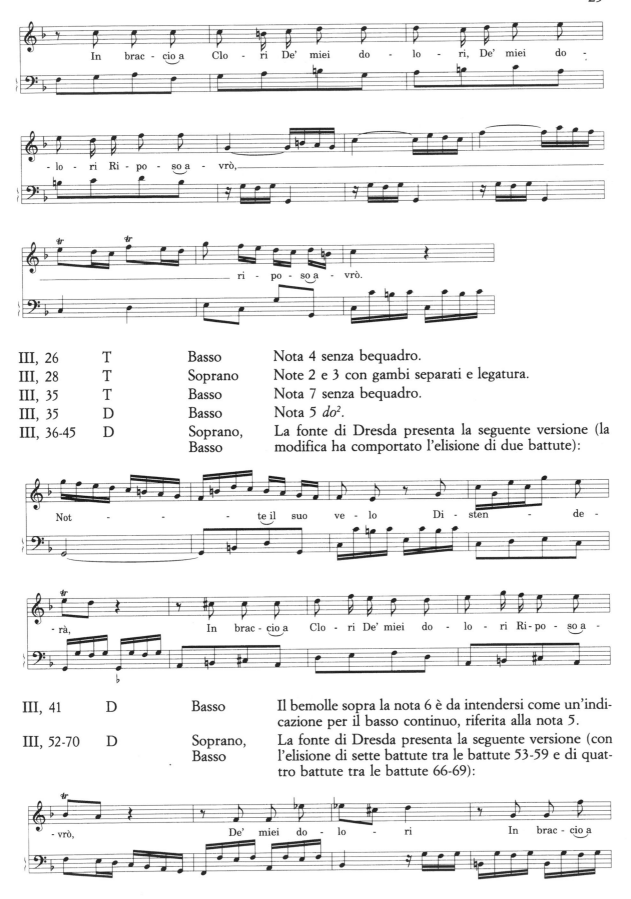

III, 26	T	Basso	Nota 4 senza bequadro.
III, 28	T	Soprano	Note 2 e 3 con gambi separati e legatura.
III, 35	T	Basso	Nota 7 senza bequadro.
III, 35	D	Basso	Nota 5 *do²*.
III, 36-45	D	Soprano, Basso	La fonte di Dresda presenta la seguente versione (la modifica ha comportato l'elisione di due battute):

| III, 41 | D | Basso | Il bemolle sopra la nota 6 è da intendersi come un'indicazione per il basso continuo, riferita alla nota 5. |
| III, 52-70 | D | Soprano, Basso | La fonte di Dresda presenta la seguente versione (con l'elisione di sette battute tra le battute 53-59 e di quattro battute tra le battute 66-69): |

III, 59	T	Soprano	Seguiamo la lezione della fonte, anche se probabilmente le due note devono intendersi come due ottavi seguiti da una pausa di quarto, come a bb. 19 e 41.
III, 66	T	Soprano	Sotto le note 1-4 «riposo», poi cancellato da Vivaldi e sostituito con «ristoro».
III, 81-86	D	Soprano, Basso	La fonte di Dresda presenta la seguente versione:

III, 95	T	Basso	In chiave di tenore dalla nota 2 alla nota 9 inclusa.
III, 99-100	T	Soprano	Manca il diesis davanti alla nota 7 di b. 99 e alle note 3 e 7 di b. 100.
III, 102	D	Soprano	Nota 3, sol³.
III, 104-120	D	Soprano, Basso	La fonte di Dresda presenta la seguente versione (la modifica ha comportato l'elisione di quattro battute):

Da Capo

Note

[1] Questa cantata è stata pubblicata in edizione moderna a cura di M. DUNHAM, in A. VIVALDI, *Cantatas for Solo Voice*, Part I, Madison, A-R Editions, 1979, pp. 39-53.

[2] Per una più ampia analisi dei problemi testuali, stilistici ed esecutivi delle cantate di Vivaldi, rimandiamo a un nostro volume monografico, in preparazione, che sarà edito nella serie «Quaderni vivaldiani» dell'Istituto Italiano Antonio Vivaldi.

[3] Si vedano anche le trascrizioni del testo – leggermente diverse dalla nostra – offerte da G. FOLENA in appendice al saggio *La cantata e Vivaldi*, in *Antonio Vivaldi. Teatro musicale, cultura e società*, a cura di L. BIANCONI e G. MORELLI, Firenze, Olschki, 1982, p. 172, e da M. DUNHAM, *Op. cit.*, Part I, pp. XVII-XVIII.

Critical Notes

The cantata Par che tardo oltre il costume, *RV 662, for soprano and continuo, has come down to us in two sources, both in the composer's hand, preserved in the Biblioteca Nazionale di Torino (Foà 27, fols 2-5) and the Sächsische Landesbibliothek, Dresden (Mus. 1-J-7, 8, pp. 96-101), respectively.[1] The first source consists of a quire of four leaves comprising two nested bifolios in oblong format measuring approximately 23 by 31 cm and containing eight pages of musical notation; only the first four staves of fol. 5v have been used. The heading "Can.:ta Del Viualdi" appears, centrally positioned, at the top of fol. 2r. Although the direction "Finis" does not appear on fol. 5v (it is present, however, in the other source), the fact that, viewed as a whole, the cantata is structurally coherent in regard to both the literary and the musical text establishes beyond doubt that this work has survived in complete form.*

Each page contains ten staves, and the music is notated on five systems of two staves; of these the upper is in the soprano clef and the lower in the bass clef, there being no indication of what type of voice and what accompanying instruments are intended. Clearly, though, this is a work for soprano and continuo.

According to researches by Paul Everett, this autograph score of RV 662 employs the same paper-type as the manuscripts of RV 657 and RV 683 (for the latter work, only in the case of the part for contralto and continuo preserved in Foà 27, fols 258-261) and would appear, from its musical handwriting, to date from the late 1720s or early 1730s.

As we saw, the second source, preserved in Dresden, is also autograph. This manuscript contains three folios measuring approximately 23.5 by 32 cm, with music written on all six pages; each page has ten staves, used as in the other score. At the top of p. 96 there appears, centrally positioned, the heading "Cantata", and slightly to the right the attribution of the work's authorship: "Del Viualdi". In the top right-hand corner of the same page we find the inscription (probably not autograph) "Nº 5nto.", which indicates the position of the cantata within the manuscript. In all probability Vivaldi prepared this manuscript after completing the version found in the Turin manuscript with the specific purpose of taking the upper limit of the vocal compass down from c''' (as in the original version) to b'' flat and simplifying some rhythmic figures. The Dresden version does not, however, constitute so much a new version of the cantata as a simplified version for the use of singers lacking the truly exceptional vocal powers of the female singer or castrato for whom the work was originally written. It is very interesting to note that in the process of making this revision Vivaldi reduced the length of the cantata's two arias; these now comprise 53 and 101 bars respectively, as against the 57 and 120 of the Turin version. All the divergences between the two versions have been recorded in the Critical Commentary. Our score follows the earlier version throughout. If performers wish to opt for the second version – as the information in the Critical Commentary enables them to do – it will be best to adhere consistently to its variant readings rather than to adopt them only selectively, which could result in an unsatisfactory mélange *lacking the integrity of either version.*

Based on an anonymous text of very modest poetic worth, the cantata adopts the structure Aria-Recitative-Aria.

The first aria consists of two quatrains of eight-syllable lines; the second of two sestets of five-syllable lines, the third and sixth lines of each being tronco *(i.e., lacking the unstressed final syllable). Both arias exhibit the customary da capo; this means that the first section of each aria (first aria, bars 1-45, third beat; second aria, bars 1-93, first beat) has to be sung twice. Since we have refrained from altering Vivaldi's musical text in any way, it may help to point out that the fermata over the third beat of bar 45 in the first aria, and over the first beat of bar 93 in the second, should be ignored the first time through. Similarly, the fermata at the end of the second section of both arias (bars 57 and 120 respectively) has a relative, not absolute, value; it is up to the interpreter to use his good sense in determining the duration of the last note before the* da capo, *also taking account of whether the aria opens on a strong beat or an upbeat.*

As regards the interpretation, it is hardly necessary to remind performers of the need to vary da capo *reprises (which does not exclude the moderate application of embellishments and* fioriture *to other sections of the aria as well). Suitable points for the possible introduction of cadenzas seem to be the second beat of bar 42 and 57 in the first aria, and the second beat of bar 119 in the second aria. The*

recitative has to be sung with great facility and rhythmic freedom. It is recommended to begin trills with a distinct upper appoggiatura.

As for the continuo instruments, they should comprise a cello and a harpsichord (a performance with harpsichord alone is ruled out by the virtuosic and idiomatic writing for the cello in this cantata). The realization offered here, conceived for harpsichord, is obviously only one of many possible ones and should be regarded as a non-obligatory suggestion that the performer is free to elaborate or change at pleasure. While the continuo realization in the arias is relatively complete as it stands, that in the recitative aims only to convey to the performer the harmonic implications of the bass (the species of chord, not the modalities of its performance, which will have to conform to the richly imaginative conventions of the early eighteenth century).[2]

Other remarks on performance practice are contained in the General Preface.

The text of the cantata is given in the Italian version of these notes.[3]

Critical Commentary

T denotes the Turin source, D that of Dresden.

movement, bar	source	instrument, voice	
I	D	Soprano, Basso	*Tempo marking "And:ᵉ".*
I, 7	T, D	Basso	*Note 16 without natural.*
I, 8-9	D	Soprano	*From bar 8 note 4 to bar 9 note 2 inclusive one octave lower.*
I, 9	D	Basso	*Semiquaver rest in place of note 8.*
I, 10	D	Basso	*Semiquaver rest in place of note 1.*
I, 13	T, D	Basso	*Note 7 without natural.*
I, 13-19	D	Soprano, Basso	*The Dresden source has the following version:*

I, 18	T	Basso	*Note 14 without natural.*
I, 20	T, D	Basso	*Note 15 without natural.*
I, 21	T, D	Basso	*Note 15 without sharp.*

I, 23	T	Basso	Note 15 without natural.
I, 26	T	Basso	Note 14 without natural.
I, 26	D	Soprano	Only D has the trill on the last note.
I, 27-31	D	Soprano, Basso	These three bars replace bars 27-31 of the Turin source in the Dresden source (where they are bars 26-28):

| I, 34-35 | D | Soprano | The Dresden source has the following version: |

| I, 36-45 | D | Soprano, Basso | The Dresden source has the following version: |

| I, 47 | T, D | Basso | Note 14 without natural. |
| I, 49 | D | Basso | The Dresden source has the following version of the first half of the bar: |

I, 52	D	Basso	Quavers D, d in place of notes 8-11 in the Turin source.
I, 53	D	Basso	Note 7 d.
I, 54	D	Basso	The Dresden source has the following version of the first half of the bar:

| I, 55 | T | Soprano | Note 14 without flat. |

I, 56	D	Soprano	*The Dresden source has the following version:*

II, 7	D	Basso	*Note 2 unfigured.*
III, 14	D	Basso	*Note 5 c.*
III, 19	T	Soprano	*Notes 1 and 2 with separate flags and joined by a slur.*
III, 20-29	D	Soprano, Basso	*The Dresden source has the following version:*

III, 26	T	Basso	*Note 4 without natural.*
III, 28	T	Soprano	*Notes 2 and 3 with separate flags and joined by a slur.*
III, 35	T	Basso	*Note 7 without natural.*
III, 35	D	Basso	*Note 5 c.*
III, 36-45	D	Soprano, Basso	*The Dresden source has the following version (shorter than the original by two bars):*

III, 41	D	Basso	*The flat over note 6 is to be interpreted as a bass figure applying to note 5.*

III, 52-70	D	Soprano, Basso	The Dresden source has the following version (with the removal of seven bars between bars 53 and 59 and four bars between bars 66 and 69):

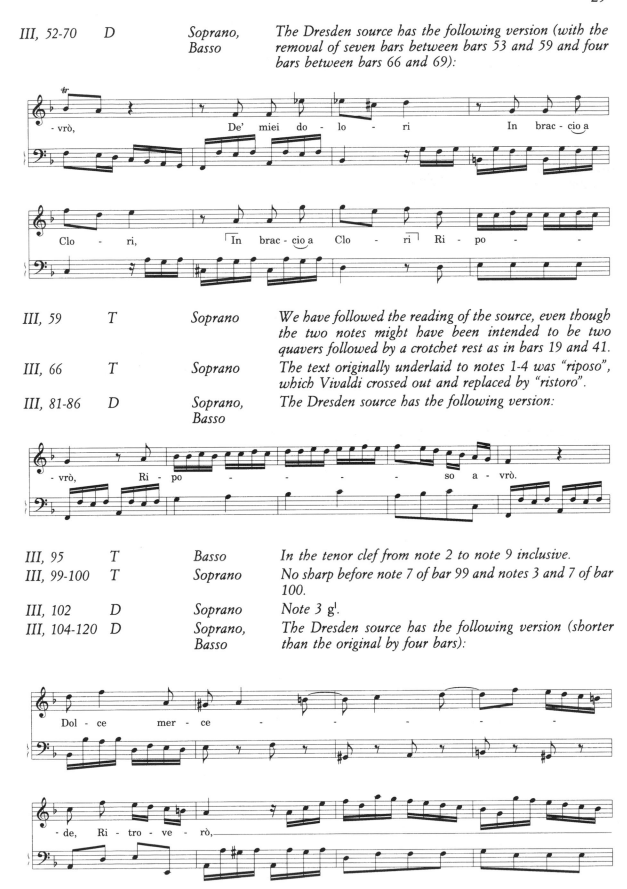

III, 59	T	Soprano	We have followed the reading of the source, even though the two notes might have been intended to be two quavers followed by a crotchet rest as in bars 19 and 41.
III, 66	T	Soprano	The text originally underlaid to notes 1-4 was "riposo", which Vivaldi crossed out and replaced by "ristoro".
III, 81-86	D	Soprano, Basso	The Dresden source has the following version:
III, 95	T	Basso	In the tenor clef from note 2 to note 9 inclusive.
III, 99-100	T	Soprano	No sharp before note 7 of bar 99 and notes 3 and 7 of bar 100.
III, 102	D	Soprano	Note 3 g¹.
III, 104-120	D	Soprano, Basso	The Dresden source has the following version (shorter than the original by four bars):

Da Capo

(Translation by Michael Talbot)

Notes

[1] *This cantata has been published in a modern edition by* M. DUNHAM *in* A. VIVALDI, Cantatas for Solo Voice, *Part I, Madison, A-R Editions, 1979, pp. 39-53.*

[2] *For a fuller analysis of the textual, stylistic and practical performing problems of Vivaldi's cantatas, the reader is referred to a monograph the editor is currently preparing; this is to be published by the Istituto Italiano Antonio Vivaldi in its series "Quaderni vivaldiani".*

[3] *See also the transcriptions of the text (differing slightly from ours) provided by* G. FOLENA *in an appendix to his article* La cantata e Vivaldi, *in* Antonio Vivaldi. Teatro musicale, cultura e società, *eds.* L. BIANCONI *and* G. MORELLI, *Florence, Olschki, 1982, p. 172, and by* M. DUNHAM, Op. cit., *Part I, pp. XVII-XVIII.*